IMAGES
of America

WOODLAND CEMETERY

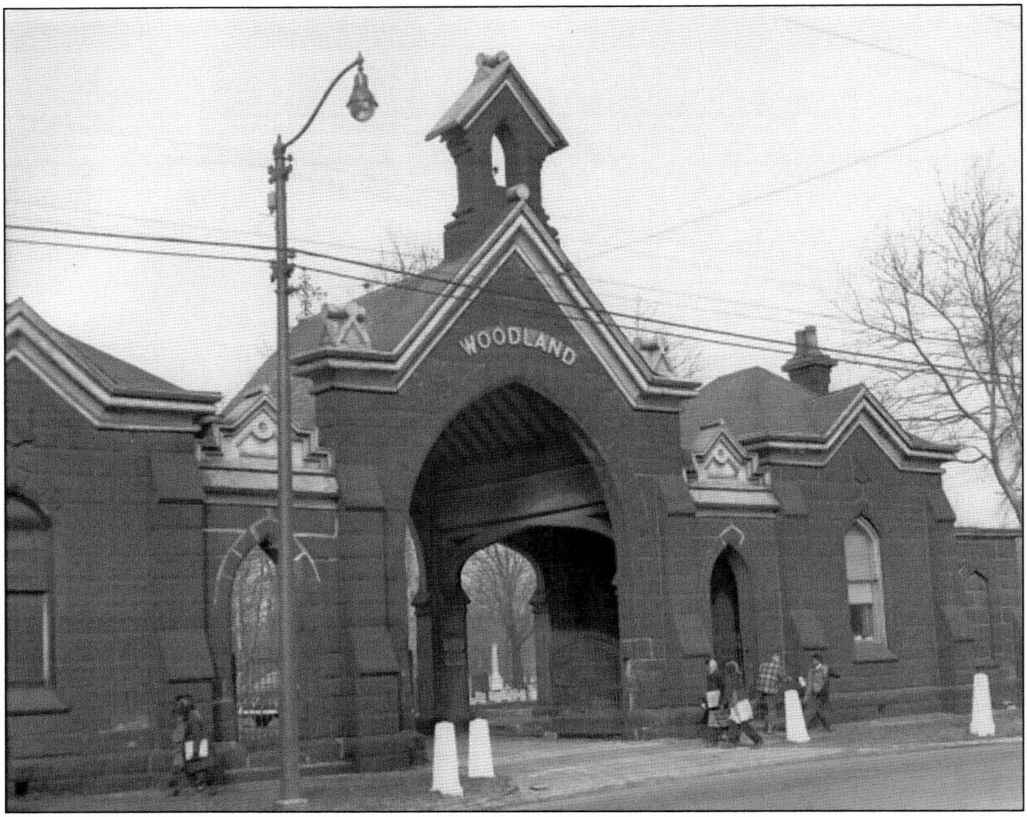

The Woodland Cemetery Gatehouse, pictured here on the south side of the cemetery at 6901 Woodland, was designed in 1870 by Joseph Ireland and deemed one of the finest post–Civil War architects. For more than 100 years, it served as an office, receiving vault, and chapel and, due to its size and structure, created an unforgettable experience of entry into the rural atmosphere of Woodland Cemetery. The original cost for basic materials including Amherst stone, in addition to other granite, was between $7,000 and $8,000. The structure included a 20-by-16-foot room on the west wing with a large stone slab floor. A 10-by-16-foot low roof annex with an entry to a basement and washroom facilities comprised the east wing. In addition, there was a room used as an office that had a basement of approximately 20 by 15 feet. The main entry arch was approximately 20 by 22 feet over an open granite floor of about 20 by 10 feet. In the winter of 1995–1996, the city dismantled the gatehouse, as it began to lean toward Woodland Avenue causing a safety concern. The pieces were numbered in the hope it could be reconstructed and placed where the old tool shed was located. In October 2011, the City of Cleveland announced that it will withdraw $2.3 million from a cemetery endowment fund, a little more than a third of the principal, to fix three old and historic cemeteries: Erie, Woodland, and Monroe Street. Woodland's gatehouse will be reconstructed, with the work scheduled to begin in 2013.

On the Cover: This photograph was taken in the early 1900s. Since the end of the Civil War, the veterans' graves at Woodland Cemetery have been honored or decorated appropriately by a number of volunteers and veteran organizations. (Cleveland Public Library Photograph Collection.)

IMAGES
of America

WOODLAND CEMETERY

Michelle A. Day and Gail Chambers
with the Woodland Cemetery Foundation

ARCADIA
PUBLISHING

ISBN 978-0-7385-9882-6

Published by Arcadia Publishing
Charleston, South Carolina

Printed in the United States of America

Library of Congress Control Number: 2012950192

For all general information, please contact Arcadia Publishing:
Telephone 843-853-2070
Fax 843-853-0044
E-mail sales@arcadiapublishing.com
For customer service and orders:
Toll-Free 1-888-313-2665

Visit us on the Internet at www.arcadiapublishing.com

No Historic spot grips our Hearts and stirs our sympathies as does a Burial Ground.

–Estella Bradburn Fisher
Memorial Day, May 30, 1930

Contents

ACKNOWLEDGMENTS

We want to express our gratitude to those that have assisted with the preservation of this historic cemetery. Without you, there would have been no need for a book regarding its history and many of its residents.

A great deal of the inspiration for my own involvement with the cemetery began with Michel Shaia, a human encyclopedia of Woodland Cemetery history, who retired as the caretaker for the City of Cleveland after 30 years of service.

In 1986, Mary H. Deal, historian, had the forethought to have Woodland Cemetery placed on the National Register of Historic Places.

The City of Cleveland must be acknowledged for supporting the Woodland Cemetery Foundation (WCF) in its endeavors to preserve these historic grounds.

The director of veteran necrology of the WCF, William Stark, has worked diligently to identify, record, and, when appropriate, obtain military markers for our resident veterans' graves. Decorating those graves for Memorial Day is a tremendous task that could not possibly be achieved without the numerous volunteers that turn out every year. Terry and Marcia Hart, along with the Boy Scouts, motivate the others that come to help.

Milano Monuments, Kotecki Family Monuments, North Coast Memorials, R&C Monuments Co., and Johns-Carabelli Co. have all graciously donated monuments.

We are grateful for the many volunteers, including "Missy," who, over the years, have donated their time to the WCF board, offered physical labor for restoration work, done some research or writing, designed our website or helped with pamphlets, and planned events, and we are especially thankful to those that attend such events when they occur.

This book would not have become a reality without the myriad of people who are involved with researching their own family histories. They shared their stories and photographs about our residents, making them come to life. Gail Chambers spent countless hours digging for facts regarding our residents so they would become more than just the dates of their births and deaths.

Those buried within Woodland Cemetery's gates are our history. The Woodland Cemetery Foundation is indebted to all of you.

The images in this volume appear courtesy of the Cleveland Public Library Photograph Collection (CPLPC), Cleveland State University Special Collections (CSUSC), and Michelle A. Day (MAD).

Introduction

Before 1831, America had no cemeteries. It is not that America did not bury its dead, but that large modern graveyards did not yet exist. The rural-cemetery-style layout of Woodland, although distinctive at the time for Cleveland, was consistent with other mid-19th century cemeteries that began to develop near cities. Woodland is now one of 12 cemeteries operated by the City of Cleveland.

Woodland Cemetery, established in 1851, has remained a historic, artistic, and cultural gem, gracing over 60 acres with a wealth of stories in the lives of over 82,000 residents, many of whom helped shape Cleveland's history. A sampling of those lives are presented in these pages, along with the history of Woodland Cemetery, the preservation work that takes place there, and hopes for its future.

Cleveland itself has grown from a community of about 15,000 to a metropolis of several-hundred thousand, its population swelled by diverse immigrant groups. The graves of that first generation of settlers—those immigrants from Connecticut who came early to seek fortunes in real estate and commerce—are found in the older sections of Woodland.

The diversity of Woodland's residents is evident with the Bohemian, German, Greek, Hungarian, African, Irish, Polish, Romanian, Russian, Scottish, Swedish, and Welsh that make up the majority of Woodland's ethnic cornucopia. Its religious affiliation has remained nondenominational. The mausoleum designs are varied, with Classical, Victorian, Egyptian, and Richardson-rustic architecture. Some are simple, while others are elaborate and ornate, with angels, obelisks, and military emblems such as eagles. In fact, Woodland was favorably recognized in *Silent Cities: The Evolution of the American Cemetery* as possessing a "profusion of well-designed monuments."

Woodland Cemetery was once the pride of Cleveland's public cemeteries. Through generous donations by the city, or through purchases, many fraternal and social organizations, such as the Freemasons, orphanages, and more, acquired lots to bury their members. Because Woodland was Cleveland's main cemetery for over 50 of the city's most dynamic years, it holds many artifacts that help with understanding the community.

Not only are two Ohio governors and one lieutenant governor laid to rest here, so is the German farmer Charles Bratenahl, the namesake of a distinguished east-side suburb. Other noteworthy residents include Lucy Ann and Holsey Gates, cofounders of Gates Mills (another east-side suburb); John P. Green, the initiator of Labor Day in Ohio; J. Milton Dyer, designer of Cleveland's city hall; Alfred E. Arthur, founder of the Cleveland School of Music; Joseph W. Briggs, initiator of the free home delivery of mail service; and Sara Lucy Bagby Johnson, the last slave to be prosecuted and returned south under the Fugitive Slave Act of 1850 prior to the beginning of the Civil War.

Veterans' graves from all branches of the nation's military and dating from the War of 1812 have been identified and are now appropriately decorated each Memorial Day. The Civil War had the greatest impact on the cemetery, with many soldiers receiving government-issued headstones and three distinct monuments being erected for the 23rd Ohio Volunteer Infantry (1865), the

7th Ohio Volunteer Infantry (1872), and the Grand Army of the Republic (1909). In June 2012, a monument was erected and dedicated to the cemetery's residents who served with the United States Colored Troops.

The idea for a new city cemetery began to evolve in 1848, as the city was running out of burial space in Erie Street Cemetery. Cleveland's leaders began to search for space for a new self-sufficient, profitable second cemetery to be located at a greater distance from neighborhood residences, assuring its use for at least 50 years. Investigation of possible sites began in July 1848, but the year ended without such a purchase. Landowner J.W. Allen twice refused, under the terms proposed, to sell his farmland on Kinsman Street and Kelly Road for cemetery purposes. Later the same year, council twice considered an offer from W.H. Otis to sell part of his farm, but no action was taken.

A cholera epidemic in 1849 made the need more evident, but the matter remained unresolved and seldom appeared on the council agenda. On June 14, 1851, the *Plain Dealer* hinted at an imminent purchase, saying, "A site is about to be purchased for a city cemetery on the plain of woodland, and to be called 'Green Lawn Cemetery.' "

City council minutes of July 22, 1851, recorded a proposition from Cleveland attorney Samuel Starkweather, an agent for Benjamin Butler, offering to sell the city 60.62 acres (part of the "Bomford tract") that Butler owned. In 1832, Col. George Bomford of Washington, DC had acquired 200 acres in Newburgh Township. He sold 100 acres to John Whipple of Providence, Rhode Island, and 60 acres to Benjamin Butler, Pres. Andrew Jackson's attorney general. The three divided the land into 40 five-acre lots just before the Panic of 1837.

The offer was accepted in concept and adopted after amendments were made and city attorneys were consulted. In August 1851, the city council voted unanimously to appropriate funds for the new cemetery—at $225 an acre—more than half of which would be issued in city bonds payable with seven percent interest to Butler over a 10-year period. The total cost would be about $23,189.

On February 26, 1852, city council allocated $40 to H.H. Blackmore for surveying the new cemetery, and in April 1852, city council approved the sale of surplus timber for improvements. By then, the population of Cleveland grew to 25,670, having an increased 20 percent from the previous year.

In October 1852, the committee on public grounds hired Howard Daniels, a well-known architect and landscape gardener, to survey and map out 20 of the 60 acres. Daniels was paid $5 a day for his services, $5 a day each for two draftsmen, $4 a day for a civil engineer, and $3 a day for an assistant for a total of $22 a day.

Early in May 1853, a committee was charged with planning the dedication ceremony for the cemetery, then located on Kinsman Street. (Kinsman Street was renamed Woodland Avenue in 1867.) City council adopted the name "Woodland" just one week before the new cemetery's June dedication. Not only did it reflect the dense grove of trees nearby (estimated to include 1,500 species), it also paid slight tribute to a romantic description of an unseen Cleveland, part of a popular 1803 pastoral poem, "Pleasures of Hope," by Scottish poet Thomas Campbell.

About 2,000 people were present on June 14, 1853, to hear Judge Starkweather deliver his address on the history of the new cemetery, which followed an opening prayer. The well-attended ceremony featured the mayor, members of city government, clergy, and a 100-voice choir.

Unlike most privately developed rural cemeteries, Woodland would profit from lot sales and fees for burials and other services. Less than a week after the dedication, a public auction was held for Woodland's several hundred lots of varied sized, priced from $8 to $400.

The cemetery's first burial occurred on June 23, 1853, for the Langshaw family's 15-month-old daughter Fanny, whose cause of death was listed as "inflammation of bowels." She is buried in Section 19. Many notable Clevelanders were buried in Woodland Cemetery, along with numerous Civil War veterans (some of whom were laid to rest on land purchased by the United States War Department in 1863).

In July 1865, a Civil War monument was erected to the 23rd Ohio Volunteer Infantry Regiment, in which future presidents Rutherford B. Hayes and William McKinley had both served. This was one of the first regimental monuments erected and dedicated to veterans of the Civil War. Another monument was installed and dedicated to the 7th Ohio Volunteer Infantry Regiment in May 1872.

In 1866, a resolution was presented to procure plans and designs for a pavilion, fountains, and perhaps a pond or two. The addition was to be constructed in the center of the cemetery at the request of many visitors. Woodland gained a stone pavilion, designed by Blackburn & Koehler, in 1866. By June 1869, the cemetery still lacked vital structures, such as a chapel for funeral services.

In 1870, Joseph Ireland, who was originally from New York but lived in the Western Reserve from 1865 to 1885, built an impressive Gothic-style stone gateway, at a cost of $7,500, on Woodland Avenue. City council had considered building it at the Quincy Avenue entrance before deciding it was more appropriate on Woodland Avenue, which shared the cemetery's name. A chapel and receiving vault were completed in 1880, and two ornamental water fountains were built in 1887. The cemetery was so ornately landscaped that courting couples often strolled the many brick paths that once were evident throughout the property.

Early in the 20th century, after its choice lots were sold, Woodland lost public favor and began to decline. Early in the 21st century, the pavilion, chapel, receiving vault, pond, and ornamental fountains were gone. During the winter of 1995–1996, the distinguished gatehouse, which had been destroyed by fire in the 1980s, was dismantled. Its stones, from local quarries, were carefully numbered and saved for future restoration.

Today, Woodland's landscape is one of grass and some sycamore trees with a few firs and other species. The curving roads and pathways are gone and grassed over. In June 2007, responding to public requests, a number of individuals formed the Woodland Cemetery Foundation (WCF) of Cleveland, Ohio. The foundation was established to help restore the cemetery, owned and managed by the City of Cleveland, to its original beauty. In addition to the goal to restoring the stone gatehouse, other projects include landscaping the grounds, installing memorial markers, assisting with funds (or acting as volunteer contractors) to repair headstones, monuments, and mausoleums, and to improve roadways. Funds received by this not-for-profit organization are used for those projects or for operational expenses.

On October 10, 2011, there was a proposal presented at the Public Works hearing to move $2.3 million from the cemetery endowment fund to restore the gatehouses at Woodland, Erie Street, and Monroe Street Cemeteries. The ordinance was approved, and the motion was forwarded to the finance committee for review at its meeting on October 24, 2011, where it was passed and signed. While it will take a number of years to fully restore all three gatehouses, the city's action has certainly offered encouragement to those foundations.

Enjoy your visit through the pages of Images of America: *Woodland Cemetery*, and perhaps you can pay us a visit in person. Please do your part in showing appreciation for this historic Cleveland icon and the surrounding environment by respecting it as the peaceful oasis that it truly is. Woodland Cemetery represents a proud past and is a cornerstone for future neighborhood revitalization as it draws visitors from the region and beyond.

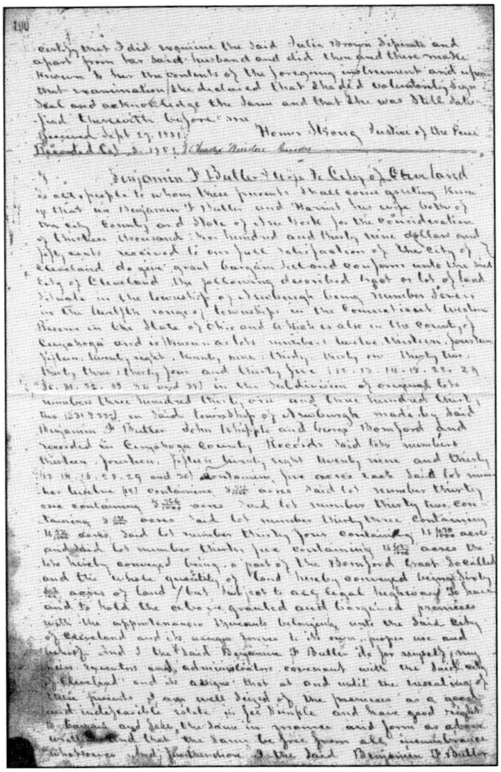

The deed transferring the land of Benjamin F. and Harriett Butler was signed on August 20, 1851. For the consideration of $13,239.50, the Butlers sold to the City of Cleveland lots numbers 12, 13, 14, 15, 28, 29, 30, 31, 32, 33, 34, and 25, containing 60.62 acres situated in the township of Newburgh, being number 7 in the 12th range of townships in the Connecticut Western Reserve in the State of Ohio in the County of Cuyahoga County in the subdivision of original lots numbers 331 and 332 made by Benjamin F. Butler, John Whipple, and George Bomford. (Cuyahoga County Recorder.)

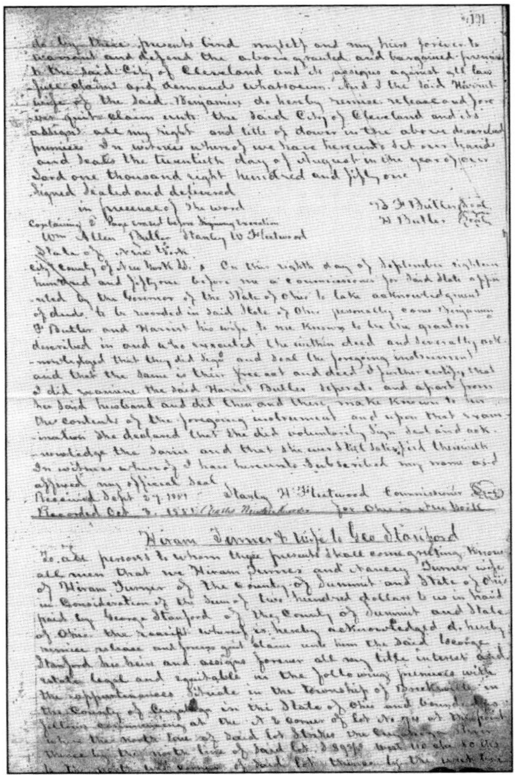

One

History of Woodland Cemetery

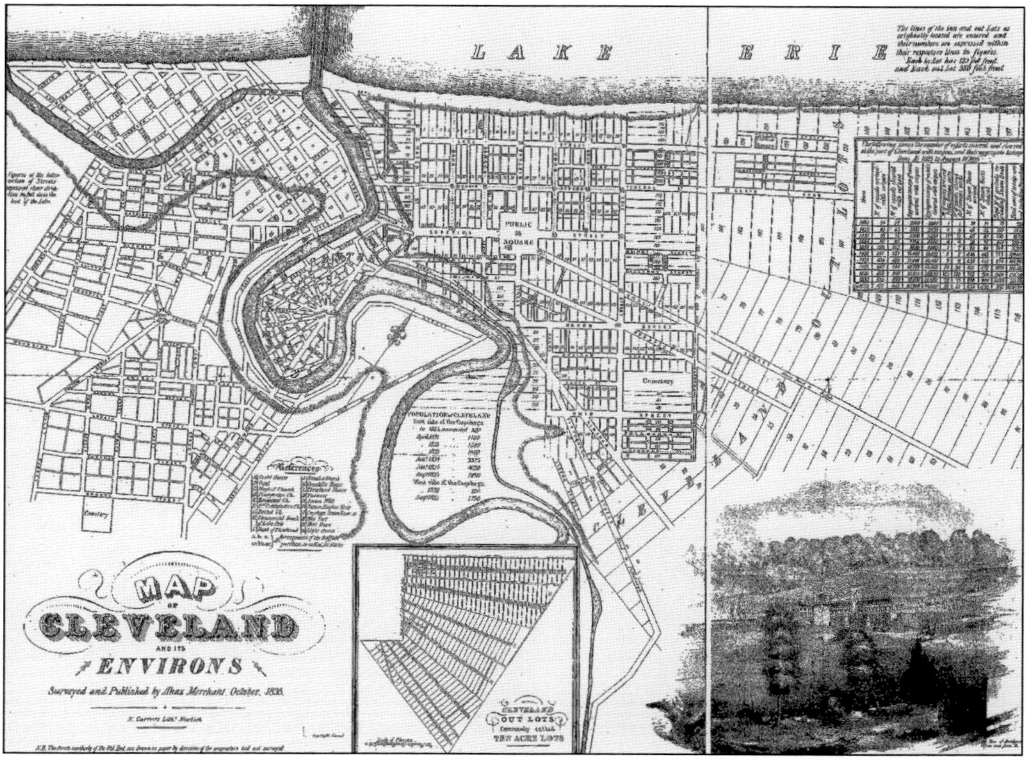

Ahaz Merchant (1794–1862) was a self-taught surveyor, builder, civil engineer, and farmer who did much for the city of Cleveland and for Cuyahoga County. Merchant surveyed most of the city's existing streets and, in 1835, published "Map of Cleveland and Its Environs," which depicted the city's entire street plan. He built several new roads (including Prospect Avenue), constructed the first horse-drawn railroad in the county, and built a fashionable five-story hotel. (CPLPC.)

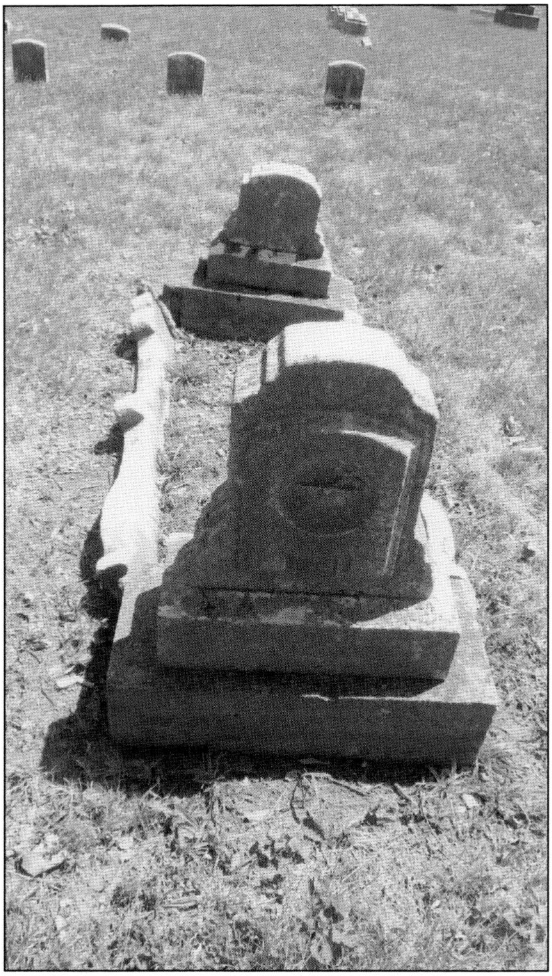

Howard Daniels was a well-known landscape architect from New York who, during the course of his career, designed six cemeteries in New York and Ohio. Among these was Woodland, 20 of whose 60 acres he laid out, in 1852, into a fashionable rural cemetery (which he called a "peculiarly American institution"). He died at the age of 41 while working in Baltimore, Maryland, and is buried at Greenlawn Cemetery in Columbus, Ohio, which he also designed. (Chuck L. Miller.)

This 1874 map of Woodland Cemetery illustrates that many of the surrounding landowners, such as Haltnorth, Foljambe, Ruffini, Haskins, Whitehead, Whipple, and Willcutt, chose Woodland as their final resting place. Note that East 66th Street was originally named Cemetery Street, while East 71st Street was named Giddings Avenue. (Ohio Historical Society.)

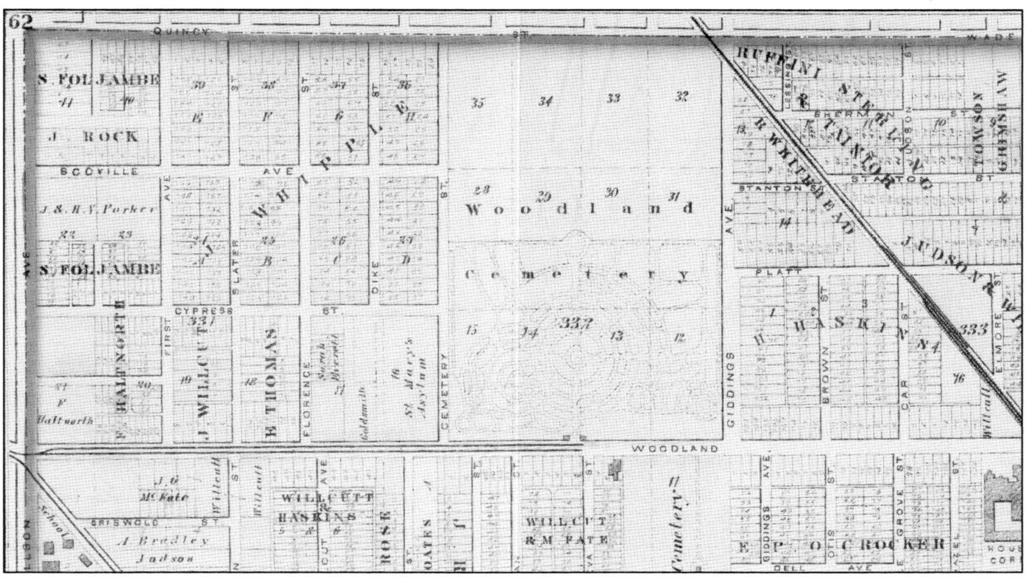

At the May 1866 council proceedings with the Committee on Parks and Public Grounds, it was authorized and adopted to procure plans and designs for the erection of a pavilion at the centre of Woodland Cemetery. Said structure was not to cost more than $2,000 when completed, but in the annual report of 1867, expenditures totaled $3,915.72. By 1869, it was suggested that a chapel be erected as an addition to the pavilion. (Ohio Historical Society/Louis Baus Collection.)

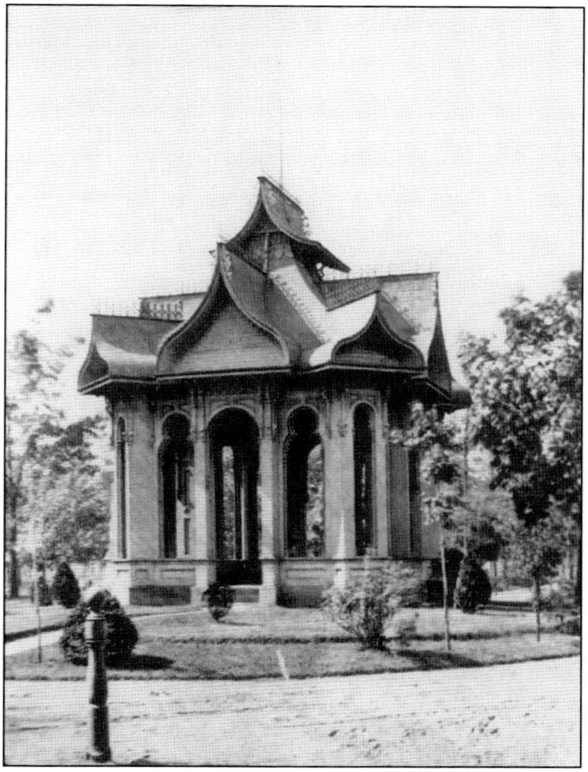

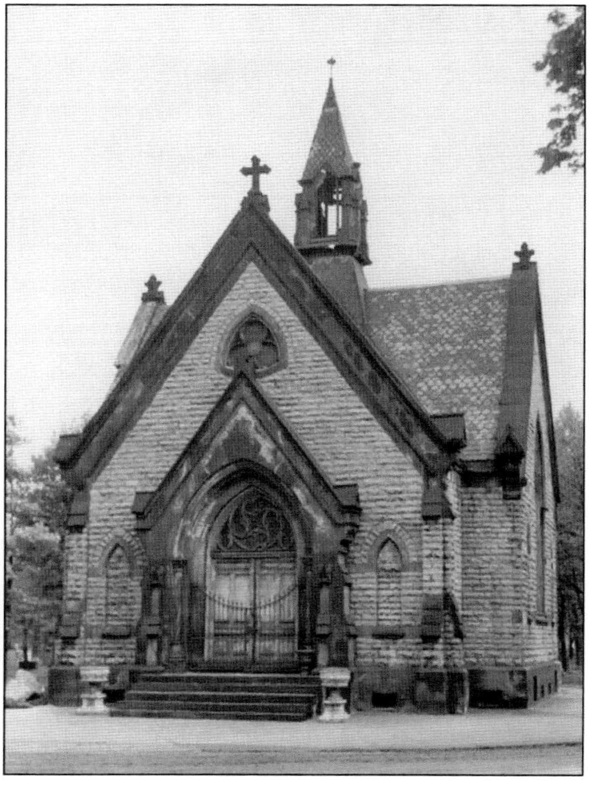

In the summer of 1881, a chapel and receiving vault—purely Gothic in design, with a 24-foot-tall spire over an arched 54-foot roof and featuring a profusion of color from the finest stained glass—was dedicated for services and funeral rites. The remains rested on a raised platform, which, following a funeral or other service, was lowered into a vault via an elevator. (CSUSC.)

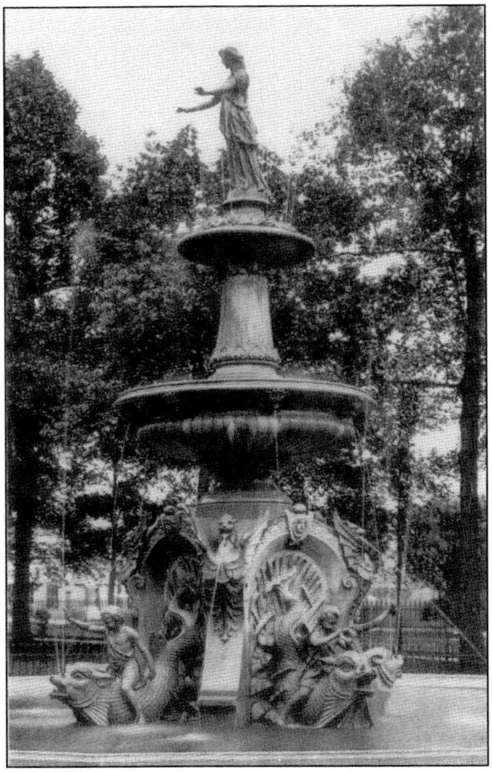

In June 1869, the cemetery trustees heard requests for one or two fountains and a pond on the grounds. It was not until 1886 that they began a search for the design of two fountains. George Rackle, a German sculptor educated at the Royal Academy, and owner of Rackle Artstone in Cleveland, was one of many to submit bids. By the fall of 1887, the two ornate and sizable fountains were complete. They were made of precast concrete, and these images are all that remain. (CSUSC.)

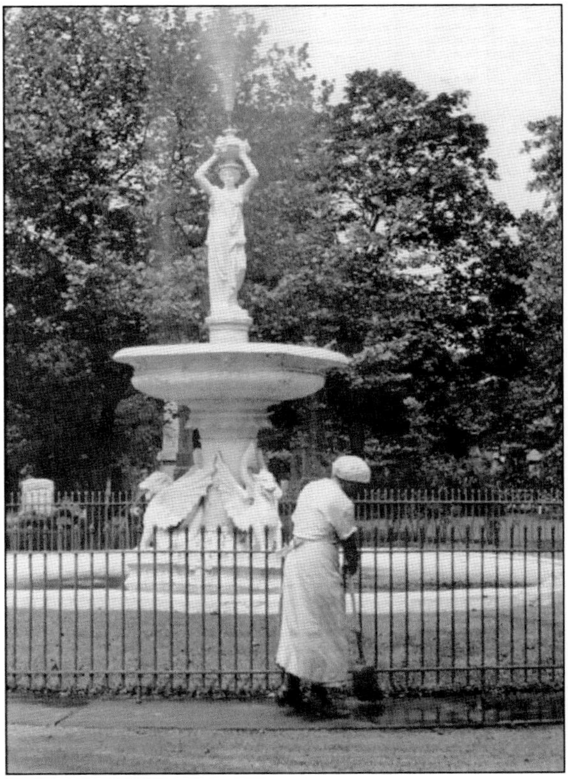

Two

Resident Diversity

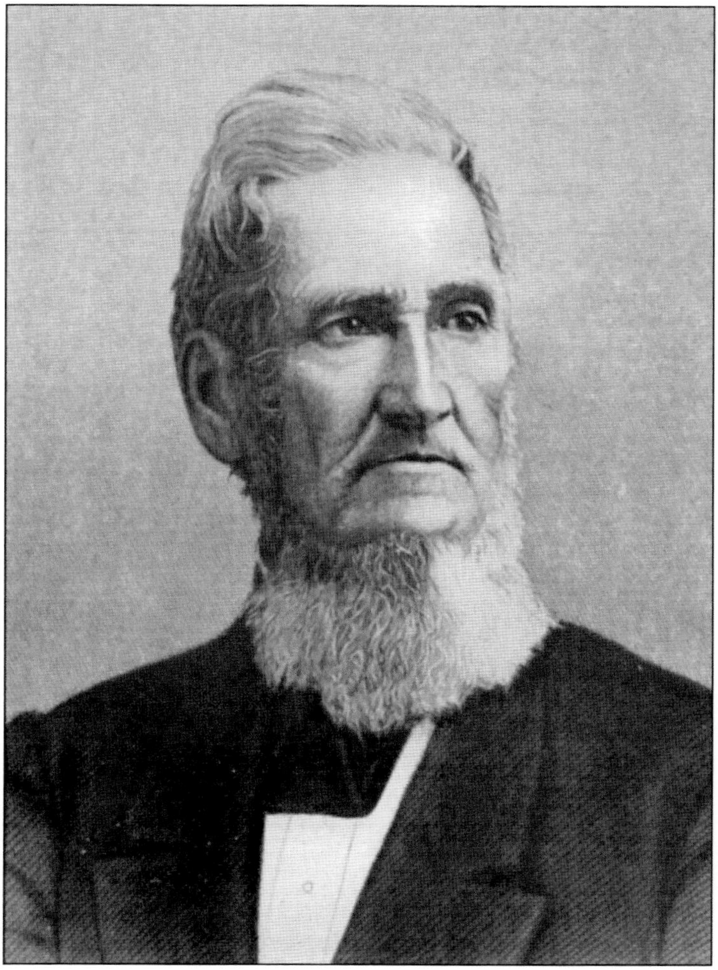

Gov. Reuben Wood, Ohio's 21st governor, came to Cleveland to practice law in 1818 and remained a leader in Ohio law and politics until his death in 1864. Wood served in the senate from 1825 to 1830 and sat on the Ohio Supreme Court as a judge from 1833 to 1847. A Democrat, he was Ohio's governor from 1850 to 1853, which was a crucial time in Ohio's history as a new constitution had just been approved. (CPLPC.)

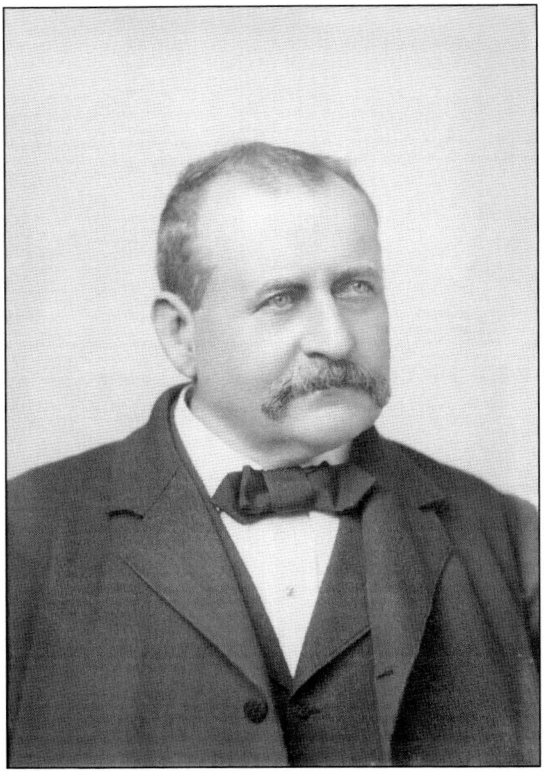

Robert Blee (1839–1898), said to be a "kind and simple man," rose to be superintendent of the Columbus & Cincinnati Railroad (the "Bee Line") in 1888, after 38 years as a brakeman and conductor. Blee was Cleveland's police commissioner from 1875 to 1879 and mayor from 1893 to 1895. During his term he supported harbor improvements and the building of docks to maintain the city's position as a Great Lakes port. He never married. (CPLPC.)

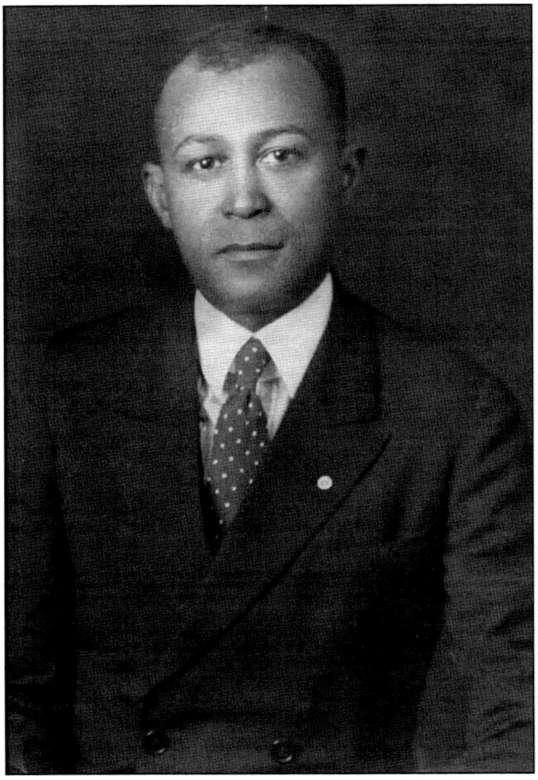

William Napoleon Alexander (1887–1945) was a Pullman porter for over 20 years. He worked 400 hours a month, traveling extensively throughout America, and took much pride in being a respected servant to passengers with a myriad of needs. Per family lore, he told his family not to spend money on a headstone, which he felt would be a waste of money. (Frances Kelley.)

William Clifford (1862–1929), a native Clevelander, was a black Republican politician admired for speaking his mind. An Ohio legislator, elected twice to the Ohio House, he played an important role in electing Marcus A. Hanna to the US Senate in 1898 by casting the deciding vote. He served in the auditor's office of the War Department in Washington, DC, where he lived with his wife, Carrie, and their two sons. (Rosemary Clifford McDaniel.)

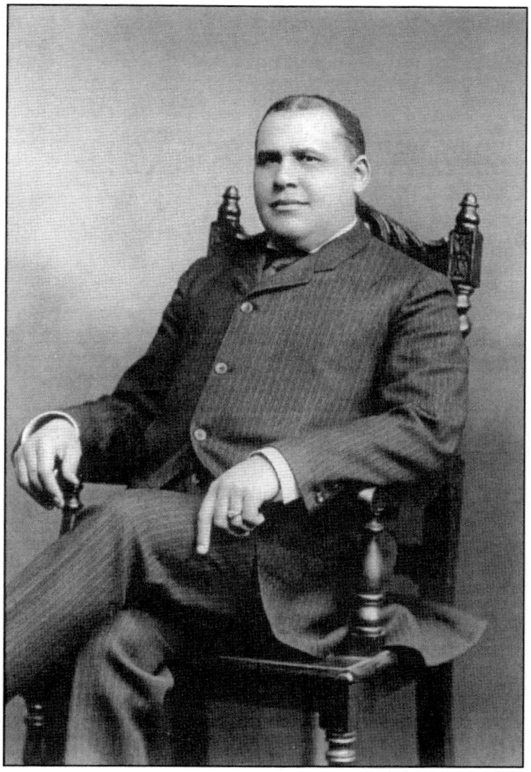

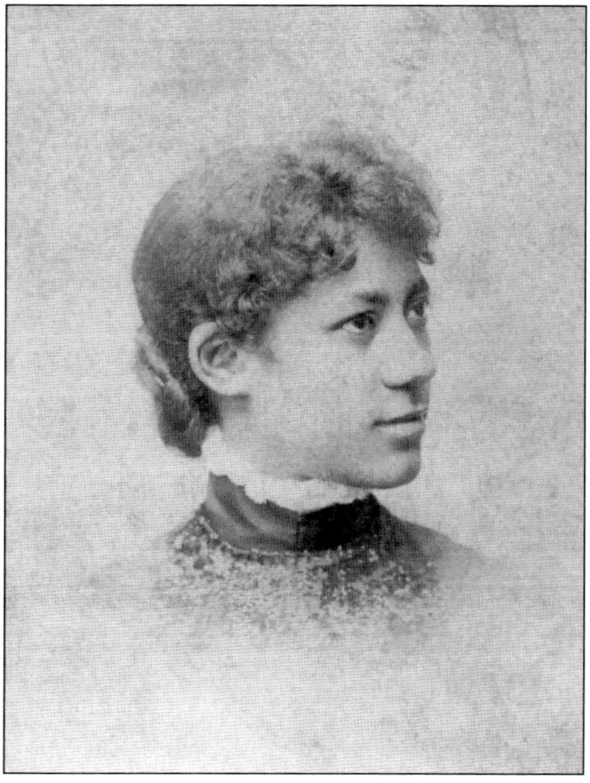

Carrie Clifford (1862–1934) was a teacher before her marriage to William Clifford. Carrie then poured her energy, organizational skills, and writing abilities into women's and civil rights. Her essay, "Cleveland and its Colored People," was published in *Colored American* in July 1905. Carrie was admired as a woman who worked ceaselessly for the rights of all black people, even recruiting members for the Niagara Movement (a predecessor to the NAACP). (Rosemary Clifford McDaniel.)

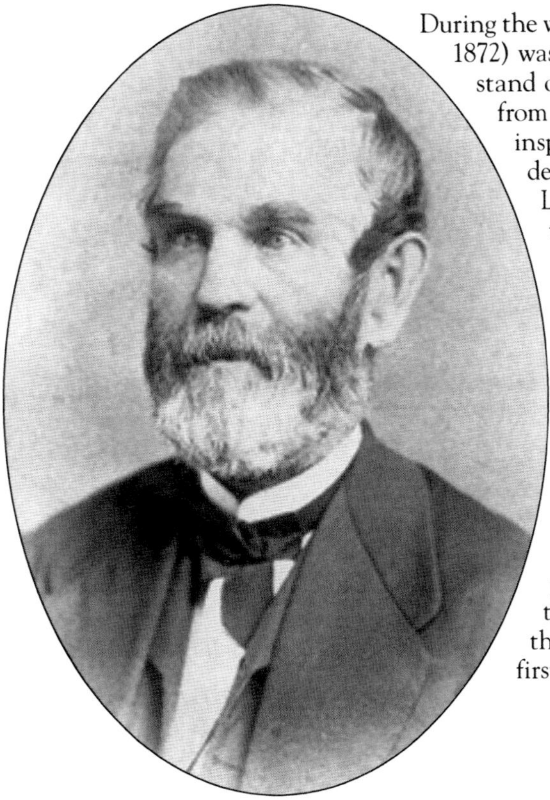

During the winter of 1862–1863, Joseph W. Briggs (1813–1872) was dismayed to see how many women had to stand out in the cold for hours to pick up letters from their loved ones away at war. Thus, he was inspired to initiate and organize the free home delivery system. On March 5, 1863, President Lincoln signed a bill to become effective that July, authorizing free mail delivery. In 1864, Briggs was appointed special agent to implement the new system and was later promoted to national superintendent. He was given the responsibility of organizing the free mail delivery in 52 cities in the United States. This was a huge undertaking, as city sidewalks had to be paved, the streets had to be lit, the houses had to be numbered, and street names had to be placed at intersections. Briggs traveled around the country for the next 10 years indoctrinating postmasters in his system. He also designed the first letter mailbox and helped to design the first mailman's uniform. He was America's first letter carrier. (CPLPC.)

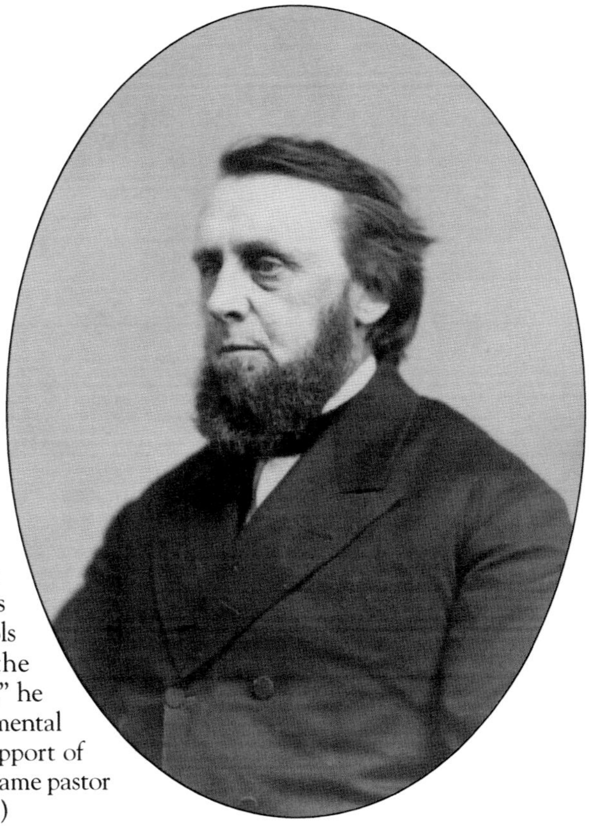

Anson Smyth (1812–1887), a Presbyterian minister, became interested in the public school system while affiliated with a church in Toledo. He worked with other professional educators to reconstruct Ohio's public schools and served as superintendent of Cleveland Public Schools from 1863 to 1866. Remembered as the "Father of the Cleveland Public Library," he is credited with its creation and was instrumental in getting legislature to authorize the support of libraries through taxation. In 1872, he became pastor at North Presbyterian Church. (CPLPC.)

German-born Adam Beilstein (1828–1896) arrived in Cleveland in 1849, where he established a successful tailoring business at 350 Central Avenue. He married Julia Rauch in 1850; they had four sons (one of whom died young) and a daughter, Elizabeth. Sons Julius and John became tailors while their brother Louis became involved with the Detroit Steel Railway Company. Elizabeth worked as a dressmaker before marrying Martin Eitel. Family members are buried in the Beilstein mausoleum. (Richard Eitel.)

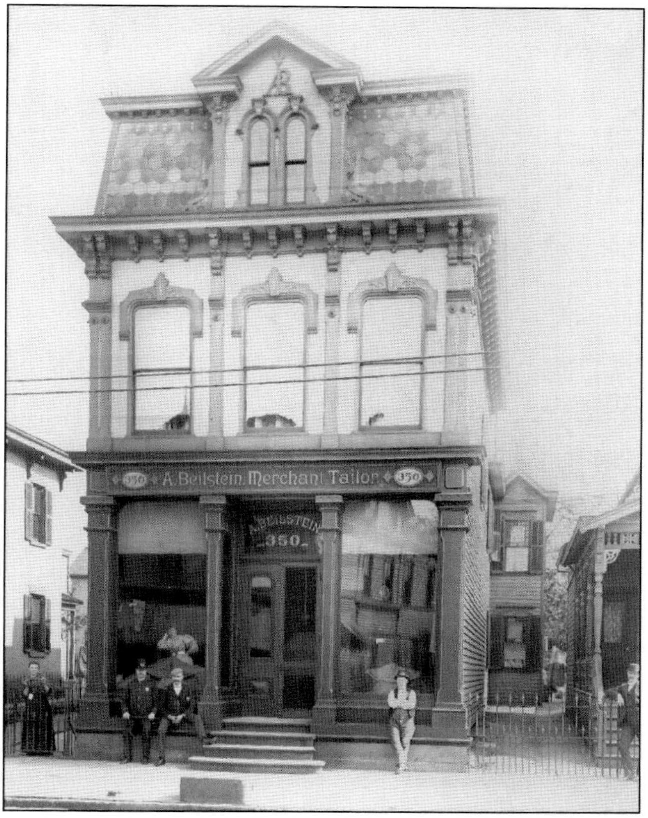

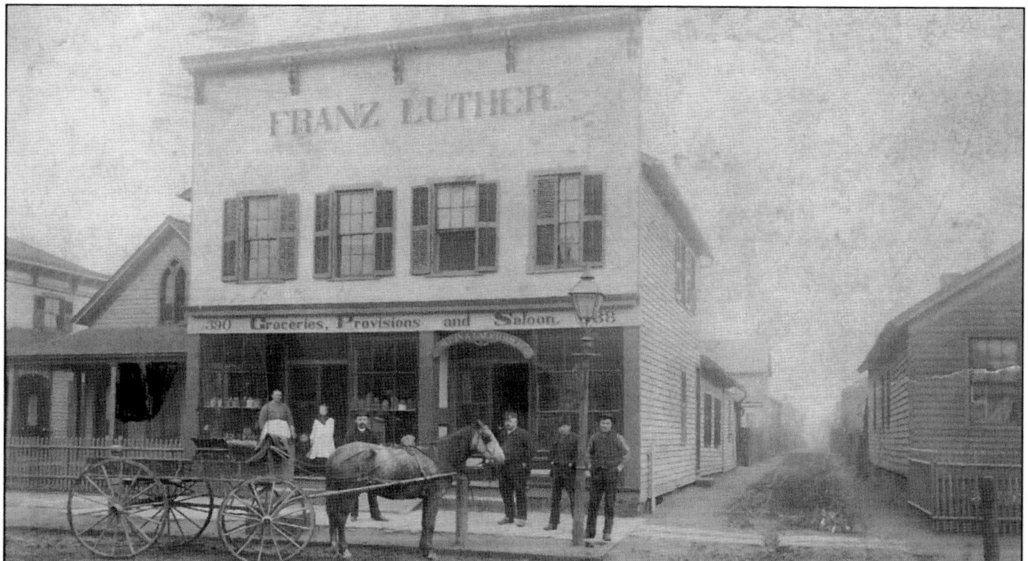

Franz Luther, born in Germany in 1831, arrived in New York in 1867. He traveled to Cleveland in 1870 and married Magdalena Boesel, also originally of Germany. Together they reared seven children at their home at 362 Orange Avenue. During the 1880s, they owned and operated a grocery with provisions and a saloon. The general store was located on Orange Avenue, near the current site of the federal post office. (Bill Luther.)

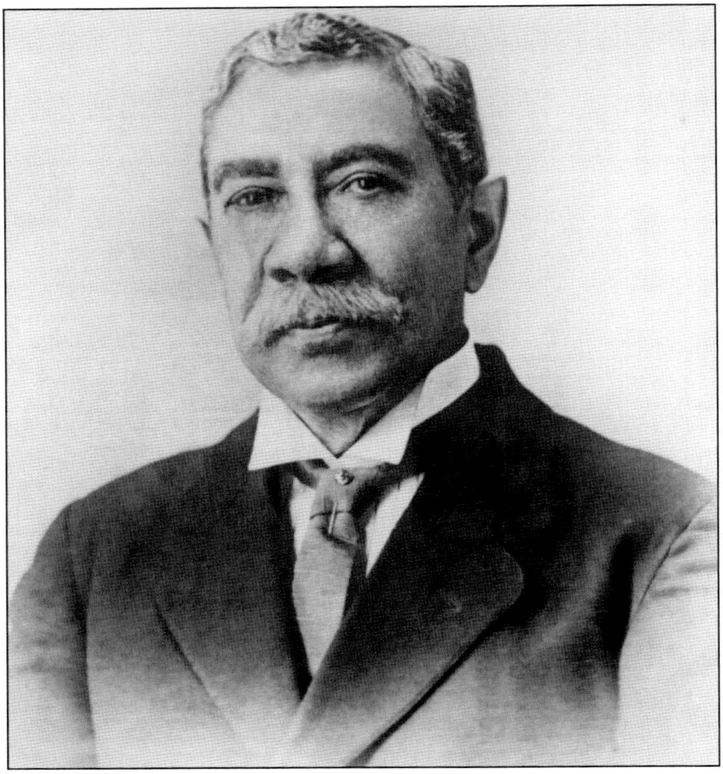

John Patterson Green (1845–1940) is known as the "Father of Labor Day" because of legislation he proposed in 1890 as an Ohio state legislator. He married Annie Walker and had four children. He was a lawyer and a Republican politician who, in 1892, became the Ohio senate's first black member. He was the US postage stamp agent from 1897 to 1905 and compiled stories of his life. John died from injuries sustained in a car crash on the eve of Labor Day. (CPLPC.)

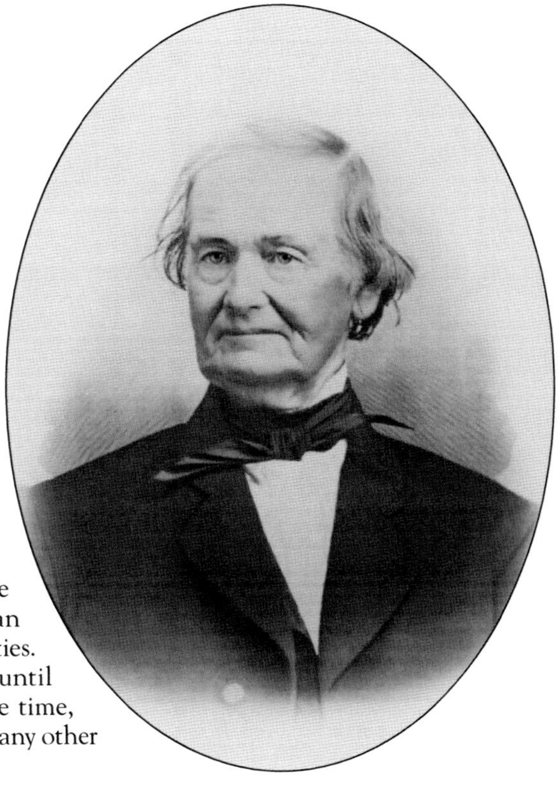

Levi Johnson (1786–1871) began his legacy in Cleveland in 1806 by building houses and barns for new settlers in Cleveland and Newburgh. He went on to build ships (including a steamship), the first courthouse and jail, the first stone lighthouse, and an inn; by 1838, he was the owner of 96 properties. His stone house, where he chose to live until his death in 1871, stood until 1909. At the time, Johnson had lived in Cleveland longer than any other person. (CPLPC.)

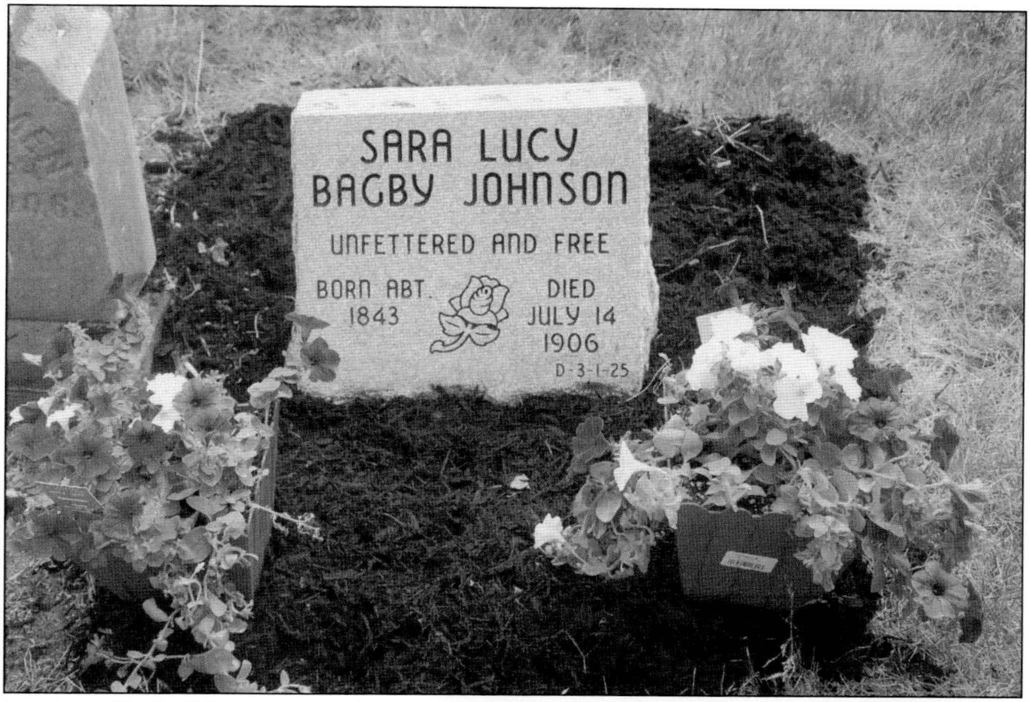

Sara Lucy Bagby Johnson was the last slave to be prosecuted under the Fugitive Slave Act of 1850. Lucy, who had escaped from Wheeling, Virginia, in October 1860 to become free, was returned to her owner, William Goshorn, in January 1861. Goshorn tested Cleveland to see if they would enforce the federal law, even though it was much discouraged. When Lucy was legally freed in 1863, she returned to Cleveland, where she married. (MAD.)

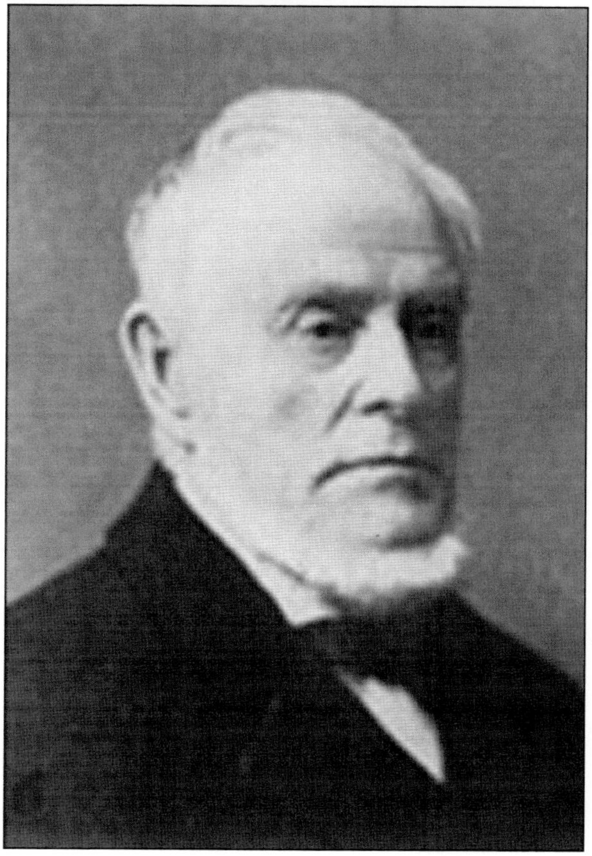

Seth Alden Abbey (1798–1880) moved from New York to Cleveland in 1830, where he operated a tavern. By 1836, he was involved with incorporating the City of Cleveland. He joined the Civil War at the age of 63 as a first lieutenant in the 2nd Ohio Cavalry and served for the duration; he was also a city marshal and a judge of police court. He married twice and had nine children. (Christopher Mentrum.)

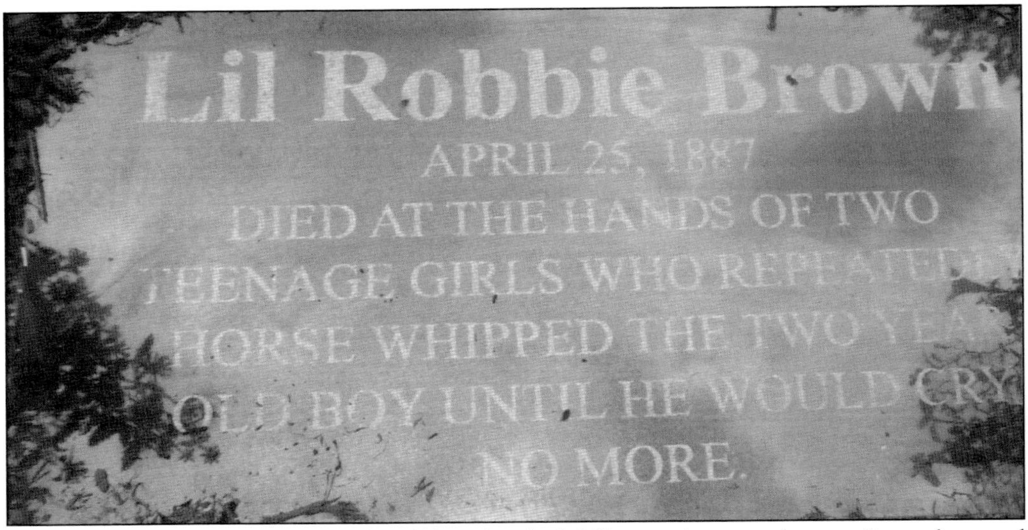

Robbie Brown was a two-year-old toddler who died following beatings by two "impudent and uncontrollable girls" in his foster mother's home. Neighbors heard the beatings and Robbie asking for food; he weighed only 18 pounds when he died. Both girls were sentenced to the state penitentiary in Columbus for 10 years. In 2011, this memorial and epitaph were donated by Edward Kotecki III in remembrance of this innocent child. (Marian Pledger.)

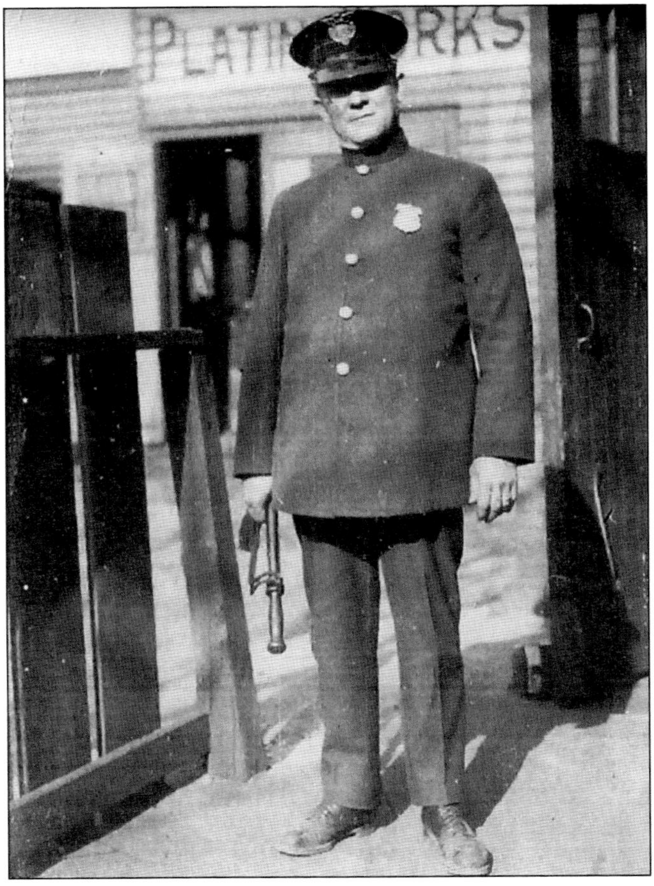

Otto Ziska (1883–1940) joined the Cleveland Police Department in 1918. On May 15, 1929, his 5th Emergency Squad responded to the Cleveland Clinic following a huge explosion with numerous dead and injured. He repeatedly entered the burning building through the thick, heavy smoke and gases to rescue those who were trapped. This heroic action led to severe medical problems for Ziska, as he had inhaled large amounts of poisonous gases emitted from burning x-ray films. (Otto Ziska.)

John Brough (1811–1865) was a journalist, newspaper publisher, and railroad president. He served as a member of the Ohio House of Representatives from 1838 to 1839, state auditor from 1838 to 1845, and as the 26th governor of Ohio. He would have run for reelection in 1865, but he developed gangrene after suffering a bad fall. He died before his term was completed, having given "full efforts to serving his state." (CPLPC.)

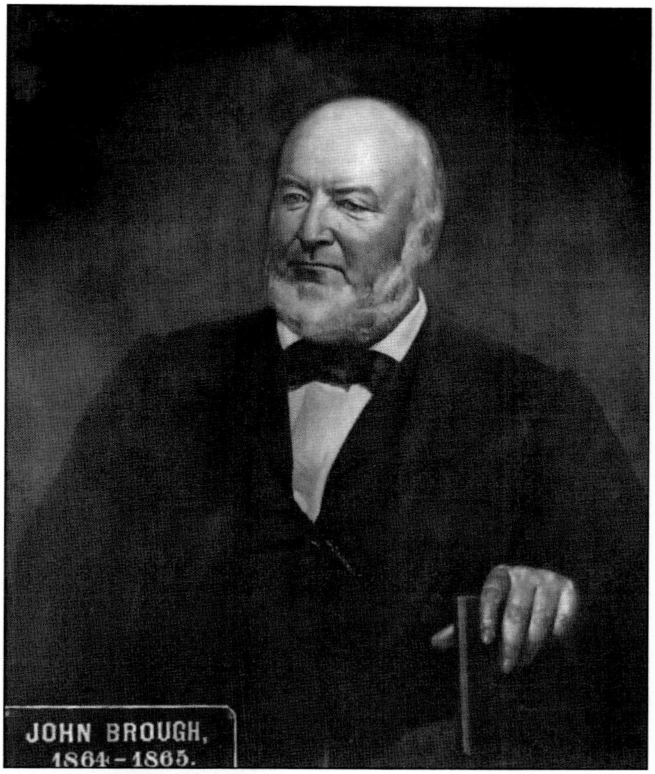

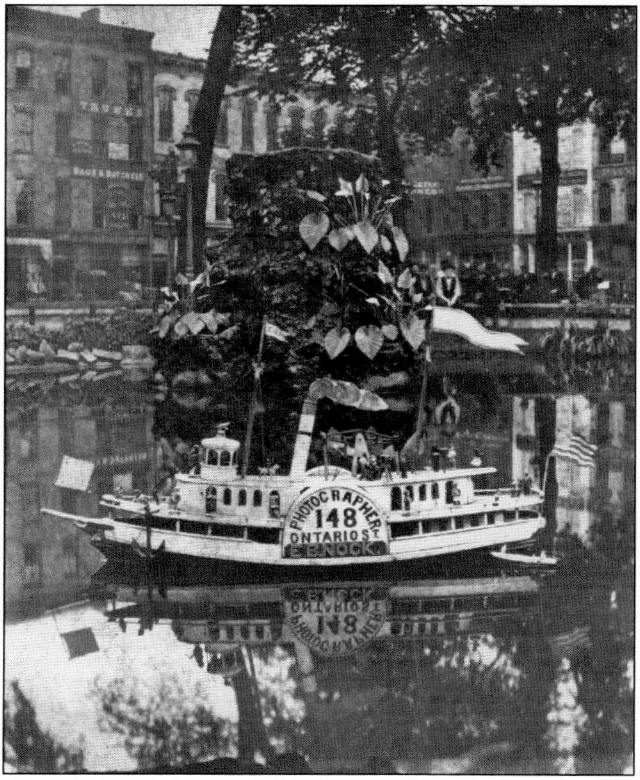

Edward B. Nock, a Cleveland photographer from 1865–1900, convinced the city to allow him to float a three-foot paddle-wheel riverboat model in a pond in Public Square, which was built in the 1870s. An advertisement for his business was prominently displayed on the paddle wheel, which moved in a circle near a waterfall. Moving figurines, including a photographer taking pictures while the captain performed a wedding, were visible on the boat. It was eventually given to the Western Reserve Historical Society. (Shovlin family collection.)

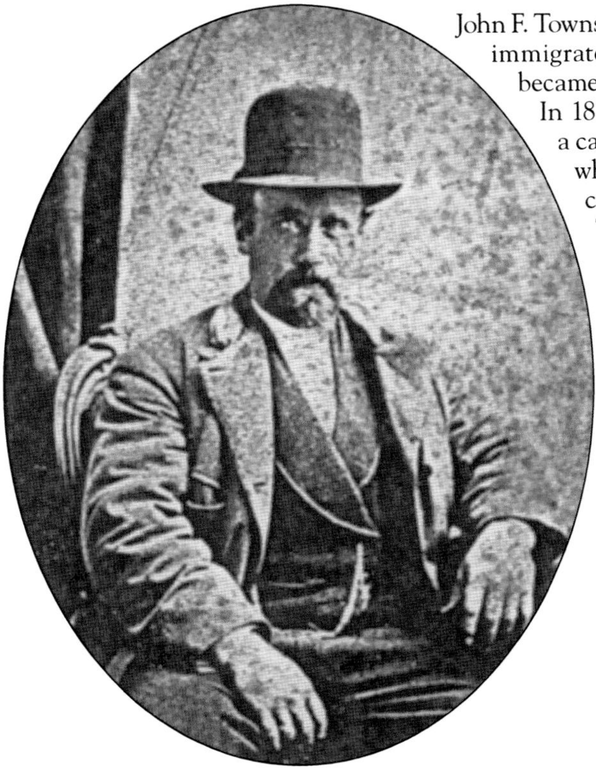

John F. Townsend, a seaman born about 1840 in Wales, immigrated to the Cleveland area in 1868. He became part owner of a scow schooner, *Saginaw.* In 1875, he was returning to Cleveland with a cargo of sulfur for the infant steel industry when a sudden gale caused the schooner to crash against the wharf near Ashtabula. Townsend got his crew to shore safely, but he had breathed in the poisonous sulfur; he died in 1876 from the damage to his lungs. (Mary Ellen Chambers.)

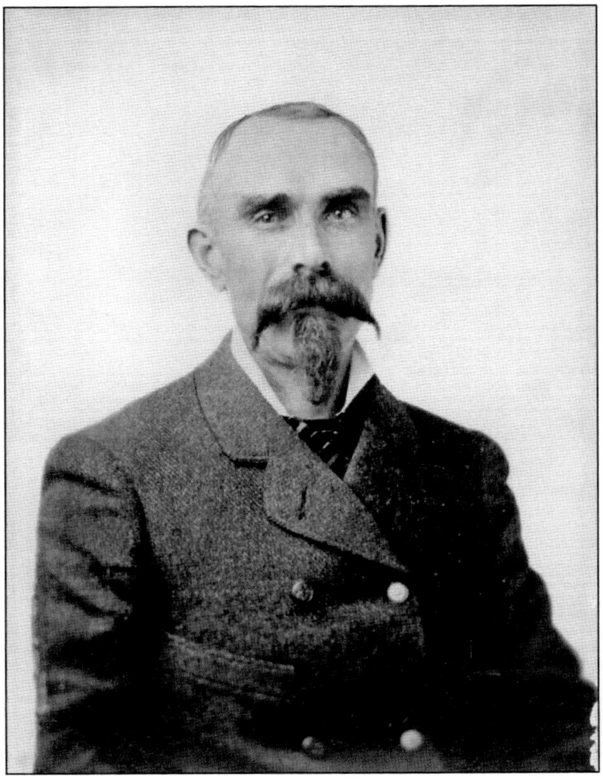

John James Kneale was born in Cleveland in 1846 to parents from the Isle of Man. John, his father, and his grandfather were all carpenters. After joining Company A, 66th Regiment of the Ohio Voluntary Infantry, Kneale fought at Atlanta and Savannah, Georgia. He had three sons, only one of whom survived to adulthood. Kneale spent his final years in the Ohio Soldiers' and Sailors' Home in Sandusky. He died in 1910 while on furlough at his brother's house in Cleveland. (Jennette White.)

Thomas Quayle became a noted pioneer shipbuilder of the Great Lakes, after arriving in Cleveland from the Isle of Man in 1827. Quayle married twice and had eight children survive to adulthood. Three of his sons were active in Thos. Quayle & Sons, which built some of the largest wooden ships on the lakes. Thomas, an initial member of the Mona's Relief Society, served two terms as its president. (CPLPC.)

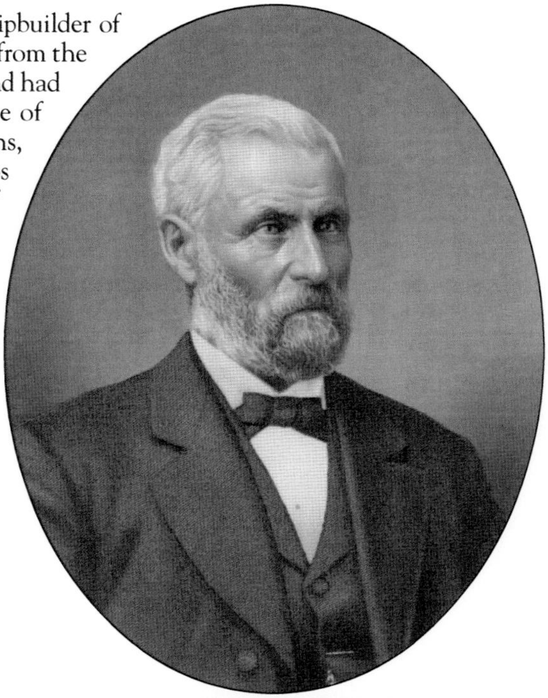

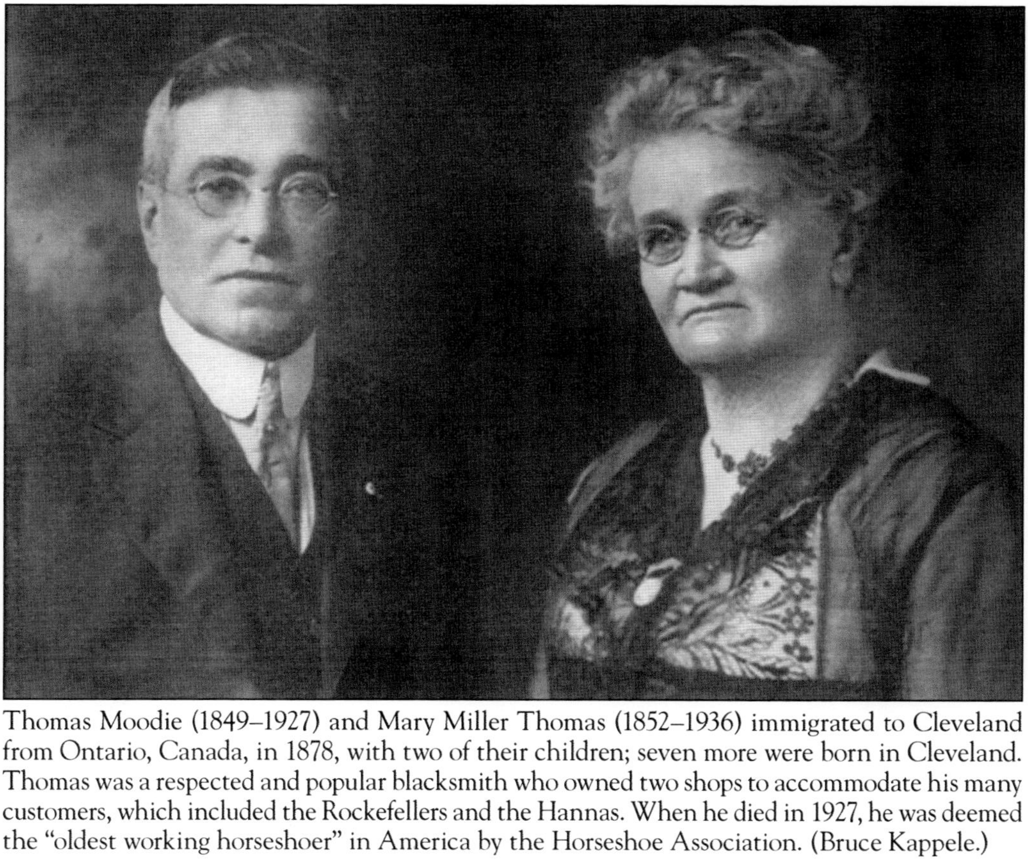

Thomas Moodie (1849–1927) and Mary Miller Thomas (1852–1936) immigrated to Cleveland from Ontario, Canada, in 1878, with two of their children; seven more were born in Cleveland. Thomas was a respected and popular blacksmith who owned two shops to accommodate his many customers, which included the Rockefellers and the Hannas. When he died in 1927, he was deemed the "oldest working horseshoer" in America by the Horseshoe Association. (Bruce Kappele.)

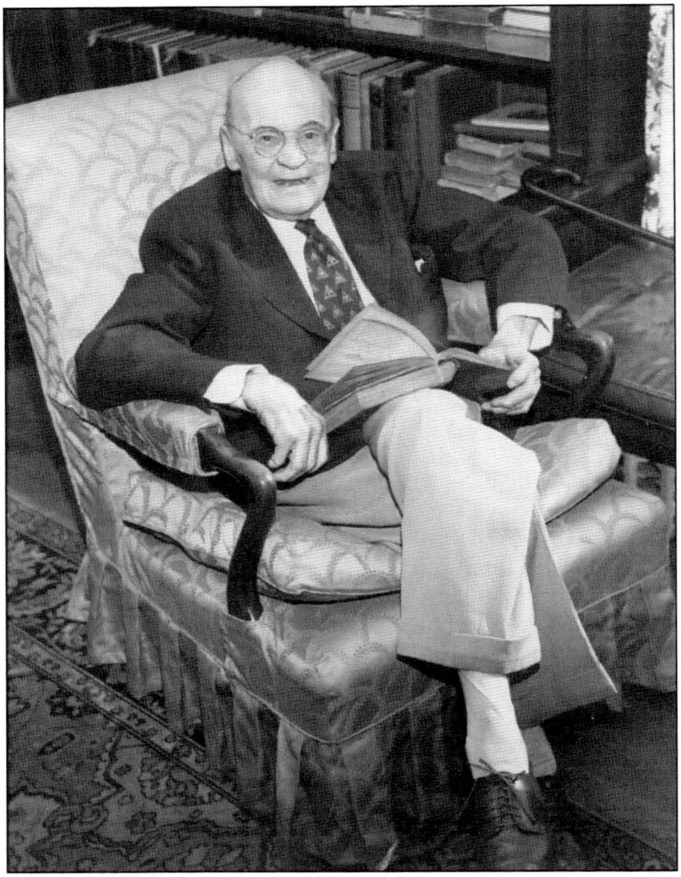

J. Milton Dyer (1870–1957) was a prominent architect who studied in Cleveland and Paris. He excelled in all types of architecture: residential, ecclesiastical, industrial, and public buildings. The majority of his work done between 1900 and 1911 was once featured in a 19-page article in the *Architectural Records*. Among his designs were Brooklyn Savings & Loan, the Tavern Club, Cleveland City Hall, and the US Coast Guard Station on Whiskey Island. (CPLPC.)

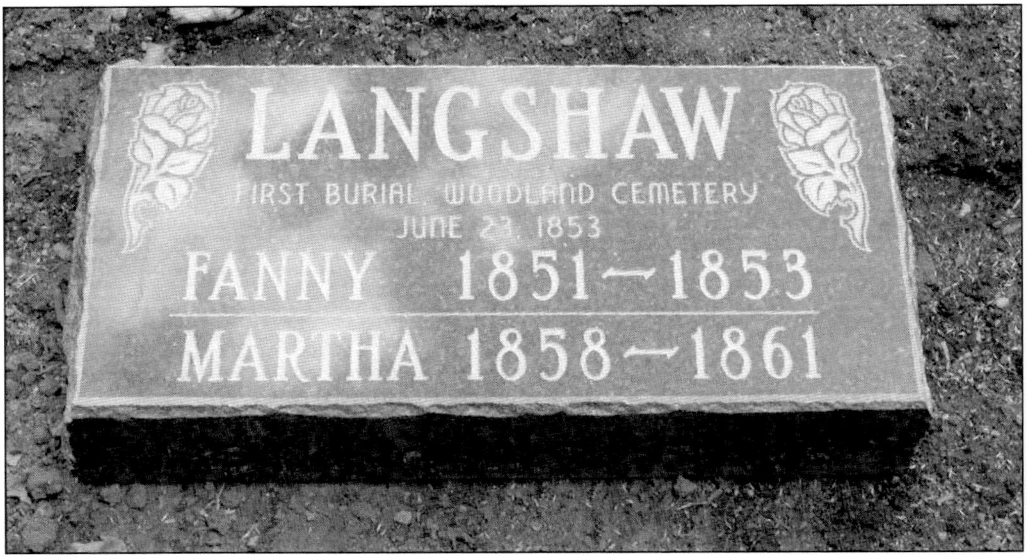

Fifteen-month-old Fanny Langshaw, born with her twin, Stephen, on October 6, 1851, was, sadly, the first person to be buried at Woodland Cemetery following its dedication on June 14, 1853. Her parents, Stephen and Hannah, emigrated from England and had a total of 11 children. Fanny's twin, Stephen, married and left many descendants in the Cleveland area. (MAD.)

Alexander Forbes (1824–1914) became a pioneer contractor and builder in Cleveland. In 1849, at the time of the Gold Rush, he crossed the plains to the Pacific coast where he engaged in mining in Stockton, California. He married Jane Maize in 1852. Forbes built homes and the old Union Depot and, in 1880, he was supervising carpenters on the railroad. He continued his prominence as a building contractor by erecting business blocks in Cleveland. (Beth Forbes Sterosky.)

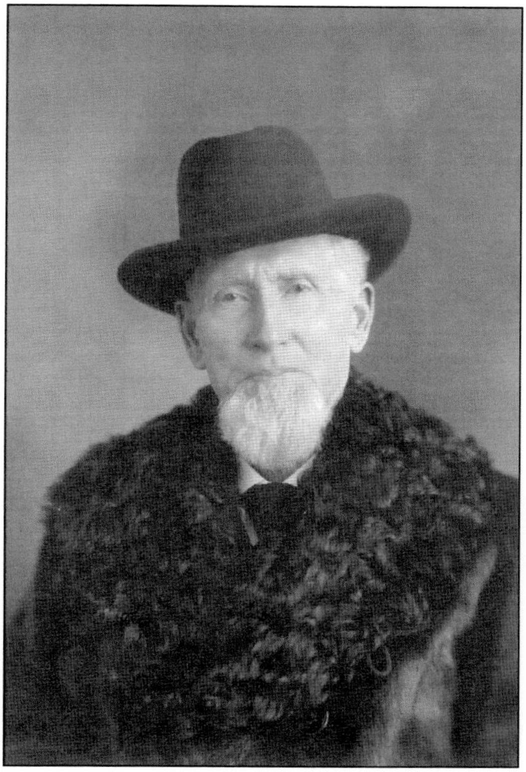

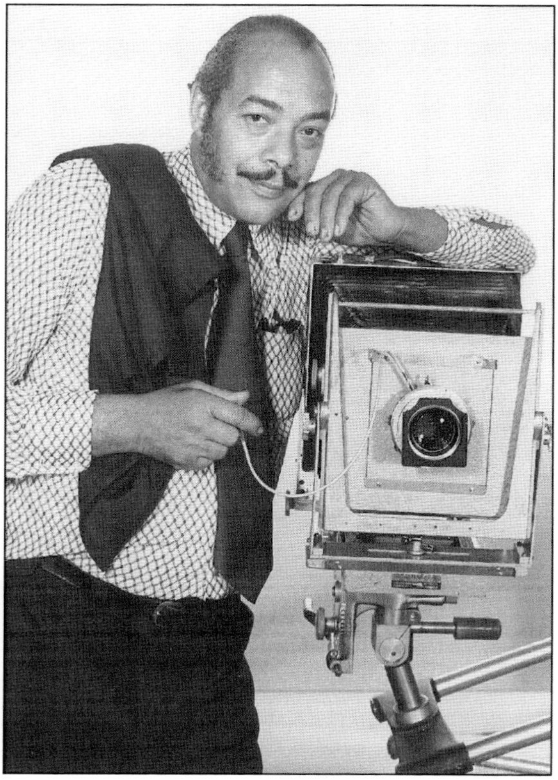

James "Jimmy" Gayle (1920–1991), described as lighthearted and never unhappy, was one of the first successful African American photographers in the field. A musician in the US Navy during World War II, he began his career in photography as a freelancer while working at a studio processing film. *Ebony*, *Jet* and the *Call & Post* newspaper bought his work. In 1967, he was hired at the *Cleveland Plain Dealer*, where he worked for 22 years. (Gina Gayle.)

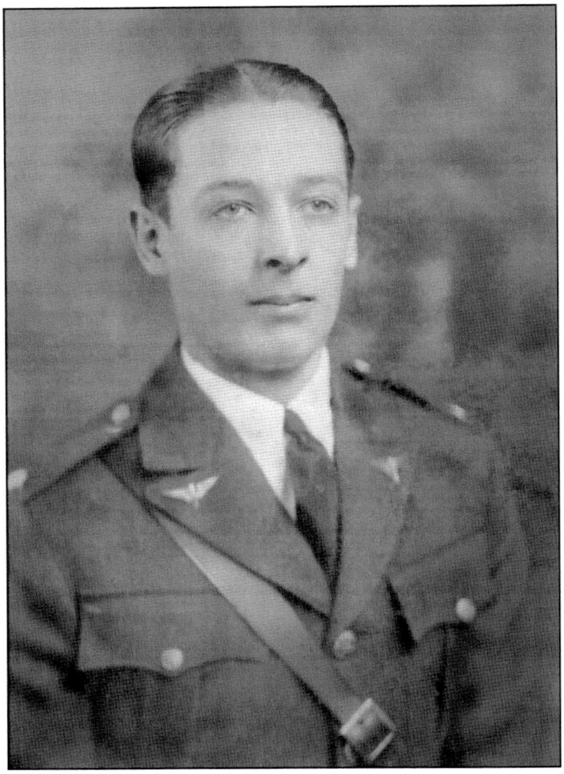

James Douglas Cleveland, a 26-year-old airmail pilot with a passion for flying, crashed his biplane into Nittany Mountain, Pennsylvania, in the early morning of May 24, 1931. The Cleveland to New York mail-delivery route was one of the most difficult and dangerous because of the Allegheny Mountains and the unpredictable weather. Forty years after the crash, his brother William Bingham Cleveland, MD, memorialized Jamie with a granite obelisk at the site of the crash, where there is also a pile of stones topped with plane remnants. A trail to the site was forged by local Boy Scouts and can still be hiked. (Katherine and William Cleveland.)

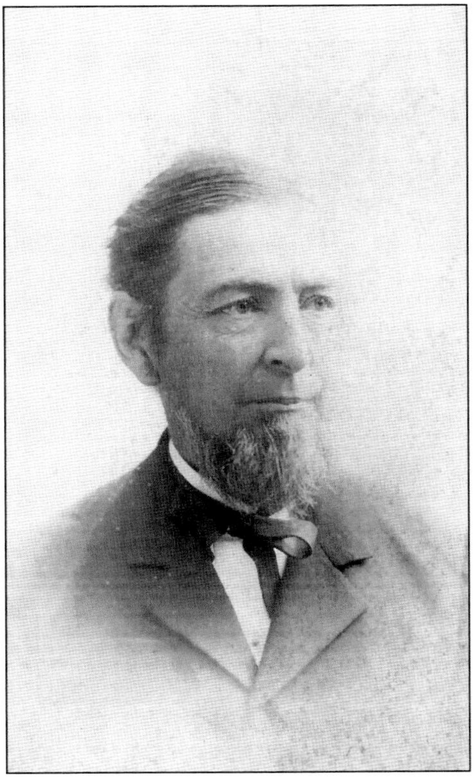

Judge James Douglas Cleveland (1822–1899) was admitted to the bar in 1843 and served as justice of the peace, city clerk, and a member of the Board of School Managers. Cleveland was a clerk of the Court of Common Pleas, an editor for the *Plain Dealer*, a deputy clerk of the US District Court and a police court judge. He was a member of the Corporation of the Case School of Applied Science, serving as president of its board of trustees for 10 years. His article "The City of Cleveland Sixty Years Ago," published in the *Cleveland Leader* and in the *Annals of the Early Settlers Association*, recounts his observations in 1835 when he arrived in Cleveland with his family. His wife was Charlotte Jane Bingham, daughter of Charlotte Mellen Kent and the Honorable James Hervey Bingham, statesman and close friend of Daniel Webster. (Katherine and William Cleveland.)

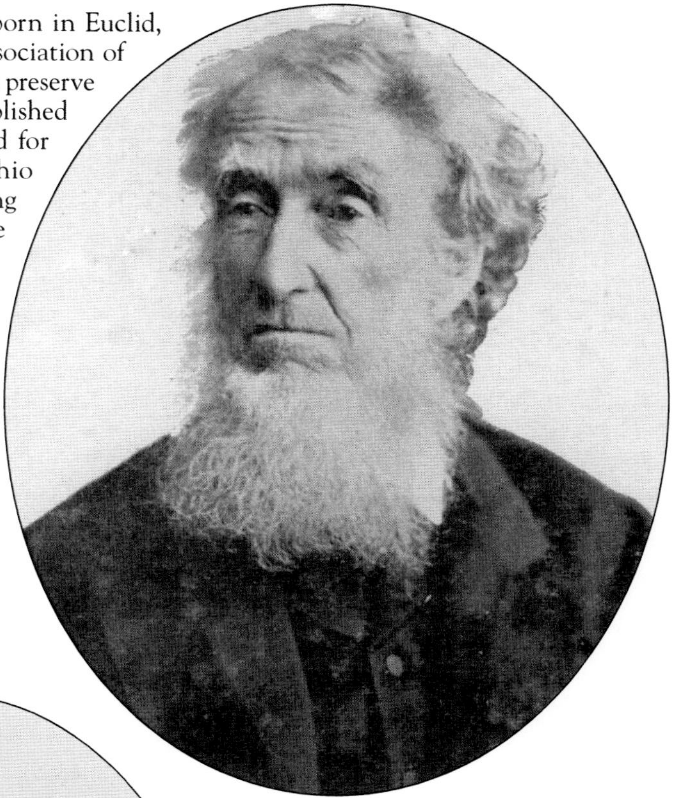

Hiram Addison (1818–1898), born in Euclid, founded The Early Settlers Association of the Western Reserve in 1879 to preserve historical information; an established 40-year residency was required for membership. He taught in Ohio and Pennsylvania before settling in Warrensville, where he wrote to newspapers regarding abolitionism, social causes, temperance, and the plight of poor, urban children. For the latter, he established the Fresh Air Camp, becoming known as "Father Addison." (CPLPC.)

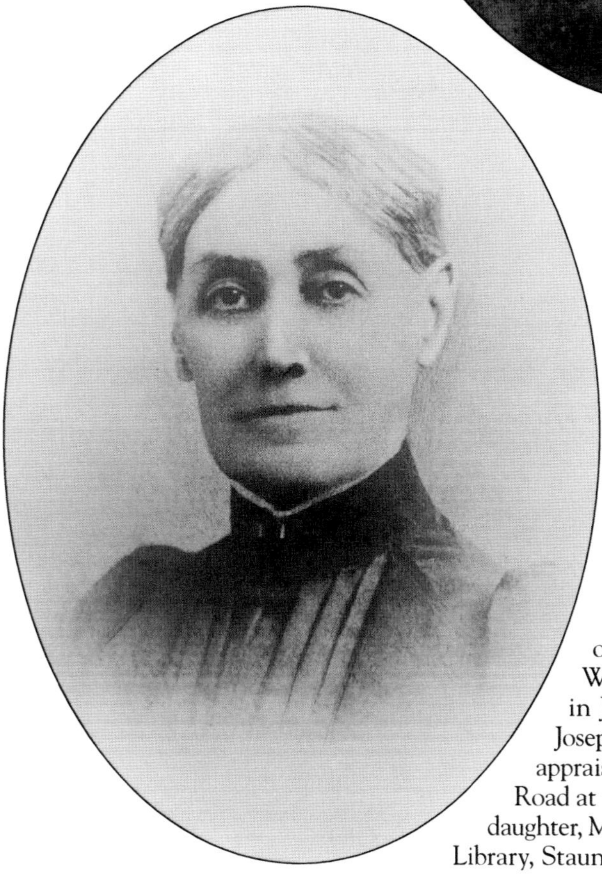

Ann Elizabeth Wilson Begges (1824–1905), known as "Aunt Lizzie" to the 28th president, Thomas Woodrow Wilson (1856–1924), was one of nine siblings of the president's father, Joseph Ruggles Wilson. They were from Steubenville, in Jefferson County. Ann married Adam Joseph Begges from Pennsylvania, who was an appraiser at the customs office located on River Road at the dock. They had a son, Henry, and a daughter, Mary Jane. (Woodrow Wilson Presidential Library, Staunton, Virginia.)

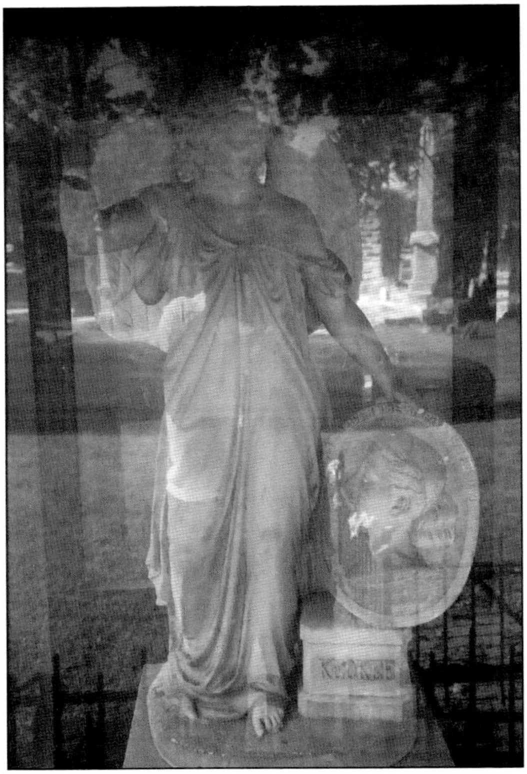

Mary Keokee Monroe (1844–1866), beloved daughter of Nelson and Mary Monroe, was given the Indian name *Keokee*, meaning *idol of their hearts*. She was showered with affection and all the benefits of material wealth, yet she died at age 17 of scarlet fever. This Italian statuary was the first work of art placed in a local cemetery and was encased in glass. The inscription reads, "she blooms in the field of night." (Jennifer Leder.)

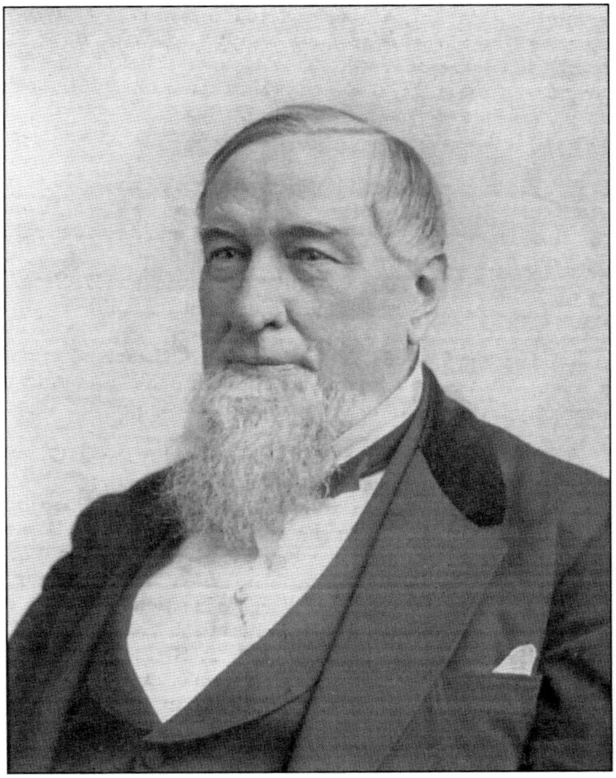

Stoughton Bliss (1823–1896) lived in Cleveland all his life. He was a city marshal, a post office clerk, a partner in a hat and fur business, and he also engaged in the making of malt for several years. He served as a colonel during the Civil War. When he came home, this reserved and honorable businessman bought interest in the Diamond Stone Quarry in Berea, which resulted in his fortune. (CPLPC.)

Johann Heinrich Beck (1856–1924), born in Cleveland and educated in Europe, became a noted conductor, composer, teacher, and violinist. He revered music and loved Beethoven. Beck led local orchestras, directed the Detroit Symphony (1895–1896), wrote an opera, organized the Schubert String Quartet in 1877 and later the Beck String Quartet, which gave frequent concerts during the 1880s. His *Lara* overture was included in a concert given by the Cleveland Orchestra in 1919. As a man, he was known to be genuine, sincere, and faithful. (CPLPC.)

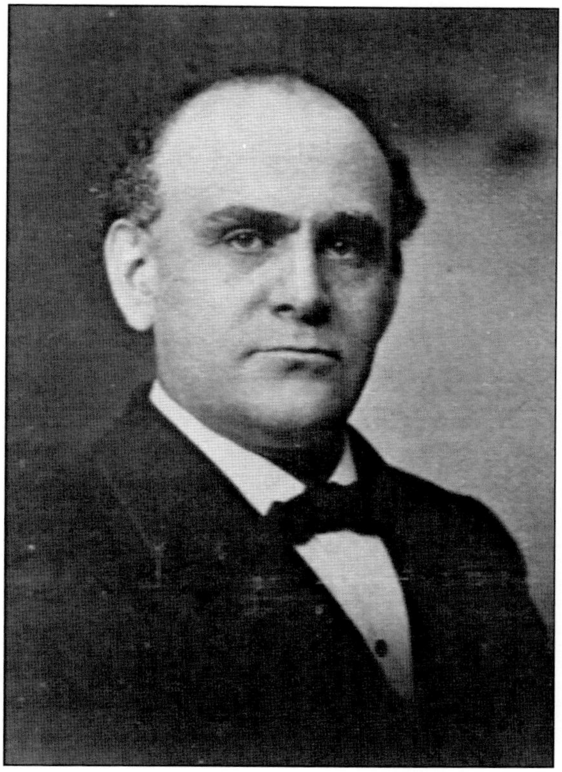

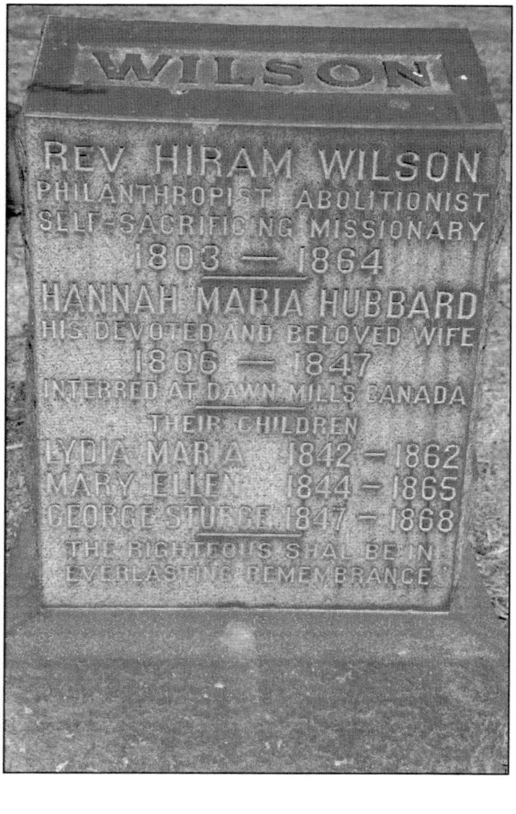

Hiram Wilson (1903–1864), an ardent abolitionist and distinguished minister, received a Theology degree from Oberlin College in 1836. A grant was bestowed upon him to look into the conditions of 20,000 free slaves living in refuge in northern Canada. Wilson established the American Missionary Association night school in St. Catherine's, Ontario, where, in December 1850, 3,000 blacks arrived, fleeing the Fugitive Slave Act. His work with Harriet Tubman is well known. (MAD.)

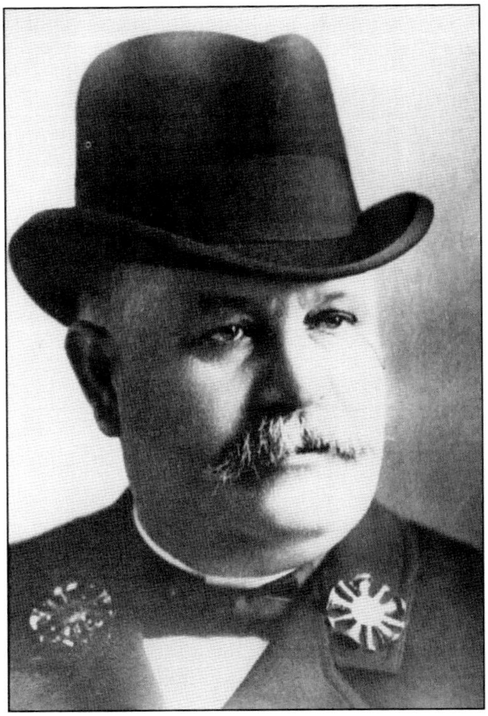

Chief James W. Dickinson (1836–1902), a native of Vermont, became a popular chief of the Cleveland Fire Department following his promotion from first assistant fire chief by the Board of Fire Commissioners on December 22, 1880. He had been very active in the volunteer fire department of Cleveland, first as a torch boy, then rising through the ranks to take command of Cataract Hand Engine No. 5 as foreman. Dickinson joined the paid department in 1863, and in 1864 he became engineer of Engine Company No. 2. He then served during the Civil War as a musician in the famous Leland's Band before returning to Cleveland where he was credited with organizing insurance and pension plans for his firemen and their families. In December 1877, while he was the assistant chief, he married Donna Z. Needham. The couple had two sons. It was noted that when Dickinson retired in 1901, he had completed a half century of service to the Fire Departments of Cleveland. (Western Reserve Fire Museum & Education Center.)

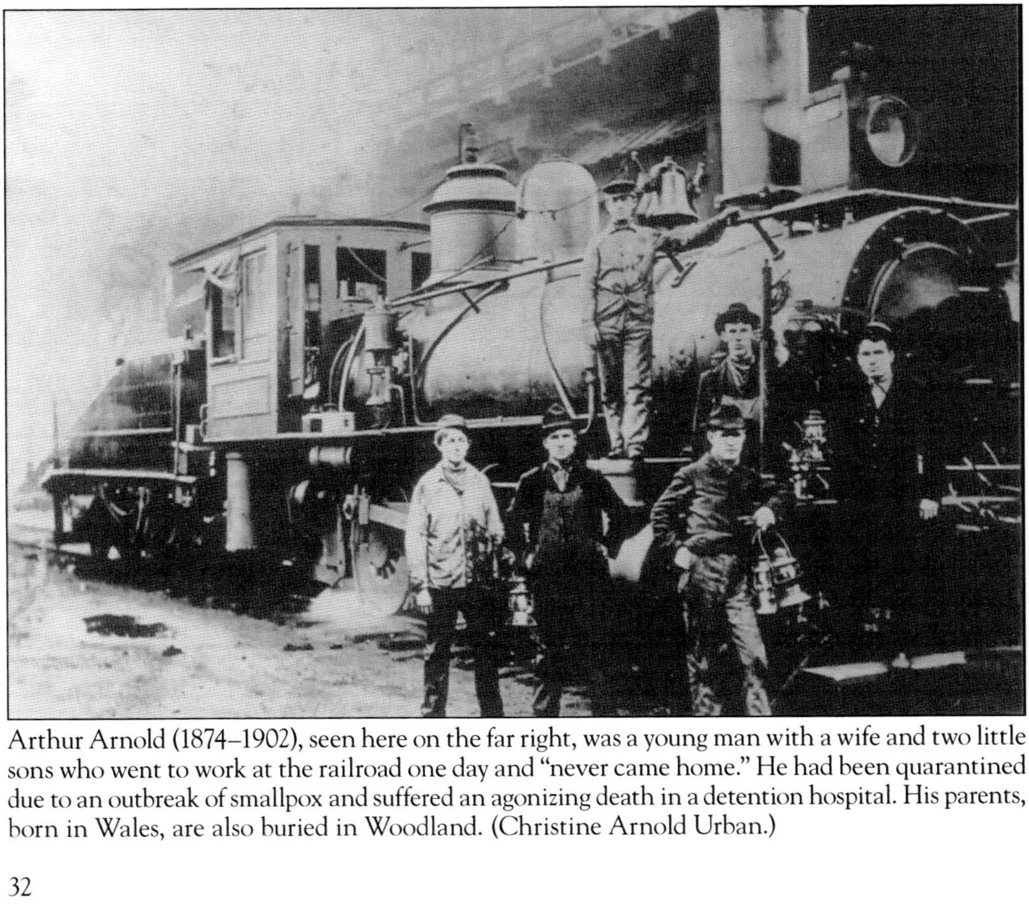

Arthur Arnold (1874–1902), seen here on the far right, was a young man with a wife and two little sons who went to work at the railroad one day and "never came home." He had been quarantined due to an outbreak of smallpox and suffered an agonizing death in a detention hospital. His parents, born in Wales, are also buried in Woodland. (Christine Arnold Urban.)

Margaret Craine Gawne (1827–1910), from the Isle of Man, was remembered as a woman of lovable traits who had enjoyed good health most of her life. Margaret was married to John Gawne, a well-known contractor. They had a total of 14 children, 9 of whom survived her. (Pat Manwell.)

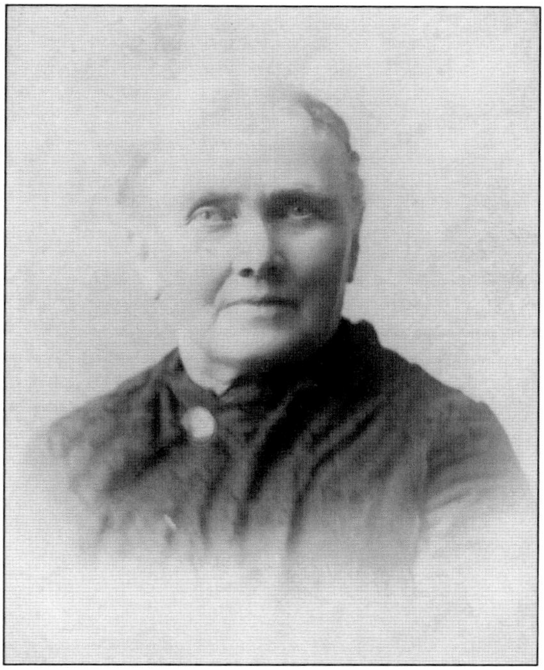

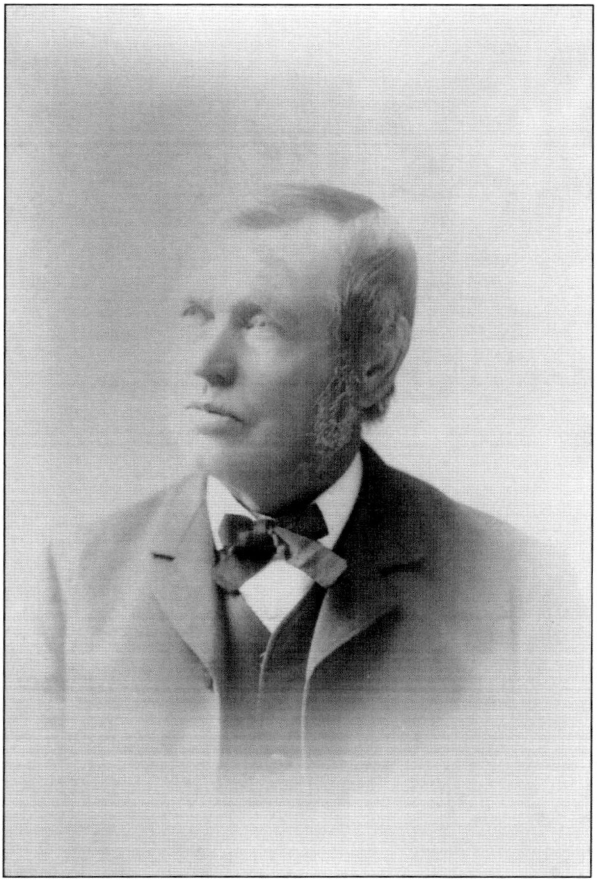

John Thomas Gawne (1847–1906), born in Isle of Man, was well known as a brick mason in several Cleveland construction businesses. The family businesses built the Fairmount Reservoir in Shaker Heights in 1885, as well as the original infirmary on Scranton Road. He was a member of the Elijah Grand Lodge of Perfection (Masons), and he and his family were active in Mona's Relief Society, which offered assistance to fellow immigrants from the Isle of Man. (Pat Manwell.)

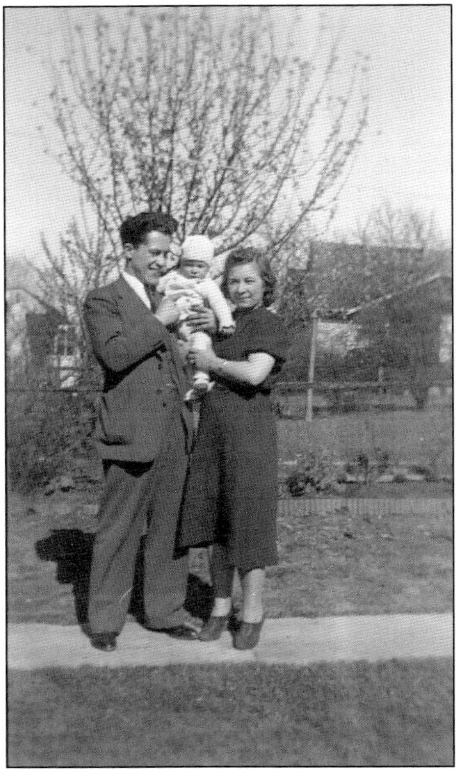

Julius Herman Day Jr. (1912–1943) and Irene Mitro (1911–1978) were married on May 26, 1934, in Cleveland, when Julius was working in one of the local steel mills. Julius, who was born in Poland, became a naturalized citizen in 1939. He died at the age of 31, leaving his wife pregnant with their third child. (MAD.)

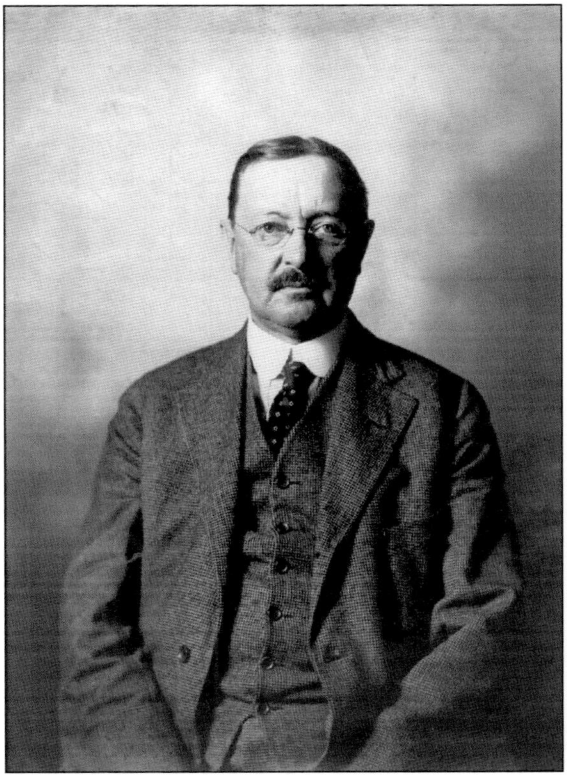

William Bingham Cleveland (1862–1929) was an inventor with 23 patents to his credit by 1919. He was the founder and president of several companies, including Forest City Electric Company, later named Forest City Machine & Forge Company, and Electric Railway Improvement Company. He loved his country home in Newbury where he kept his bird dog kennels. In 1948, the state purchased the property, which is now Punderson State Park. At age 41, Cleveland married Ocie Browne Coppedge of Stanton, Tennessee. They had six children. (Katherine and William Cleveland.)

Lydia Gawne Kermode (1855–1893), daughter of John and Margaret Craine Gawne, lived in Cleveland all of her life. She married James Kermode in 1871 and bore five children before they divorced in 1884. She died of pneumonia at the age of 38. (Pat Manwell.)

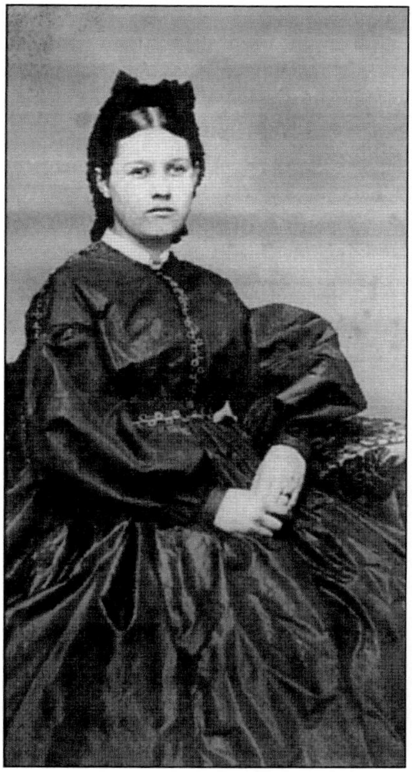

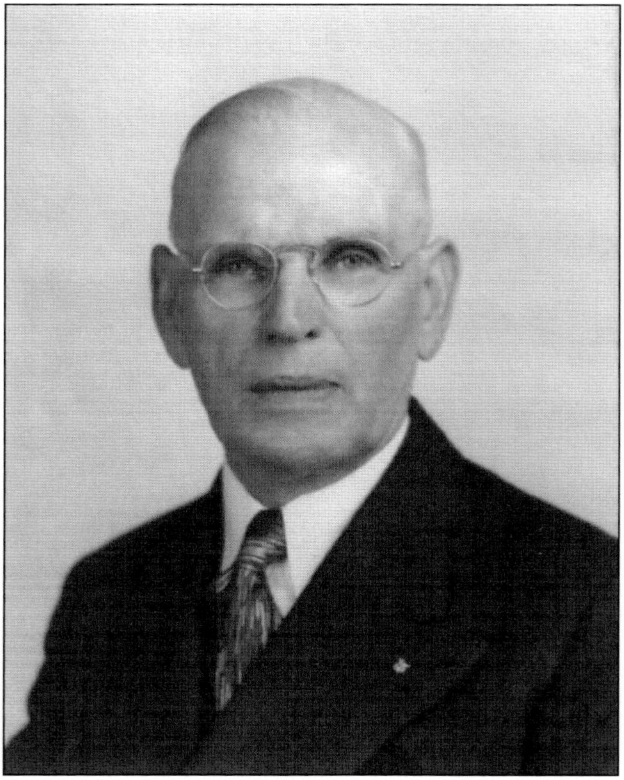

William Richard Cubbon (1871–1947), a Cleveland native, was a director on the board of the Savings & Loan Company since 1939. He was interested in home decor and antiques. Cubbon served as the supreme vice president of a fraternal insurance organization, was past master of Forest City Masonic Lodge, and was an active member of Webb Chapter, Al Koran Shrine and Al Sirat Grotto. He married Francis M. Kneale, who died in 1944. (Pat Manwell.)

George and Charlotte Tolhurst were natives of Kent, England, being born in Leeds 1800 and Maidstone 1799, respectively, and marrying at All Saints Church, Maidstone, in 1823. George's parents were psalm singer/musician Henry Tolhurst and Ann Sweetlove. Charlotte's parents were Charles Waghorne and Charlotte Bailey. In 1832, George and Charlotte immigrated per *Hudson* to the United States and settled in Cleveland, Cuyahoga, Ohio, on Ontario Street. George, a boot and shoe maker, became one of seven amateur instrumentalists to form the Cleveland Harmonic Society 1835. He was naturalized in 1840. George and Charlotte subsequently lived on Kinsman, Parkman, and Webster Streets, Cleveland. Their closest relative and beneficiary was a nephew named Frederick Tolhurst, who immigrated in 1846 and was a Baptist minister in Cuyahoga County. (G. Hall and J. Dalrymple.)

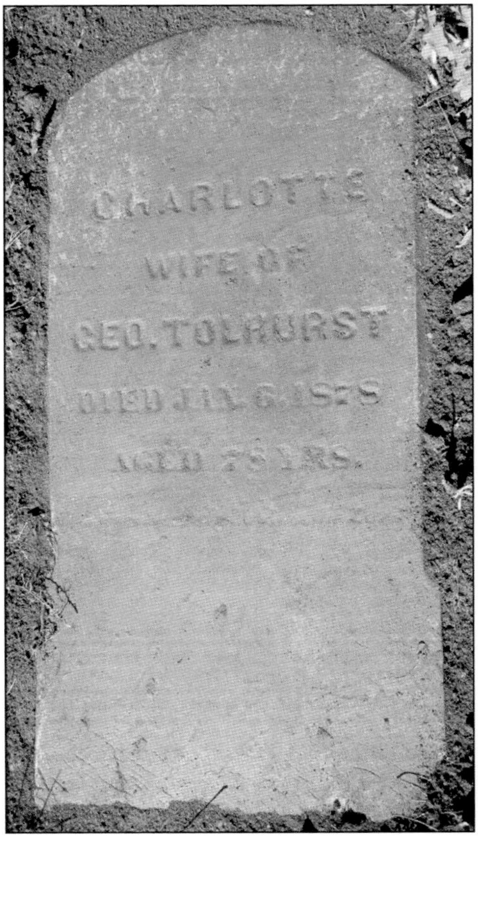

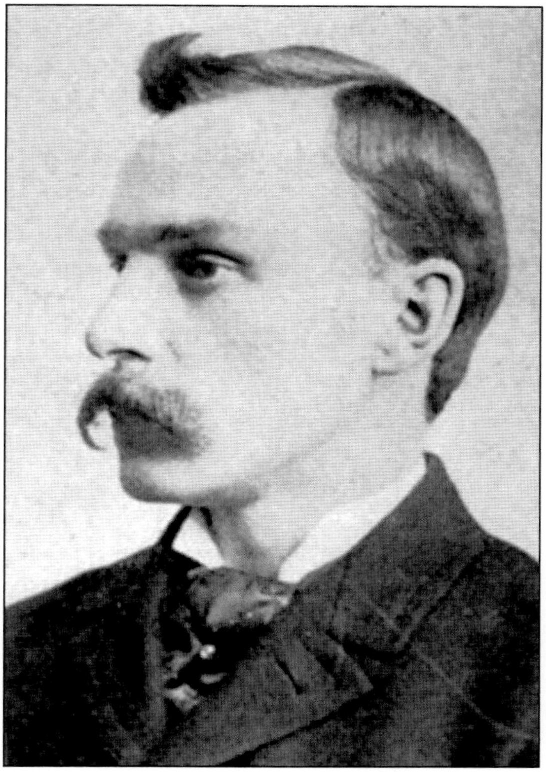

John Marvin Freese (1859–1911), born in Cleveland, was an architect with Hall & Freese in Columbus, Ohio, from 1885 to 1906. He designed the Franklin Park Conservatory there in 1895. Freese served as a sergeant in Company C1, Regiment US 1 in the Army. His parents, a brother, and two younger sisters (who died from diphtheria in 1878, just twelve days apart), are buried in Woodland. (Cecilia Eppink/Columbus Public Library.)

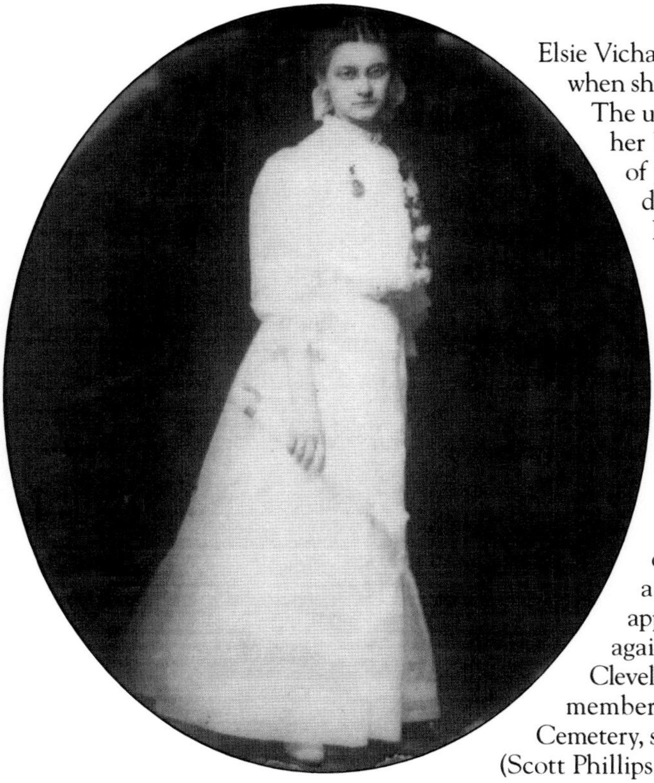

Elsie Vicha (1900–1915) was only 14 years old when she was struck down by heart disease. The unusual locket shown here, given to her by an aunt, was her favorite piece of jewelry. Elsie and her sister Bessie, daughters of Joseph K. and Anna Knechtl Vicha, were both members of The Busy Bee Club in the old Croton neighborhood. The Vicha and Knechtl families were among the earliest of the Bohemian (Czech) immigrants to settle in Cleveland. The Knechtl family was among the first 12 Bohemian families in 1852, with the Vicha family following in 1860. Elsie's father, Joseph K., was a key leader of the early Union movement, an active Free Thinker, and as an appointee of Mayor McKisson, fought against sweatshops and child labor in Cleveland. With over 164 additional family members resting eternally in Woodland Cemetery, she will never be alone or forgotten. (Scott Phillips.)

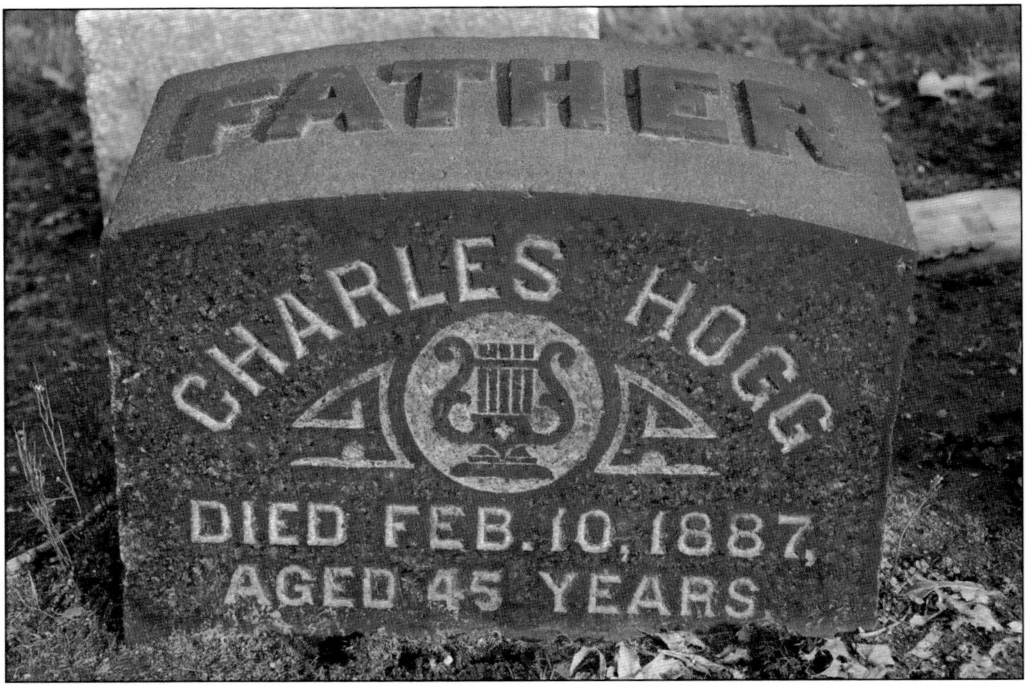

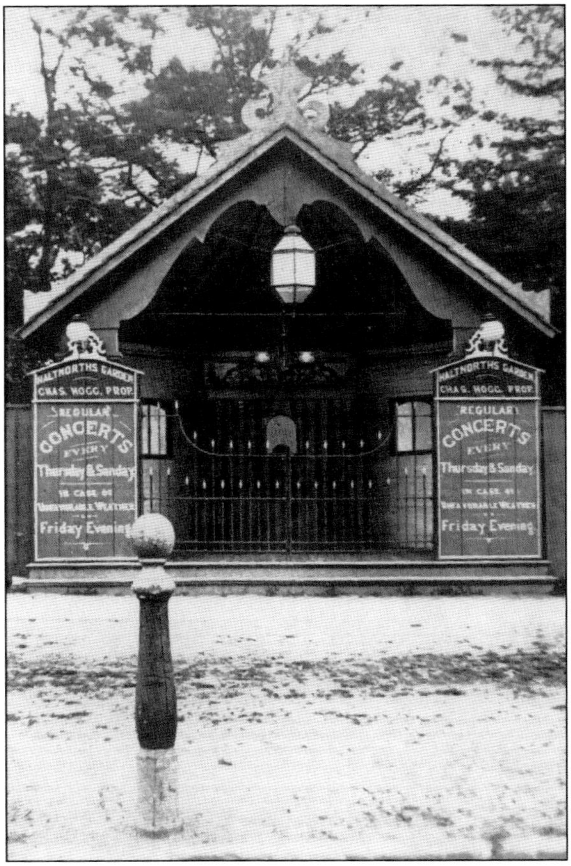

Charles Hogg (1842–1887) was 45 when he died after months of suffering from paralysis and pain. He had studied music, enlisted for several years, managed a lager-bottling works, and then opened Cleveland's Haltnorth's Hall and Garden, where he introduced the concept of outdoor concerts. He often entertained guests with what was considered to be one of the best tenor voices in the city. His wife continued to manage the establishment following Hogg's death. (MAD.)

Frederick Haltnorth (1825–1882), born in Germany, was known as an entrepreneur in Cleveland. Frederick was already a successful brewer when he opened Haltnorth Gardens, a popular beer garden on Woodland Avenue, where one could enjoy a picnic or an opera while socializing over beer. In 1864, he accepted an offer of $120,000 for his brewery, which was producing 12,000 barrels annually. His second wife, Gertrude Lembeck (1815–1899), survived him. (Ohio Historical Society/Louis Baus Collection.)

Sarah Adams Estabrook Thatcher (1820–1909) was one of the first volunteers, and the last survivor, of the Northern Ohio Sanitary Commission, which was established at the onset of the Civil War. As a young woman, Sarah became the first female librarian in the country before marrying Peter Thatcher Jr., a well-known Cleveland architect, in 1849. They had three children: Peter, John, and Annie. Sarah's gracious and generous influence continues today through the efforts of her numerous philanthropic endeavors. (Ohio Historical Society/ Louis Baus Collection.)

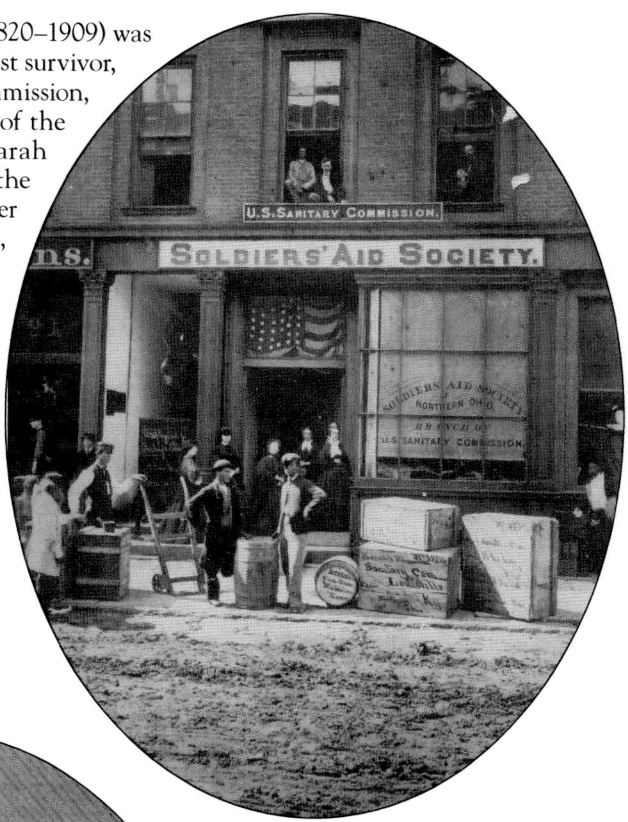

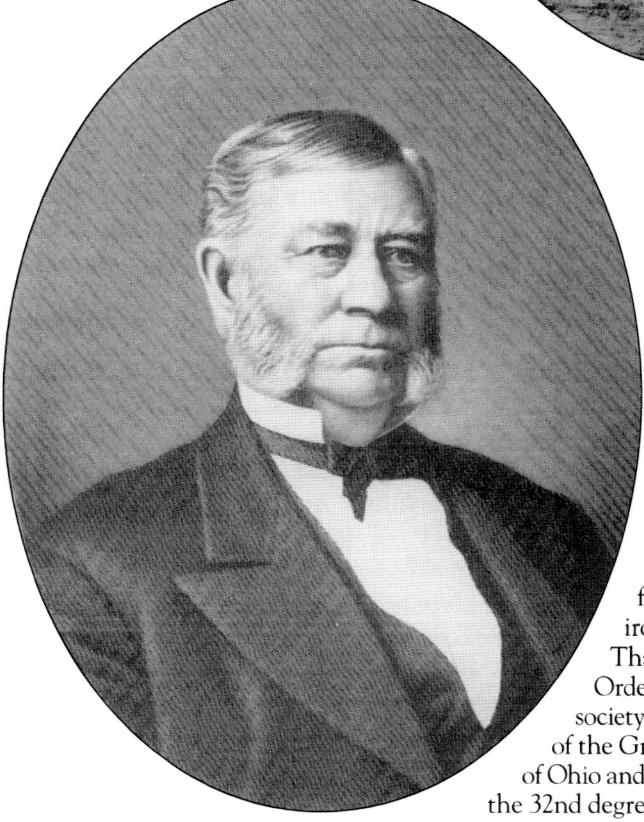

Peter Thatcher Jr. (1812–1880), a well-known architect and a genial gentleman who never actively sought political office, was appointed to several offices of public trust. He is also remembered for patenting and manufacturing iron roofing, which was very durable. Thatcher was initiated into the Masonic Order in 1854; he rapidly advanced in the society, eventually becoming grand treasurer of the Grand Command of Knights Templar of Ohio and passing through the Scottish Rite to the 32nd degree. (History of Cuyahoga County.)

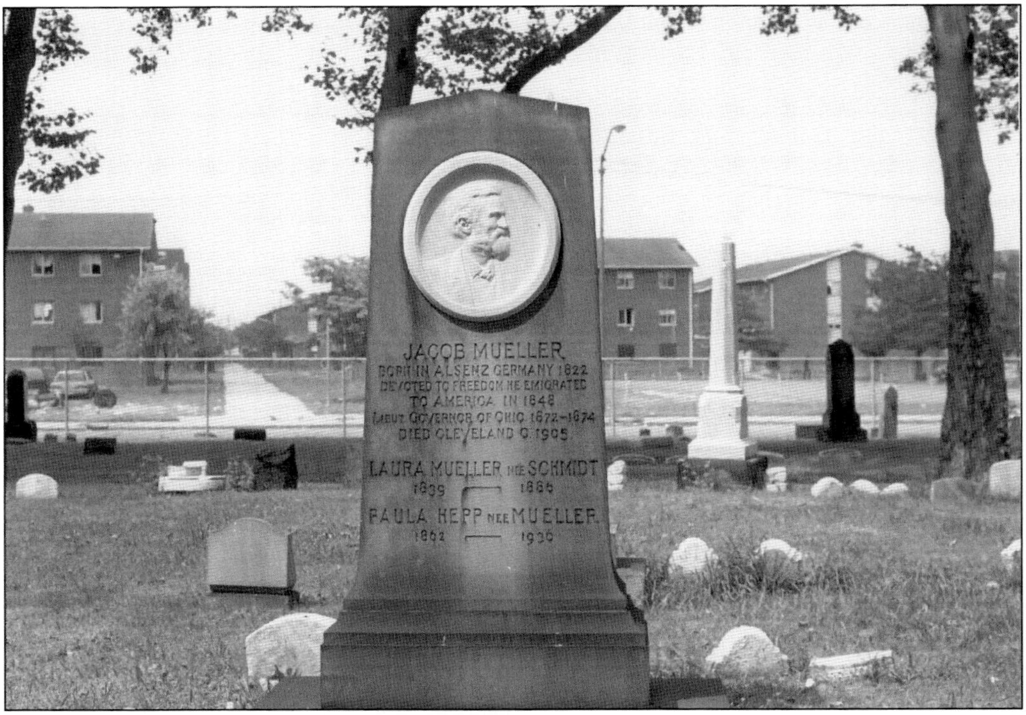

Jacob Mueller (1822–1905), after fleeing his native Bavaria in 1849, studied law and English and earned admittance to the Ohio bar in 1854. In addition to practicing law, Mueller established the German Insurance Co.; was a partner in printing the first (and only) 1¢ daily German newspaper in Ohio; and was active in local, state, and national politics. He was lieutenant governor of Ohio from 1872 to 1874 and also served on the city council. (Early Settlers Association of the Western Reserve.)

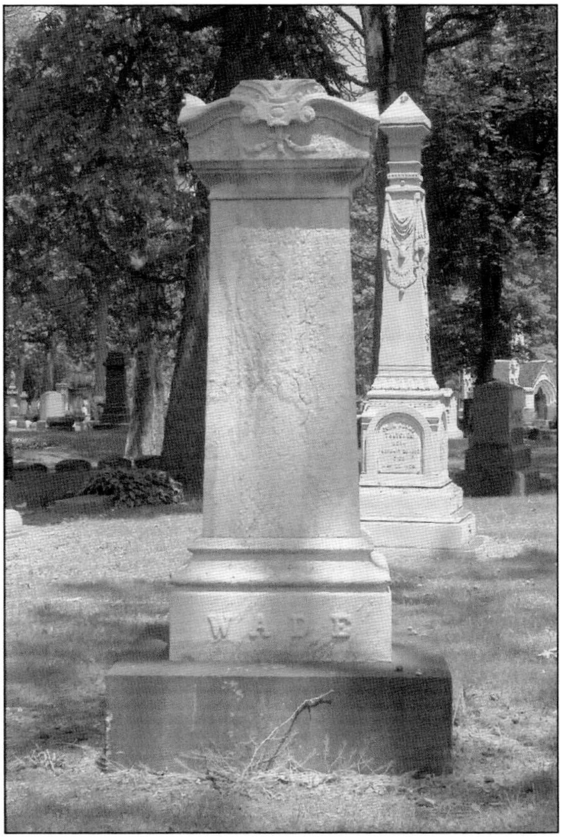

Edward Wade (1802–1866) was known as an argumentative and eloquent opponent of slavery at a time when abolitionism was frowned upon. He was admitted to the bar in 1827, practiced law, and was justice of the peace in Ashtabula County before moving to Cleveland in 1837. He was a prominent leader in the Free Soil Party and was elected as a candidate to the 33rd, 34th, 35th, and 36th Congresses (1853–1861). (MAD.)

George B. Senter (1827–1870) was "universally esteemed" as a councilman, mayor, and military leader during the Civil War. He was a staunch supporter of the Union cause and, in 1861, invited President-elect Abraham Lincoln to visit Cleveland, which he did. As mayor in 1865, Senter proclaimed a day of mourning to honor the assassinated president. He later practiced law and held interest in a wholesale wine and liquor business in Cleveland. (MAD.)

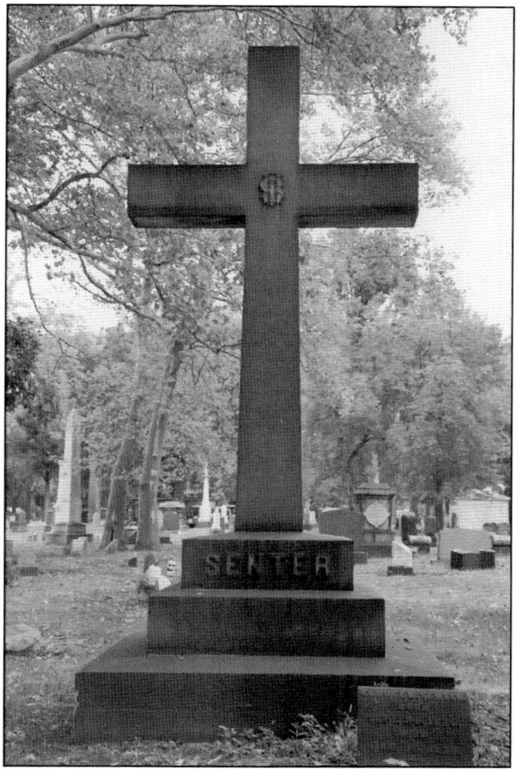

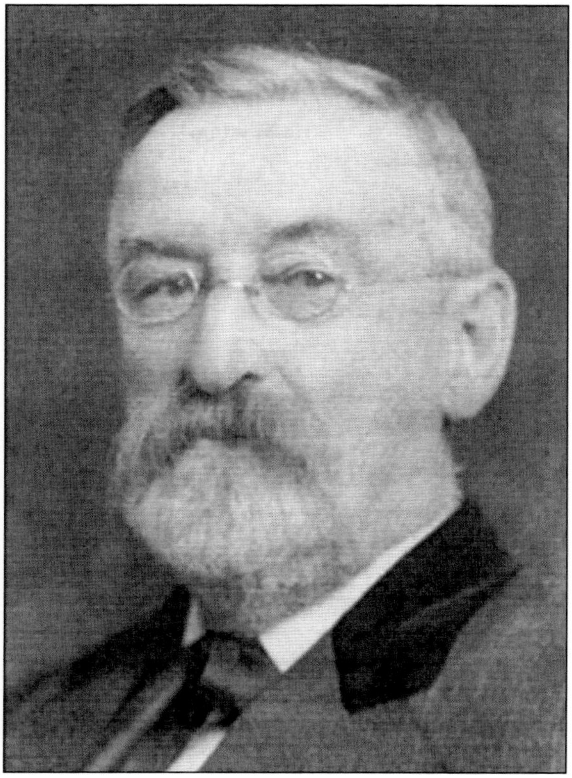

John Harrington Farley (1846–1922) was regarded as "a most pleasant man" and was known as "Honest John." He served as a Democratic member of city council for three terms (1871–1877) and as Cleveland mayor (1883–1885 and 1899–1901). He was also a competent and successful banker, being a founder of Central National Bank. An active and energetic man, he admired the "science" of boxing and played cribbage and checkers to keep his mind engaged. (CPLPC.)

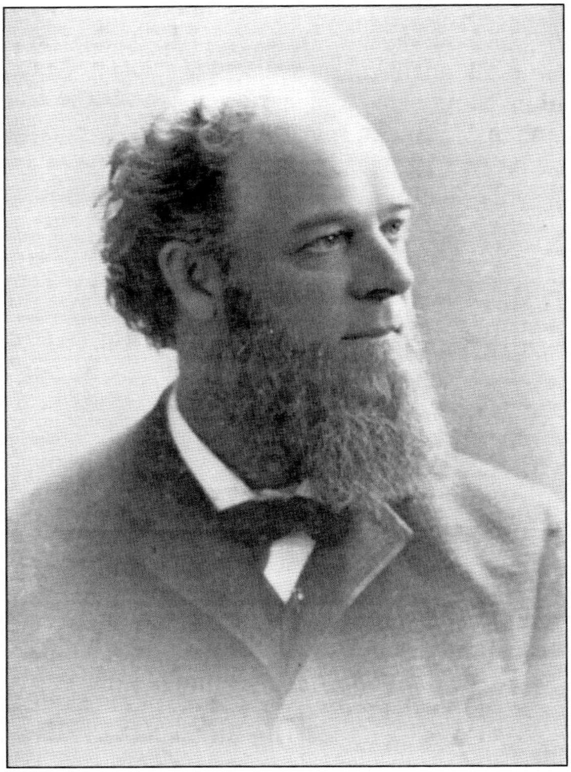

George William Gardner (1834–1911) was a businessman, councilman, and a mayor of Cleveland. He became a sailor at the age of 14, built the largest grain elevator on the Cuyahoga River, was the first commodore of the Cleveland Yacht Club, and owned several successful business enterprises. While in public service, "he felt it was his duty as a citizen to respond to every demand made upon him by fellow citizens." (CPLPC.)

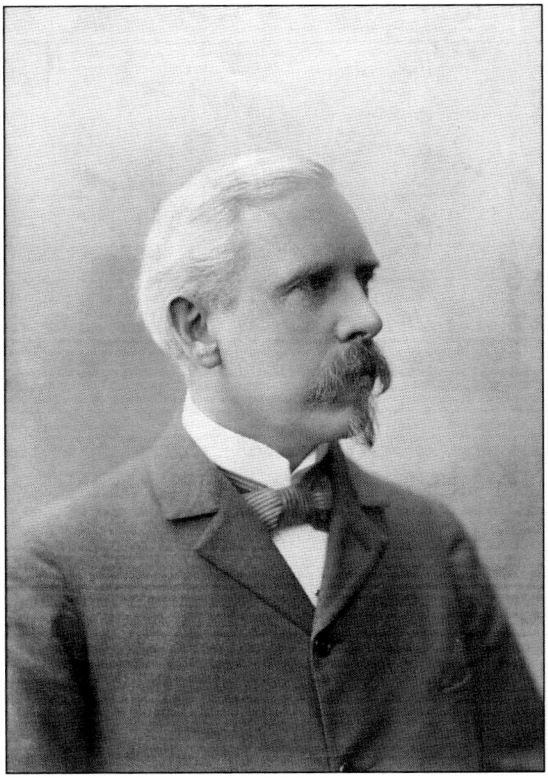

Alfred F. Arthur (1844–1918) was a noted tenor, cornetist, conductor, educator, and compiler at a time when musical concerts were a social event. In 1873, he founded the Cleveland Vocal Society, which he conducted through 29 seasons. In 1875, Professor Arthur founded the Cleveland School of Music, to which he dedicated a great deal of his time. As a composer, Arthur wrote songs and three operas, authored technical studies, and compiled two hymnals. (CPLPC.)

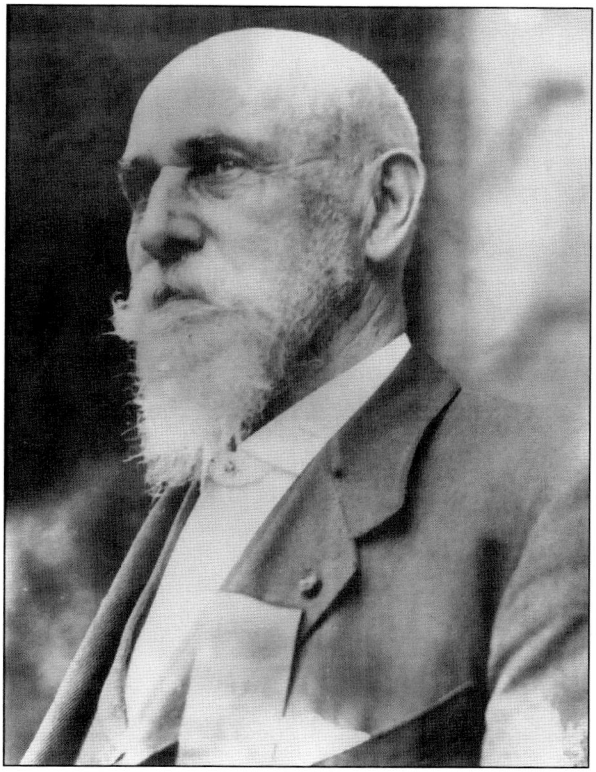

John N. Frazee (1829–1917) became Cleveland's first police chief in 1852, charged with protecting 67,000 people. He was a corporal in the Cleveland Grays before the war broke out and left his law enforcement position to enlist in April 1865, serving as a lieutenant colonel with the 84th and 150th Ohio Infantries until mustering out in August 1864. From 1870 to 1885, he was captain, commanding the active company of the Cleveland Grays. Frazee ran a successful laundry business until his retirement in 1888. (Cleveland Police Museum.)

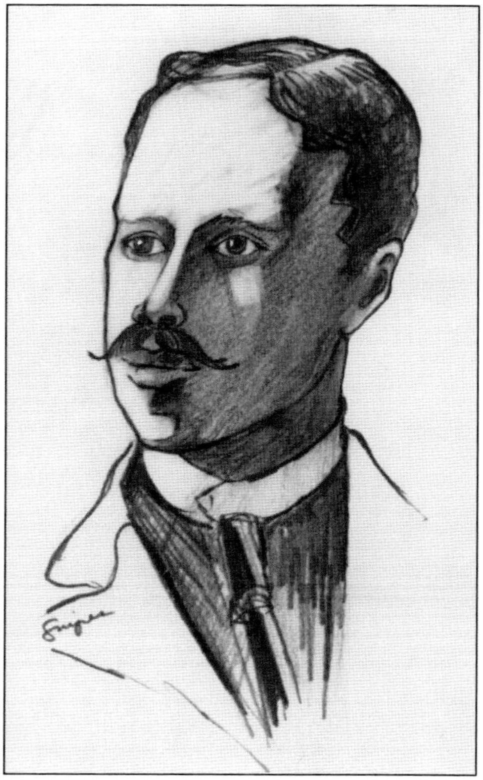

Samuel Clayton Green (1872–1915) was an enterprising African American businessman whose numerous business ventures were designed to turn segregation and discrimination to his advantage. However, insufficient support from black customers caused his businesses to fail. The Leonard Sofa Bed Co. offered couches from $28 to $65; he also tried real estate and built a laundry, a restaurant, a grocery store, and a drugstore. Green was referred to as "the most successful legitimate businessman." (CPLPC.)

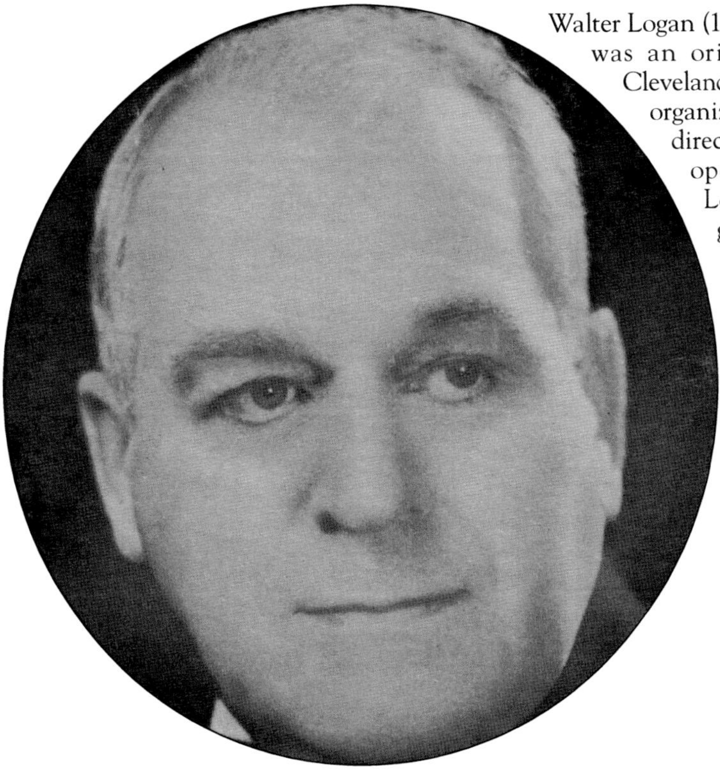

Walter Logan (1876–1940), born in Quebec, was an original violinist with the Cleveland Orchestra, which he helped organize. He was a pioneer musical director and was first to produce operas for radio broadcast. Logan was only 12 when he gave his first professional performance and only 14 when he became Cleveland's youngest conductor, leading the YMCA Orchestra. He was also the dean and head of the Cleveland Music School Settlement violin department (CPLPC.)

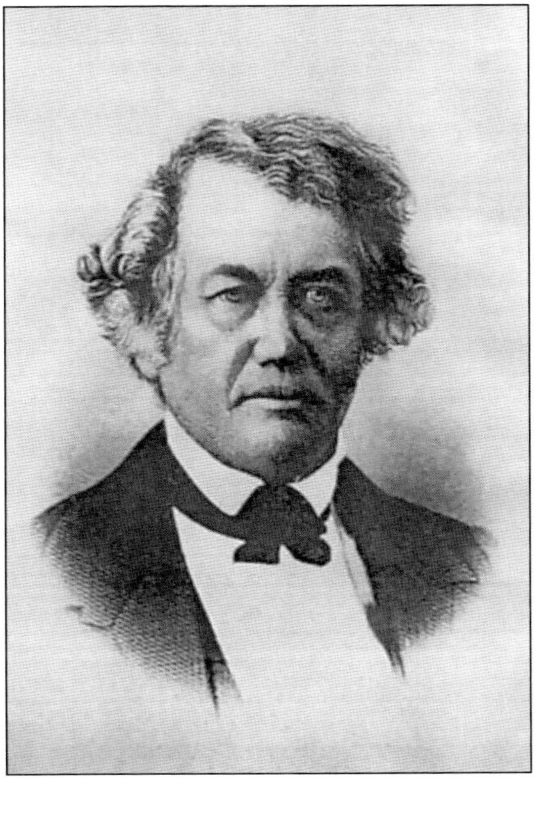

Cleveland's first physician, Dr. David Long (1787–1951), served as a surgeon during the War of 1812 and, in 1824, was elected president of a group that eventually became the Academy of Medicine. He opened a dry-goods store, built the first warehouse on the Cuyahoga River, and was the first librarian of the Library Society. David was trustee of Cleveland Village several times and sat on the first Cleveland Board of Health. (CPLPC.)

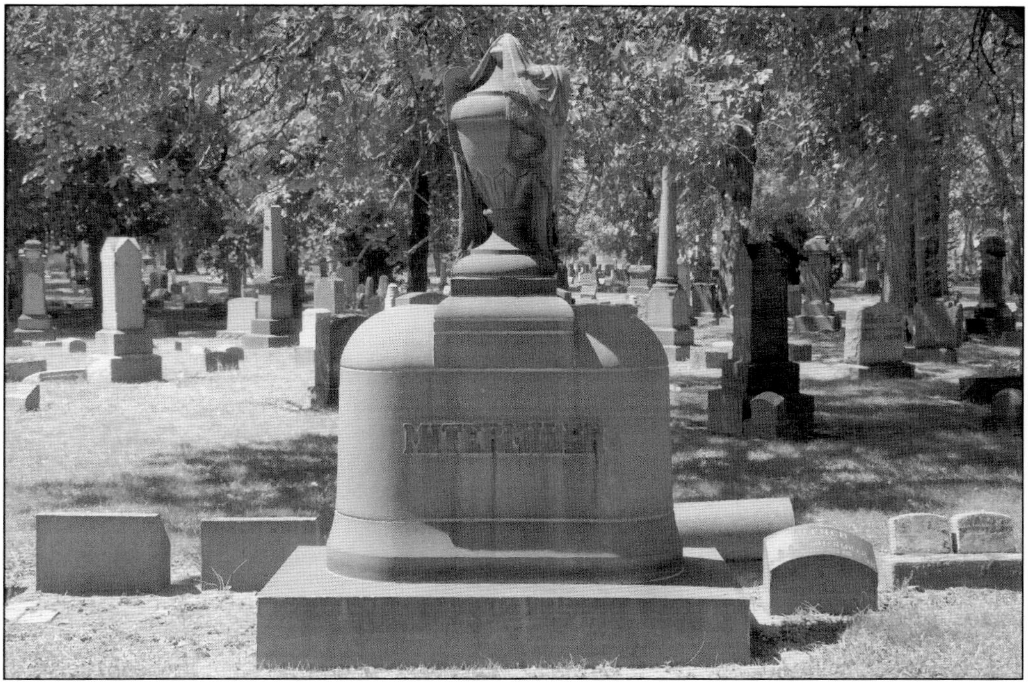

Andrew Robert Mitermiler (1840–1896), from Czechoslovakia, received his education at the University of Vienna before arriving in Cleveland in 1871. A civil engineer, he designed business blocks, social halls, and dozens of breweries, in addition to churches and housing for Czech and German residents. The first Hungarian Catholic parish church, St. Elizabeth Catholic Church, was built from his design. Many of his buildings still stood in the 1980s. (MAD.)

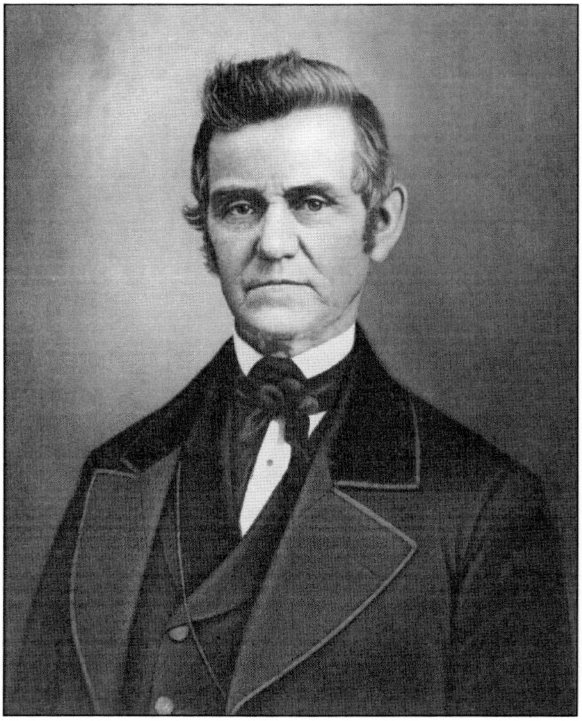

William Augustus Otis (1794–1868) practiced his religion in both his personal and business life as a leading merchant, pioneer iron industrialist, banker, and civic leader. He was instrumental in developing trade between the Western Reserve and eastern markets when, in 1825, he shipped the first Ohio wheat to New York City via Buffalo and the Erie Canal; thus, Cleveland was established as a port. (CPLPC.)

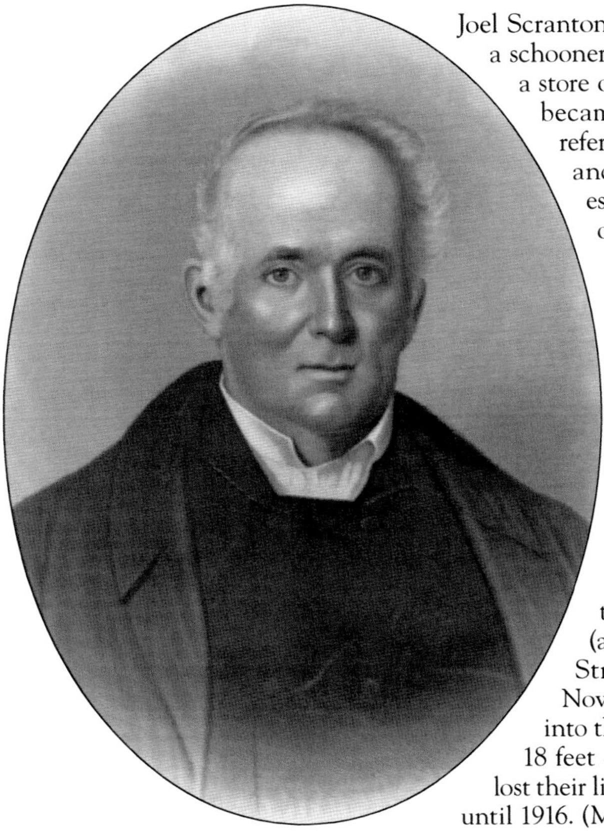

Joel Scranton (1793–1858) arrived in Cleveland on a schooner laden with leather goods and opened a store on the Cuyahoga River in an area that became known as Scranton Flats. He was referred to as unconventional, independent, and democratic. He acquired many real estate holdings. He loved reminiscing with others and was known to have a great sense of humor. He and his wife, Irene, reared four children. (CPLPC.)

Annie Stoudt Hoffman and her two young children, Harvey George (age three) and Gertrude Elizabeth "Annie" (age one), drowned in the Central Viaduct Streetcar Disaster on the foggy night of November 16, 1895. Their streetcar plunged into the Cuyahoga River, 100 feet below, into 18 feet of water. Of the 21 persons aboard, 17 lost their lives. Widowed, Albert W. Hoffman lived until 1916. (MAD.)

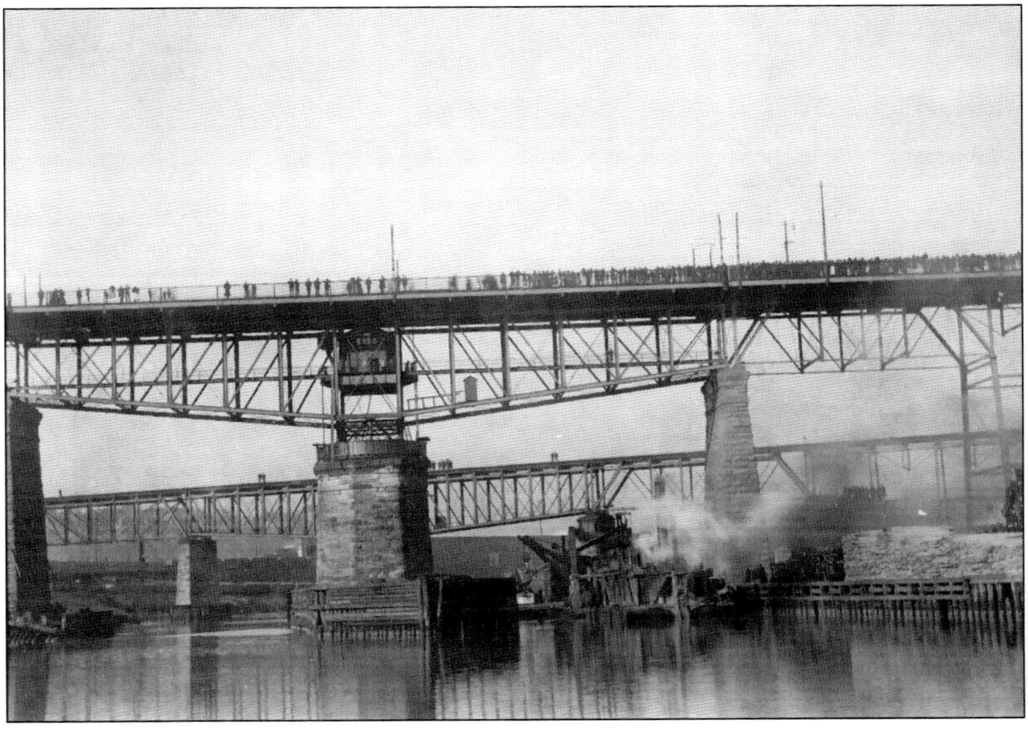

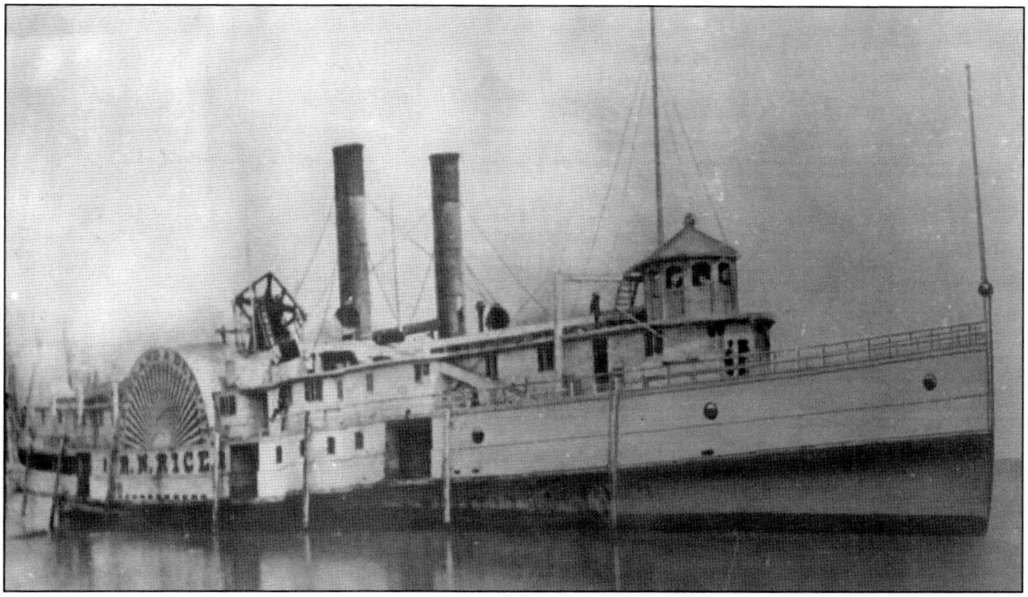

The *Morning Star*—a wooden side-wheel steamer with 38-foot paddlewheels, built in 1862—was carrying about 70 passengers in addition to its crew when it collided with the *Cortland,* eight miles north of Lorain Harbor in Lake Erie, on June 21, 1868. Both sank. Nine of the victims are buried in Woodland; a 10-year-old boy, William R. Lidstone, is among them. The above photograph shows the *Morning Star*'s sister ship, the *R.N. Rice.* (Clarence S. Metcalf Great Lakes Maritime Research Library of the Great Lakes Historical Society.)

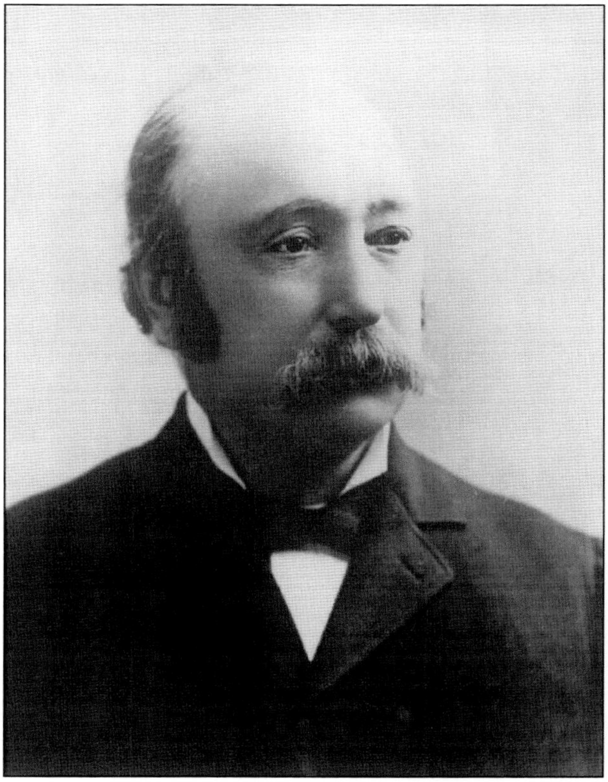

Henry Hoehn (1840–1903) was a most efficient and popular superintendent of police in Cleveland, possessing the "proper traits for an ideal peace officer." He rose through the ranks, gaining others' confidence as both gave and commanded respect. Hoehn was appointed a patrolman in 1866 and was a captain by 1883. He also served with the 20th Ohio Independent Light Artillery Army of Cumberland. (CPLPC.)

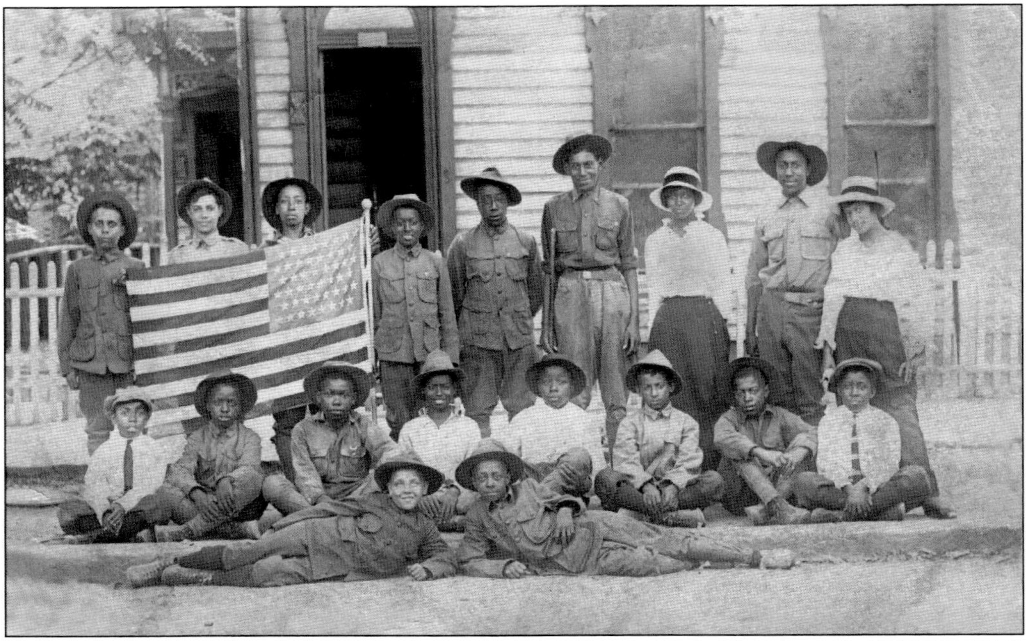

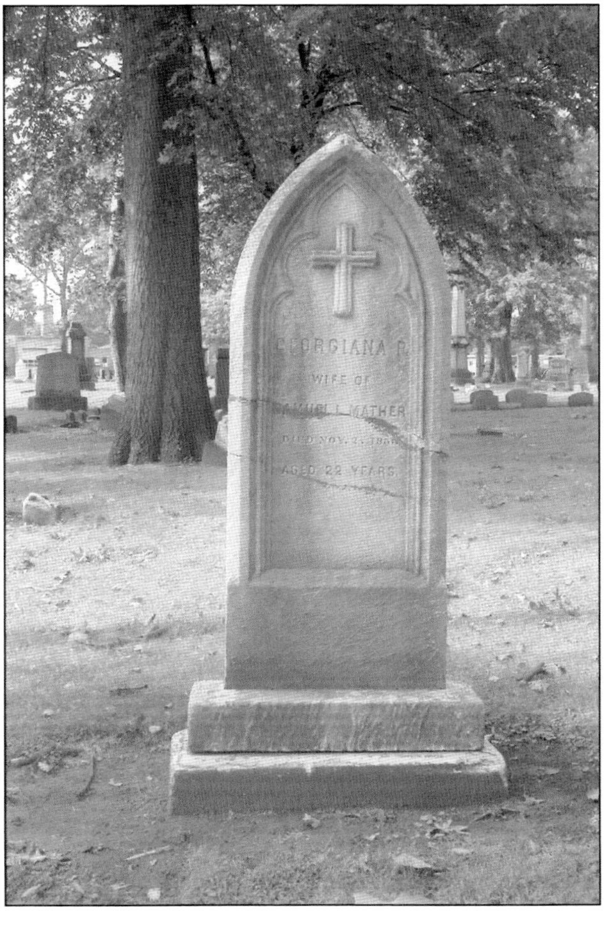

Robert Oliver Lipscomb (1898–1915) was a good student and active youth who eagerly joined the Boy Scouts of America when it was only five years old. He became a member of one of the first troops in the United States, Troop 63. Robert can be seen standing second from the right in the second row of this photograph. When he died tragically at the age of 17 in an accident, his parents chose to have the Boy Scout emblem engraved on his headstone. (Lipscomb family photograph.)

Georgiana Pomeroy Woolsen (1831–1853) came to Cleveland from New Hampshire in 1840 and married Samuel Livingston Mather in September 1850. Sadly, she died while her sons were mere toddlers, on November 2, 1853, at the age of 22. (MAD.)

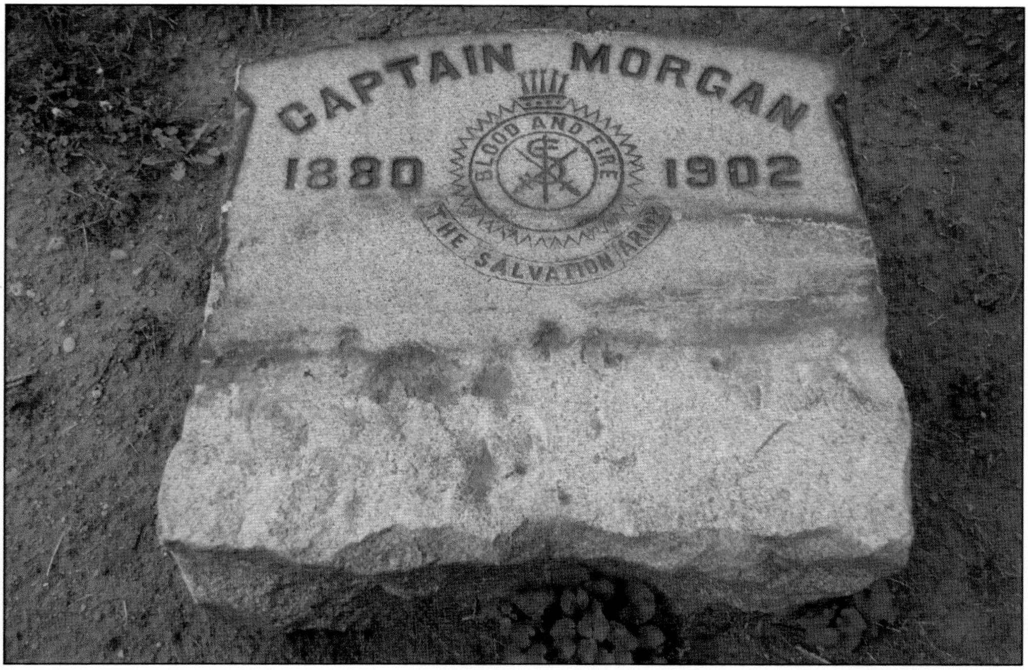

Letha Morgan, a captain in the Salvation Army, was born in Morgantown, West Virginia, and arrived in Ohio in January 1902. She trained in New York City and was assigned to Elyria and Ashtabula before arriving in Cleveland in April 1902. The religious young woman became ill with smallpox that same year and, "being perfectly reconciled and ready to go," died on December 31st at the age of 22. (MAD.)

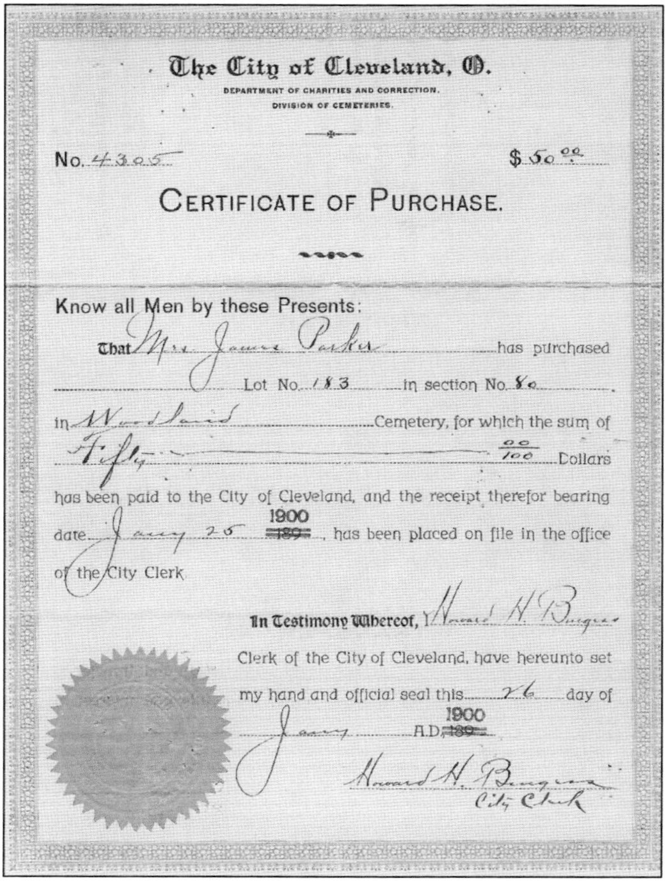

The City of Cleveland, O.

DEPARTMENT OF CHARITIES AND CORRECTION.
DIVISION OF CEMETERIES.

No. 4305 $50.00

CERTIFICATE OF PURCHASE.

Know all Men by these Presents:

That Mrs. James Parker has purchased Lot No. 183 in section No. 80 in Woodland Cemetery, for which the sum of Fifty 00/100 Dollars has been paid to the City of Cleveland, and the receipt therefor bearing date Jany 25 1900, has been placed on file in the office of the City Clerk.

In Testimony Whereof, I Howard H. Burgess Clerk of the City of Cleveland, have hereunto set my hand and official seal this 26 day of Jany A.D. 1900

Howard H. Burgess
City Clerk

This certificate illustrates that in June 1900, Lot 183 in Section 80 was purchased for the sum of $50 for James Parker, who died in January 1900 at the age of 72. He had worked as an iron molder. His wife, Leticia, and two daughters are buried with him. (Parker family papers.)

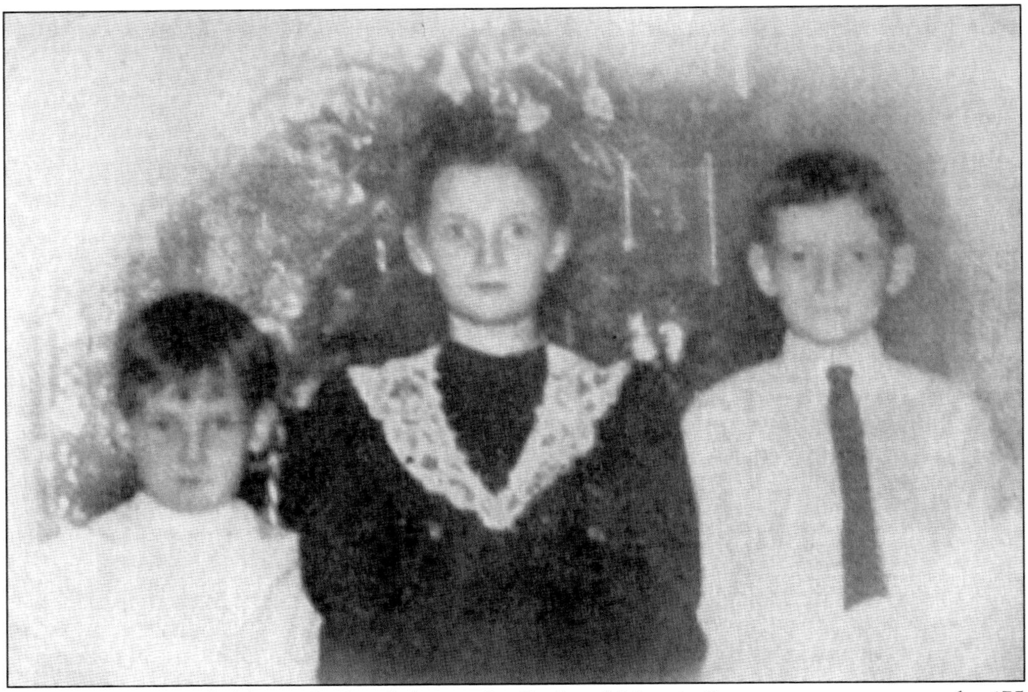

Three of the four children of a Swedish couple, Carl and Minnie Swanson, were among the 175 that died on Ash Wednesday, March 4, 1908, in a fire at Collinwood School. Pictured from left to right, Edwin (13), Hulda (11), and Fred (8) were among the victims that were crushed or suffocated as they tried to escape from the school. (Marshall Everett/N.G. Hamilton Publishing Co.)

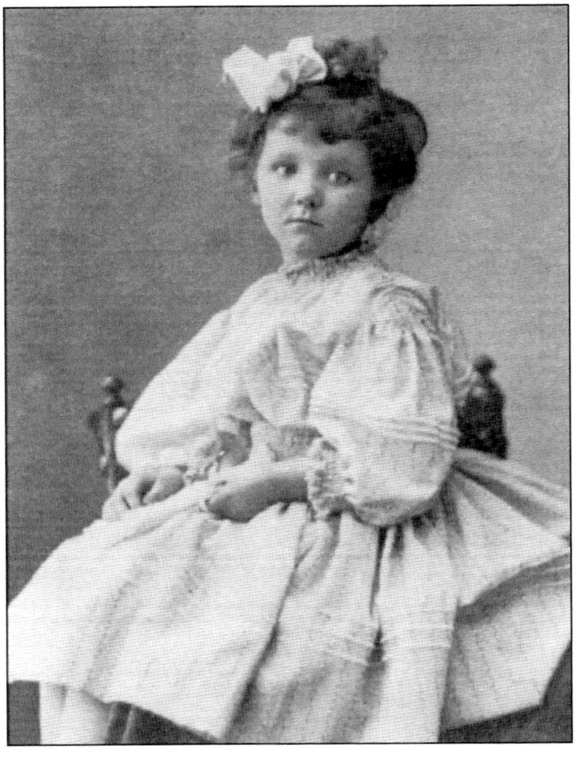

Gretchen Dorn (1897–1908), the beautiful little daughter of Frank and Gretchen Dorn, was said to be "a favorite of her teacher." She was one of the 175 killed in the Collinwood School Fire on March 4, 1908. Her father was a hero in rescuing many others, but he was unable to save Gretchen. A sister, Kae, escaped from the fire and became a well-known artist. Gretchen's parents are buried with her. (Marshall Everett/N.G. Hamilton Publishing Co.)

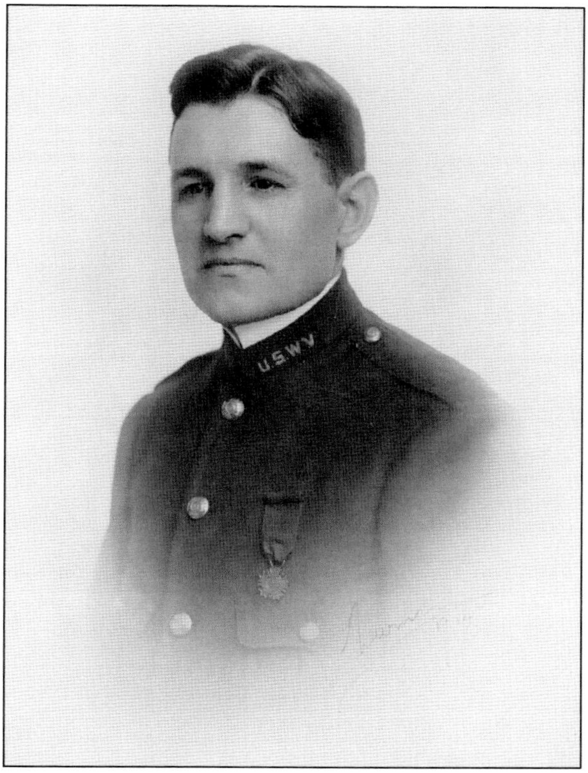

Walter Kinnear Patterson (1873–1962) was a Scotsman who held several jobs, including assistant superintendent of Woodland Cemetery, where his children loved to play. He completed his family genealogy and wrote a history of the Old Newburgh neighborhood where he grew up. In 1960, he was given the great honor of being the grand marshal of the Memorial Day parade. (Betsy Barber.)

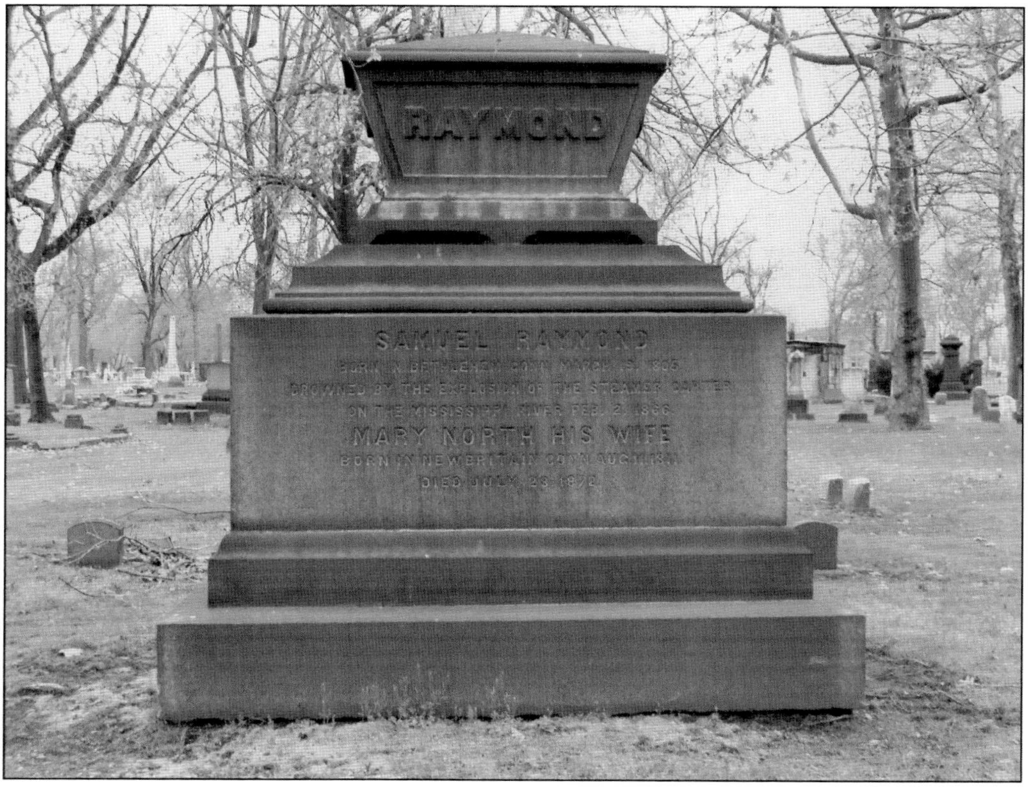

Samuel Raymond (1805–1866) and his wife, Mary North Raymond, along with some friends, were on the *W.R. Carter* steamship when her boiler exploded near Vicksburg, Mississippi, at 4:00 a.m. on February 5, 1866. Samuel was a very well-known and respected businessman and merchant in Cleveland for over 30 years. Mary survived; however, Samuel's body was never recovered. (Stanislav Zadnik.)

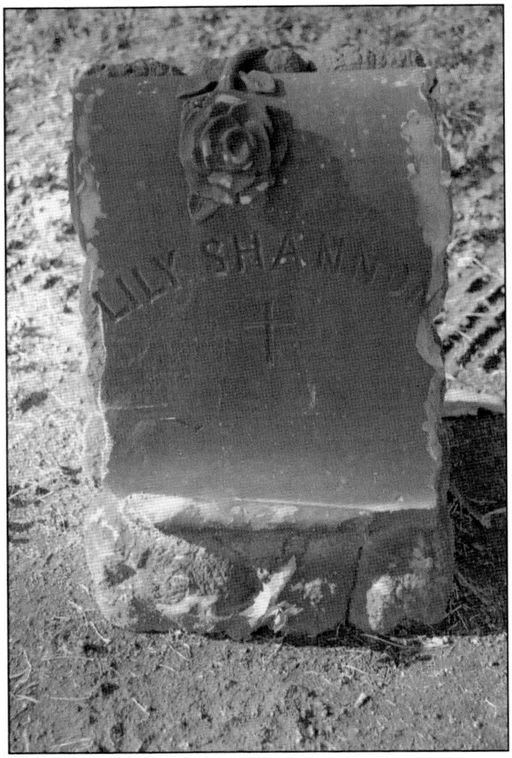

The headstone of Lily Shannon, who died at 13 months in 1885, marks the graves of her entire family; her parents, James and Mary McGinty Shannon, and her brothers, James Jr. and John, all died in a fire at their home in October 1892. James and his brother-in-law John McGinty operated a saloon on the first floor of the building, with the family living on the second floor. Everyone but the Shannon family escaped. (Gail Whitchurch.)

The purpose of a burial vault is to protect the casket from the weight of the earth and maintenance equipment. At the time of the Civil War, a grave would be lined with bricks, and the coffin placed inside and covered. In the late 1800s, companies began to manufacture two-piece concrete burial vaults. By the late 1920s, companies began to coat the vaults with asphalt to keep moisture away from the casket. (Gregory Sent.)

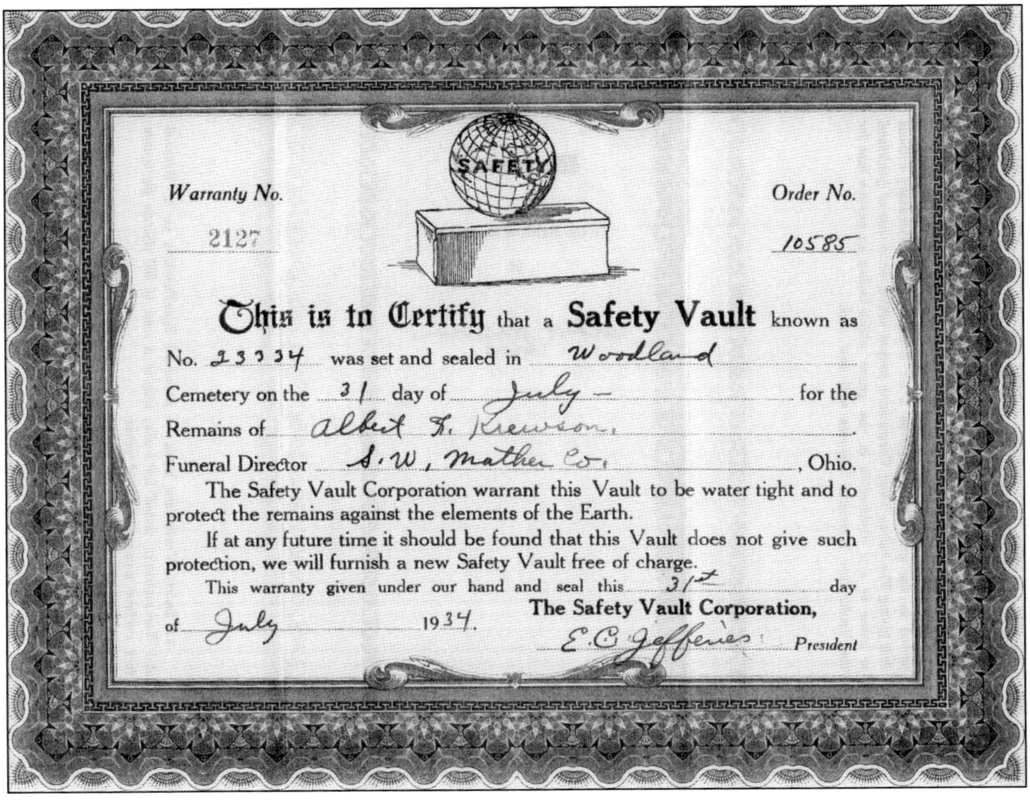

SAFETY

Warranty No. 2127

Order No. 10585

This is to Certify that a **Safety Vault** known as No. 23334 was set and sealed in Woodland Cemetery on the 31 day of July — for the Remains of Albert F. Krewson. Funeral Director S. W. Mather Co., Ohio.

The Safety Vault Corporation warrant this Vault to be water tight and to protect the remains against the elements of the Earth.

If at any future time it should be found that this Vault does not give such protection, we will furnish a new Safety Vault free of charge.

This warranty given under our hand and seal this 31st day of July 1934.

The Safety Vault Corporation,

E. C. Jeffries *President*

Albert Frederick Krewson was born in Muskingham, Ohio, on March 11, 1865. He worked first as a collector before founding Krewson Bros. with his brother Walter. They dealt in furniture, clothing, stoves, and even window shades, as the advertisement shows. Albert retired before 1920, probably because of arthritis. He died in 1934. (Gregory Sent.)

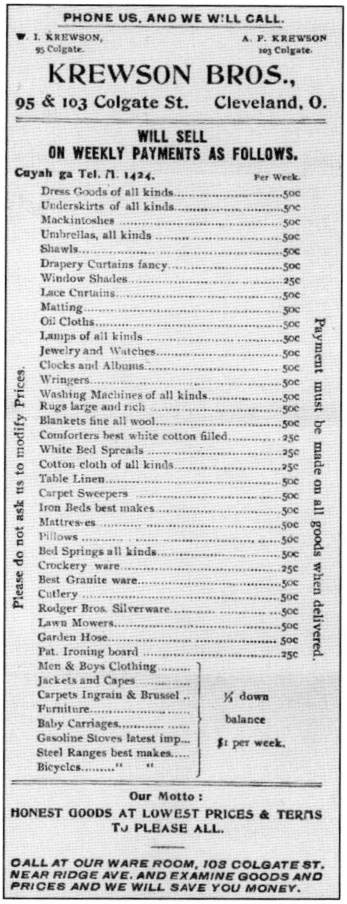

PHONE US, AND WE W!LL CALL.

W. I. KREWSON, 95 Colgate. — A. P. KREWSON 103 Colgate.

KREWSON BROS.,

95 & 103 Colgate St. Cleveland, O.

WILL SELL
ON WEEKLY PAYMENTS AS FOLLOWS.

Cuyah ga Tel. M. 1424.

	Per Week.
Dress Goods of all kinds	50c
Underskirts of all kinds	50c
Mackintoshes	50c
Umbrellas, all kinds	50c
Shawls	50c
Drapery Curtains fancy	50c
Window Shades	25c
Lace Curtains	50c
Matting	50c
Oil Cloths	50c
Lamps of all kinds	50c
Jewelry and Watches	50c
Clocks and Albums	50c
Wringers	50c
Washing Machines of all kinds	50c
Rugs large and rich	50c
Blankets fine all wool	50c
Comforters best white cotton filled	25c
White Bed Spreads	25c
Cotton cloth of all kinds	25c
Table Linen	50c
Carpet Sweepers	50c
Iron Beds best makes	50c
Mattres-es	50c
Pillows	50c
Bed Springs all kinds	50c
Crockery ware	25c
Best Granite ware	50c
Cutlery	50c
Rodger Bros. Silverware	50c
Lawn Mowers	50c
Garden Hose	50c
Pat. Ironing board	25c

Men & Boys Clothing, Jackets and Capes, Carpets Ingrain & Brussel, Furniture, Baby Carriages, Gasoline Stoves latest imp., Steel Ranges best makes, Bicycles " " — ⅓ down balance $1 per week.

Please do not ask us to modify Prices.

Payment must be made on all goods when delivered.

Our Motto:
HONEST GOODS AT LOWEST PRICES & TERMS TO PLEASE ALL.

CALL AT OUR WARE ROOM, 103 COLGATE ST. NEAR RIDGE AVE. AND EXAMINE GOODS AND PRICES AND WE WILL SAVE YOU MONEY.

Frank J. Elliot (1854–1923), born in Philadelphia, was a proud member of the United Commercial Travelers of America (UCT), a fraternal benefit society that was formed by eight traveling salesmen early in 1888. The sample case, a vital tool to a traveling salesman, became the symbol for UCT (as is evidenced on Elliot's headstone). Elliot sold soap products. He married twice but was a widower at the end of his life. (MAD.)

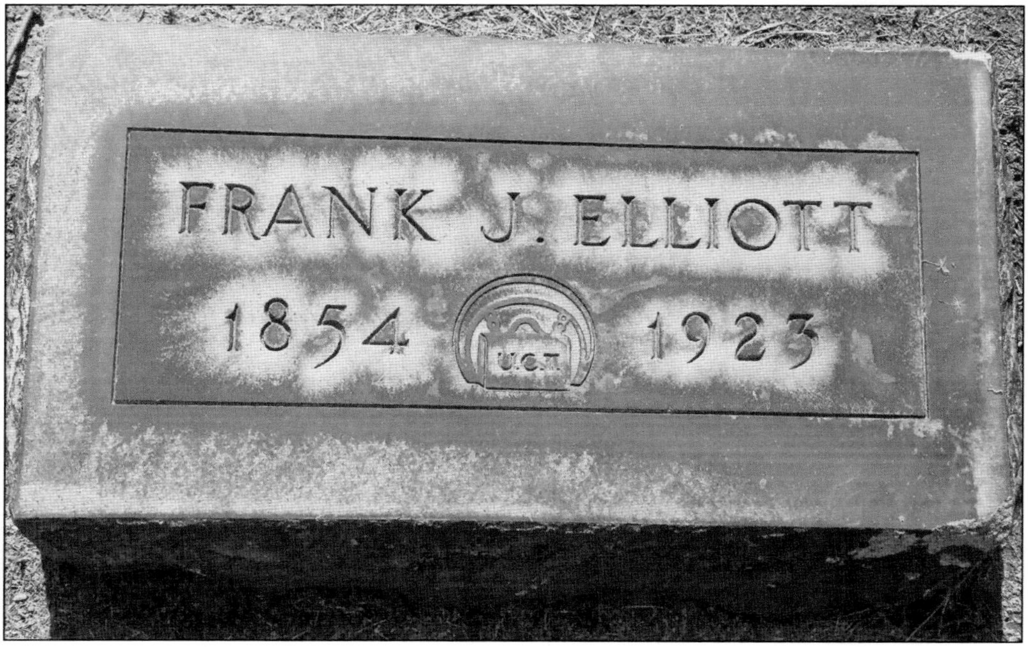

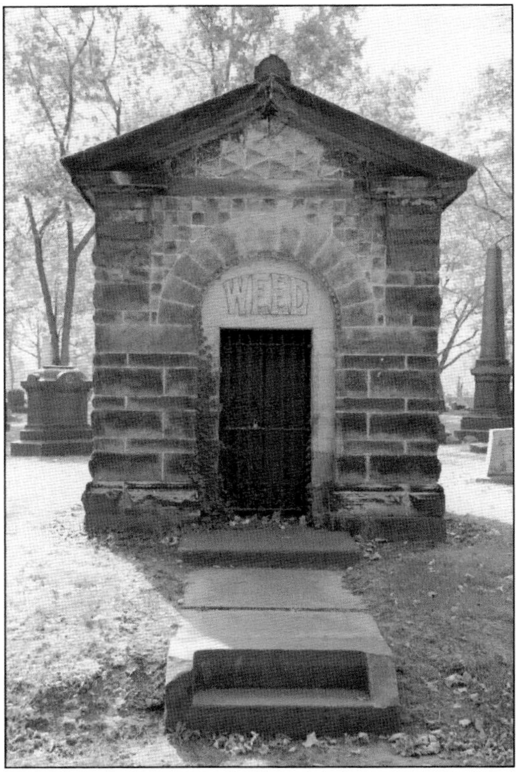

Dr. Theodore Arthur Weed (1856–1920) attended Cleveland College of Physicians and Surgeons at the University of Wooster in 1877, following an education in the Cleveland public schools. He became an allopath and owned a practice in West Park, Ohio. He married Anastasia Sarah Farnan in 1884 and they had three children while living in Rockport Hamlet, now Rocky River. Dr. Weed died of heart disease. (MAD.)

Harriet C. Fissel Adams (1861–1924) was the 63-year-old widow of William Adams living on West 36th Street in Lorain when a deadly tornado formed in Sandusky Bay. The tornado went through Lorain and Sandusky, damaging 1,000 homes and destroying many businesses. Harriet was killed by debris in a falling building. It was accepted that 85 people died that day as a result of the storm. (CSUSC.)

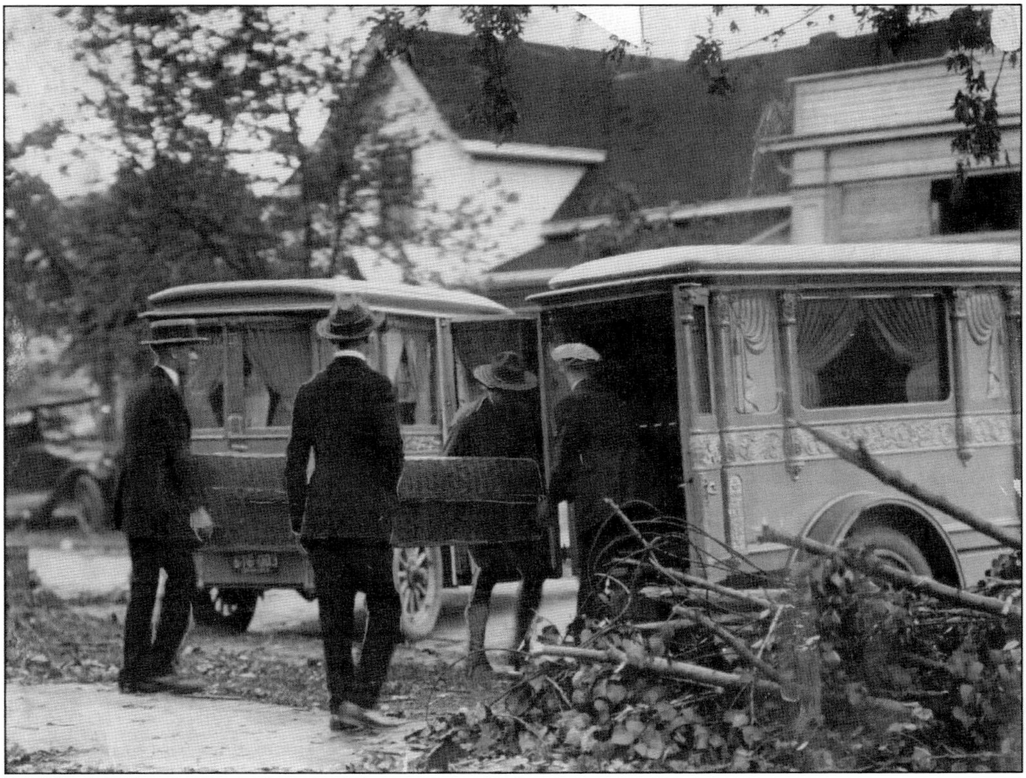

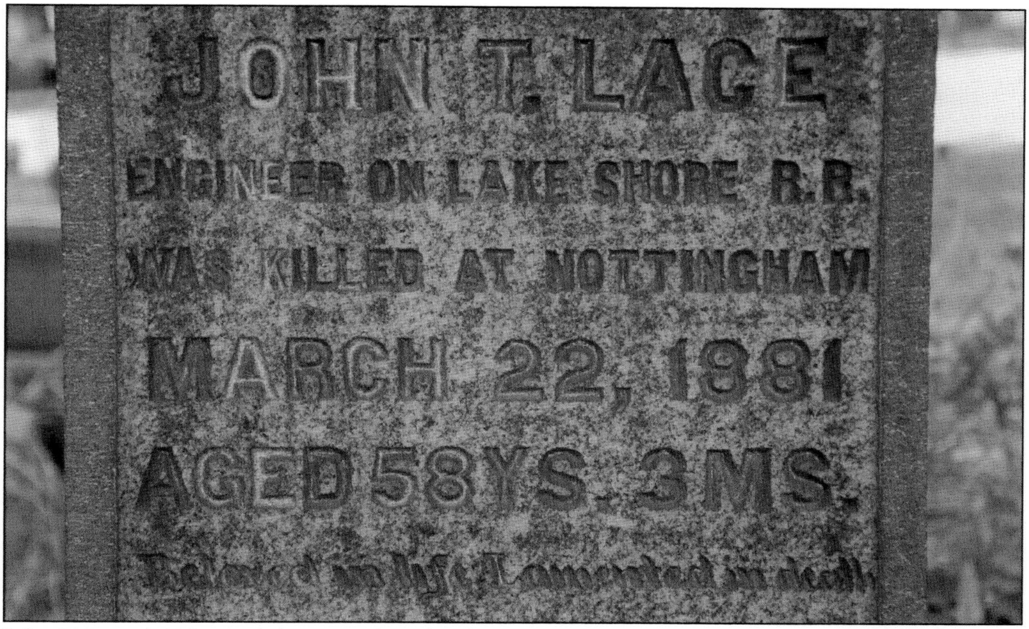

John T. Lace (1822–1881), born on the Isle of Man, married Catherine Adams. John, a locomotive engineer for the Lake Shore Railroad, was driving Engine No. 327, a passenger train, when it jumped the tracks at Nottingham and landed in a ditch. John's fireman, 23-year-old T.H. Stevenson, was also killed, and several others were hurt. John was a member of the Brotherhood of Locomotive Engineers and a Mason. (MAD.)

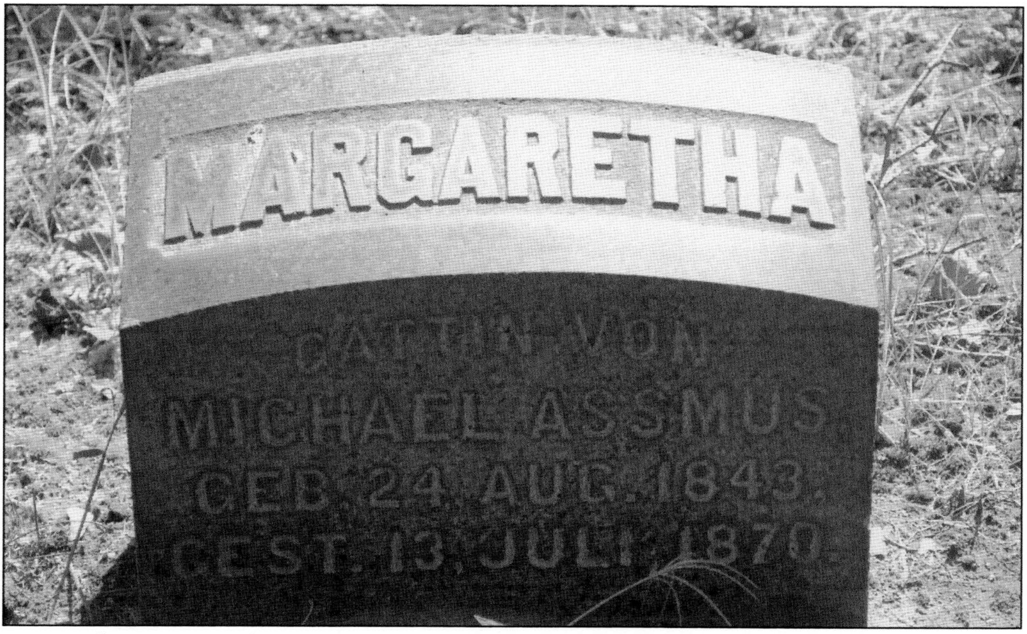

German-born Margaretha Kuentz Assmus (1843–1870) married Michael Assmus in 1864. Michael was a butcher and owned his own meat market at 260 St. Clair in the Linndale area. Their only child, a son named Michael, died of convulsions in 1867 when he was only 26 days old. After Margaretha's death, Michael remarried and had another son, Michael Jr., who also became a butcher. (MAD.)

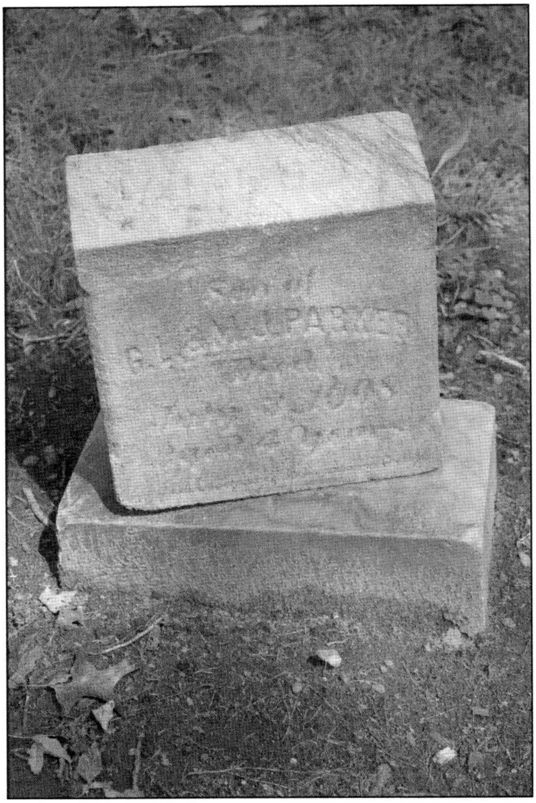

James L. "Jimmy" Parker (1904–1908), son of George and Wilhelmina "Minnie" (née Koester) Parker, went with his mother to the S.S. Kresge store on July 3, 1908, to buy fireworks for a Fourth of July celebration. A demonstration of "perfectly harmless" sparklers caught Minnie's billowy skirt on fire, which then caused a huge display to explode in flames. Minnie lost her little boy in the smoke, was herself burned badly, and was convinced to go home as she was told Jimmy had been found. When she arrived home, George had already been called to the morgue to identify his son's body. Six young women also died in that fire, which resulted in more stringent fireworks laws to be passed by August 1908 in Ohio, with more states following its lead. (MAD/CSUSC.)

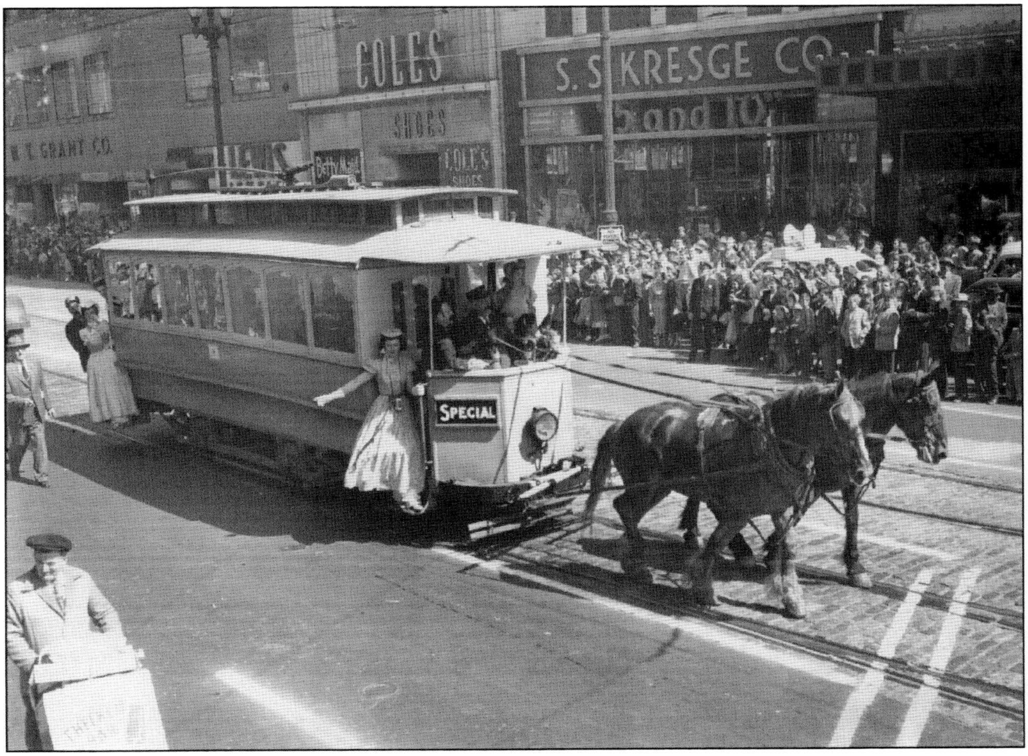

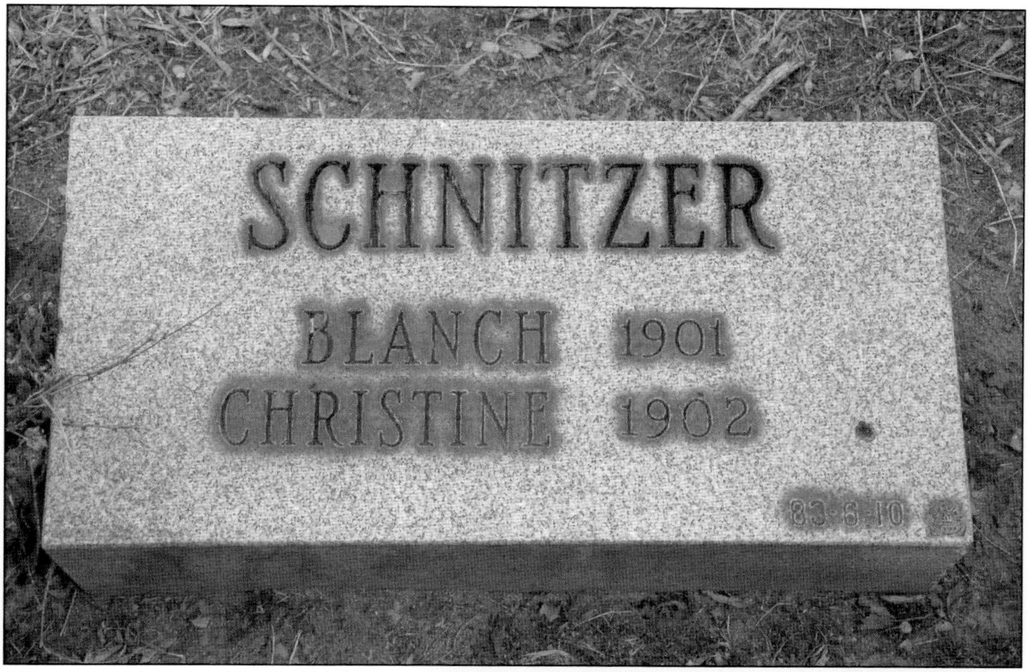

Christine Schnitzer (1886–1902) died in Charity Hospital from burns sustained in a fire at Fairmont Manufacturing Co., which produced *torpedoes*, a type of firework that was popular at the time. Two other young women, ages 17 and 18, also died in the accidental fire, which was started as an inexperienced employee was mixing chemicals. (MAD.)

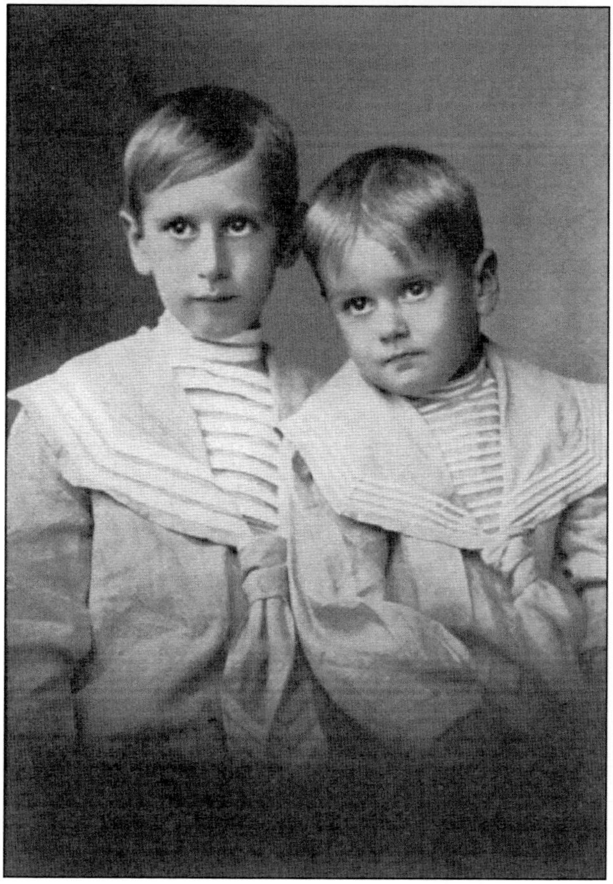

Tommy and Nils Thompson, sons of Swedish couple Otto and Sophie Thompson, died together in the Collinwood School Fire on March 4, 1908. Otto had died in a railroad accident in 1899, leaving Sophie a widow. Nils, the oldest son and "a great help to his mother," had escaped from a window of the school but, when he was unable to find Tommy, he went back into the school to look for him. (Marshall Everett/N.G. Hamilton Publishing Co.)

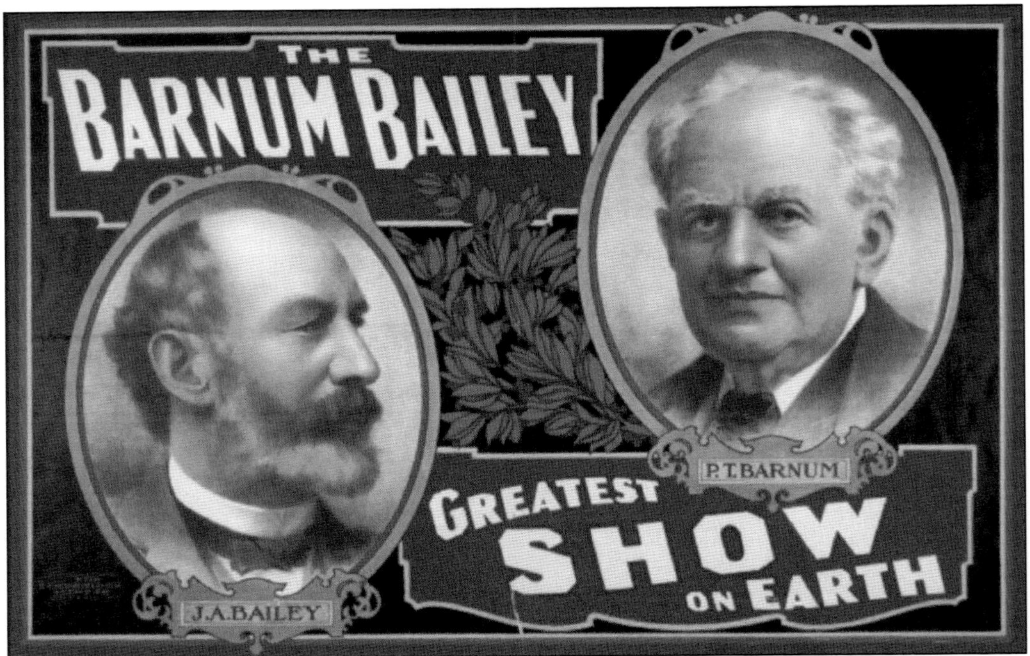

Charles Lyle, a Philadelphia-born man of around 40 years of age, arrived in Cleveland as a driver for the Barnum and Bailey Circus about a week after the Hagenbeck Circus had appeared, in May 1906. Charles was killed on May 31st at the Fairfield grounds when he was accidentally run over by one of the heavy trucks owned by the circus. His daughter agreed that the circus would pay for his burial. (New York Public Library for Performing Arts.)

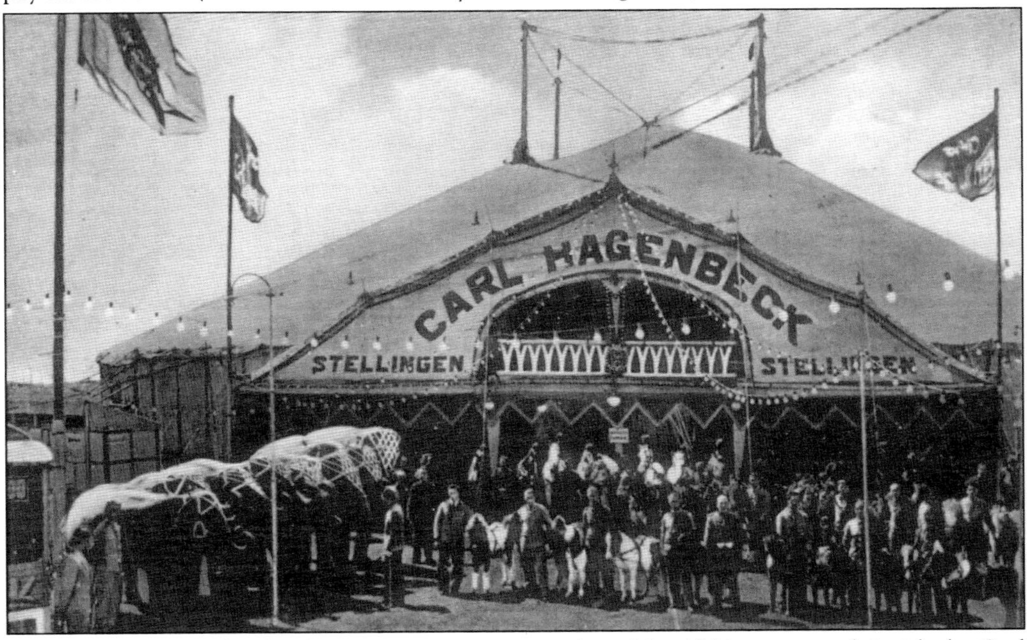

Henry Ross, believed to be about 21, came to town early in May 1906 as an attaché with the Carl Hagenbeck Circus. Henry became very ill and was diagnosed with cerebral spinal meningitis at Charity Hospital, where he died on May 16th. His burial was paid for by the circus after the authorities did not find any information regarding any next of kin. (MAD.)

Isabella Waller (1821–1903) was married first to Josiah Bate, who died in New York in 1856. She moved to Cleveland with her four children and lived with a sister-in-law, Octavia Bate, an unmarried nurse. In 1863, Isabella married Englishman William Waller. It was perhaps her relationship with Octavia that gave her an idea for improving the design of hospital beds, which earned her Patent 124,398 in March 1872. (Miami University Library.)

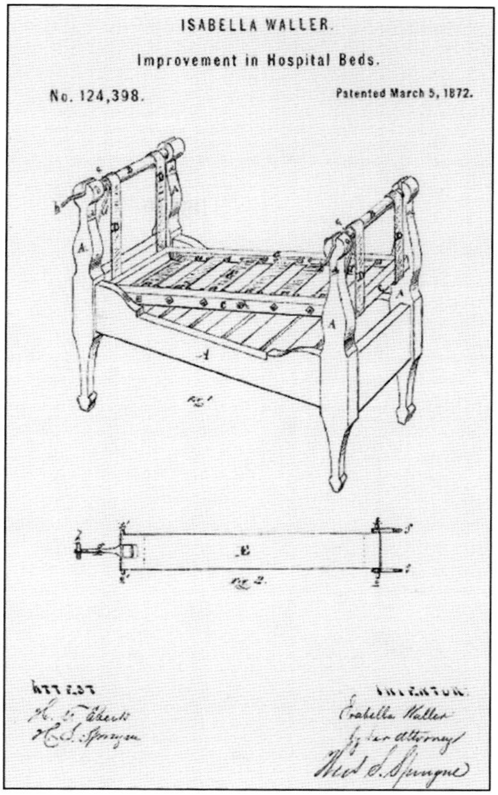

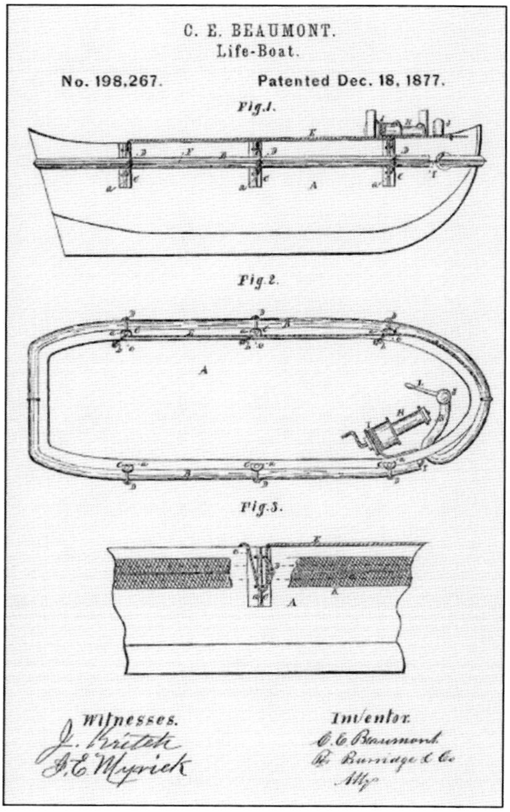

Cornelia Pease Erwin Beaumont (1839–1903) invented an improvement in lifeboats, which earned her Patent No. 198,267 on December 18, 1877. Cornelia had married Dr. William Henry Beaumont (born in London, England) in 1862, and the couple had seven children. They lived in the Newburgh area, and may have owned a floral shop as William was working as a florist in 1870, and Cornelia worked as a florist following the death of her husband. (Miami University Library.)

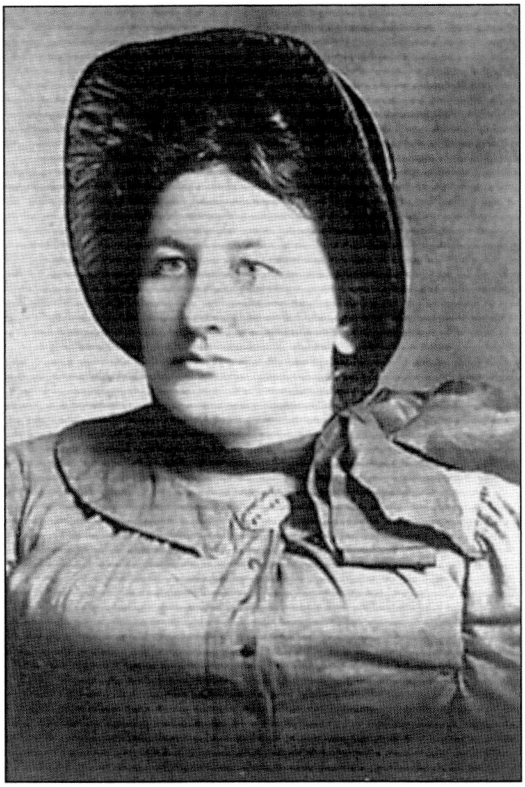

On May 9, 1869, German immigrants Henry May and Caroline "Carrie" Maria Berensmeyer (1854–1923) were married at the Zion Lutheran Church in Cleveland. Carrie had 18 pregnancies, including twins, with many of the children dying at birth or as young infants. Nine children lived to become adults. (Rene Holz.)

Henry May (1844–1922) worked as a shoemaker to support his family at the Sandusky Shoe Repairing Factory in Cleveland. Pictured below around 1910 are, from left to right, Harry E. Garber (the shop's owner), Frank Neuberger, and Henry May. (Rene Holz.)

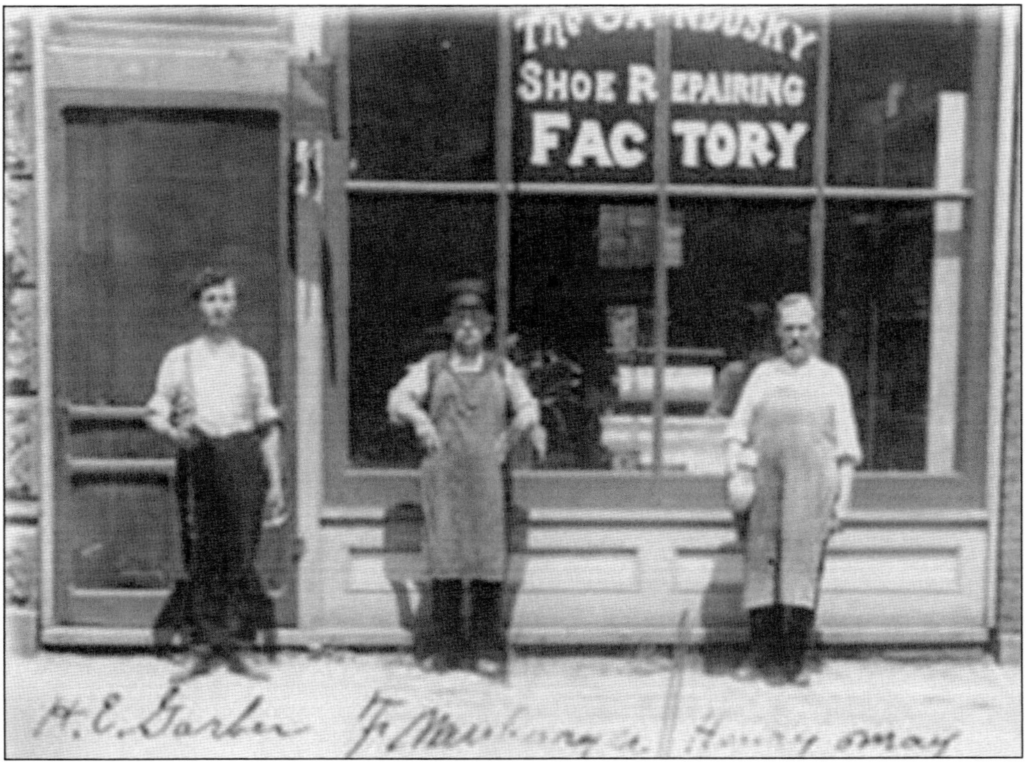

Henry Gilbert Abbey (1821–1887) was a respected attorney who practiced law in Wisconsin; panned for gold in 1849 in California; and became proficient in the knowledge of business, labor, and management. He became a lawyer-agent and assistant to Leonard Case, owner of Case School of Applied Science in Cleveland. Abbey managed the entire Case estate and negotiated with individuals and corporations as required. He married Mathilde "Amelia" Johnstone in 1859. (Cleveland Abbe and Joseph Genung Nichols.)

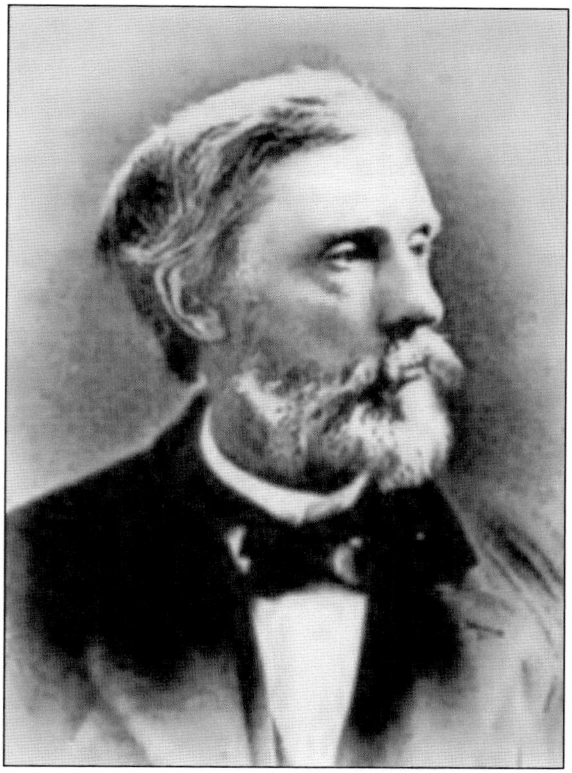

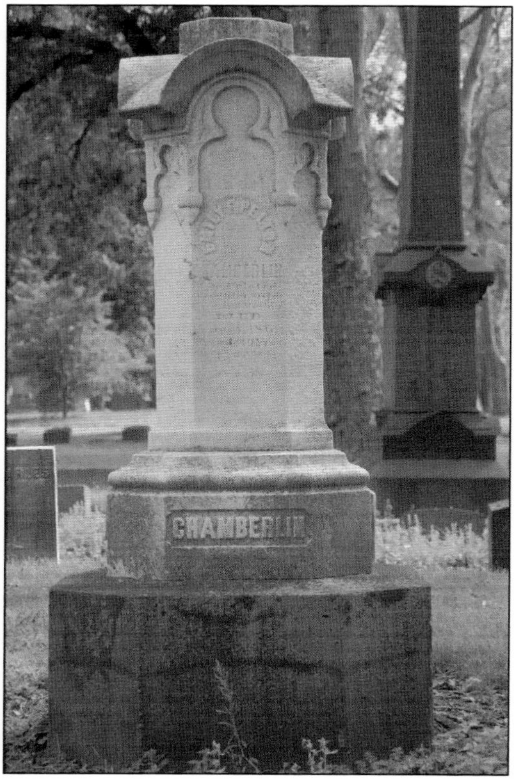

Philo E. Chamberlain (1811–1886) and his second wife, Sarah Ellsworth Chamberlain (1835–1908), had one daughter, Martha Pamela Chamberlain (1863–1884). Philo had been mayor in Akron (1845–1846), became a county commissioner in Cleveland, and began the Northern Transportation Co. on Lake Erie. In 1878, he acquired land in Michigan's Leelanau Peninsula to ensure a reliable supply of wood for his fleet of steamers, which ran between New York, Chicago, and Milwaukee. (Carolyn Barrett.)

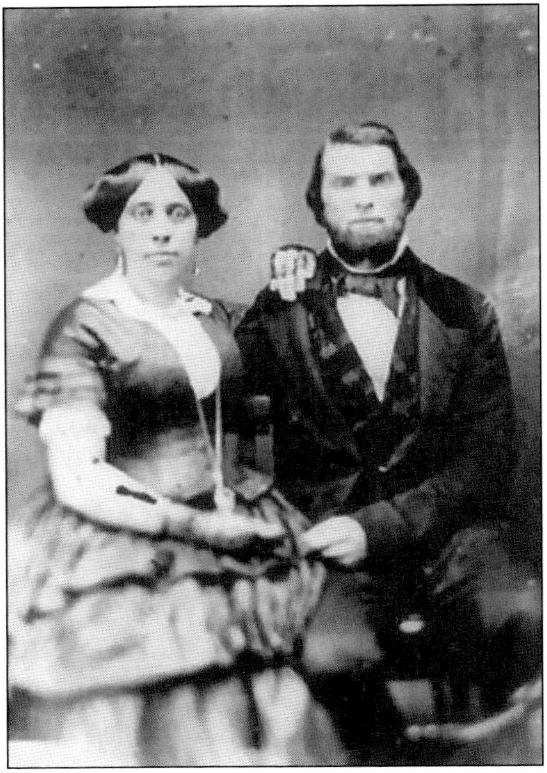

David "Brown" Alexander (1820–1860) died of tuberculosis and is buried with his second wife, Frances Ann Parnell (1822–1863). He and his first wife, Mary Ann, immigrated to America from England in 1832 and settled in Northfield, Ohio. Mary Ann, who died in 1848, is buried in Northfield with their three-year-old daughter Elizabeth. Brown was a member of the Cleveland Red Jackets (a volunteer firefighting group) and also practiced carpentry. When he died in 1860, Frances was left with two young sons, Charles and William. She worked as a dressmaker to support herself and the boys until her death three years later, in 1863. (Mary Helen Bouchard/MAD.)

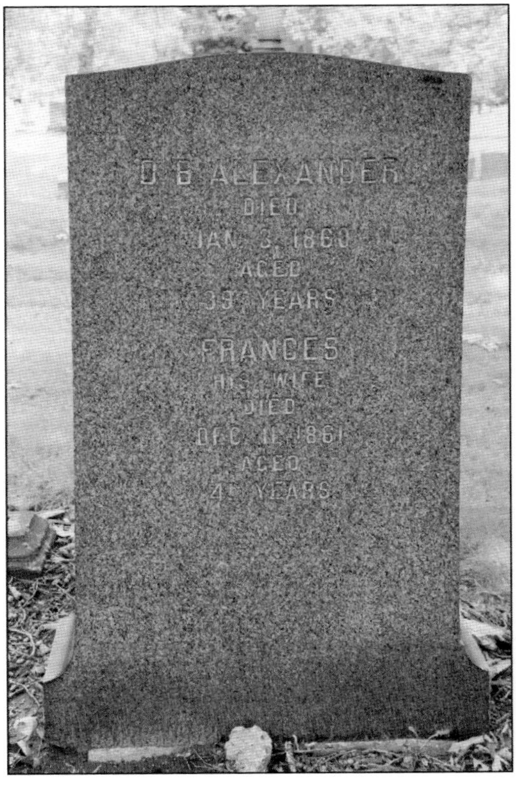

Daniel Conway (1847–1909) from Newfoundland was a marine engineer and a member of the Marine Engineers Beneficial Association for 30 years. He served in the Civil War from 1863 to July 1865 and married Minerva "Minnie" White of Oswego, New York, in 1871. The last ship he sailed as an "engineer on the lake" was the steamer *Portage*. Daniel was 62 years old when he died. (MAD.)

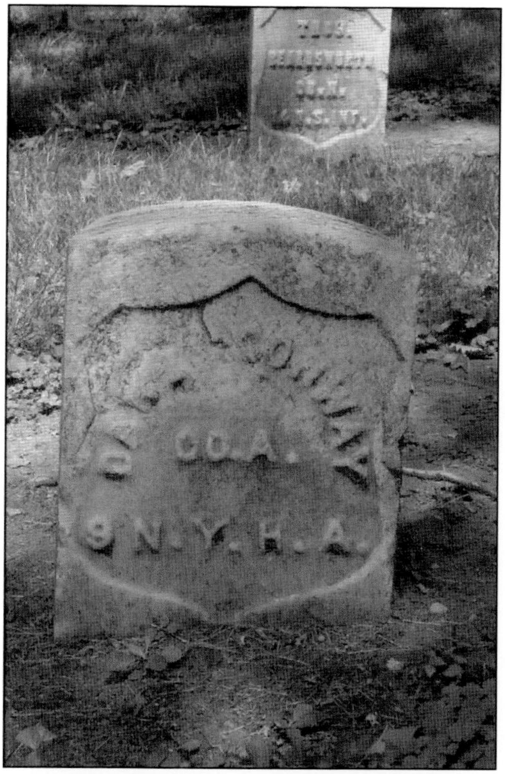

Thomas (1811–1889) and Elizabeth Hawley Cross (1812–1901) married on June 20, 1831, in Leicestershire, England, before immigrating to America on the *Kate Howe* in May 1850. They settled first in Wisconsin, but by 1900 had moved to Cleveland, where Thomas continued to work as a farmer. The couple had 14 children. At the time of Elizabeth's death in 1901, there were 20 grandchildren and four great-grandchildren. (Nancy Gavin Koester.)

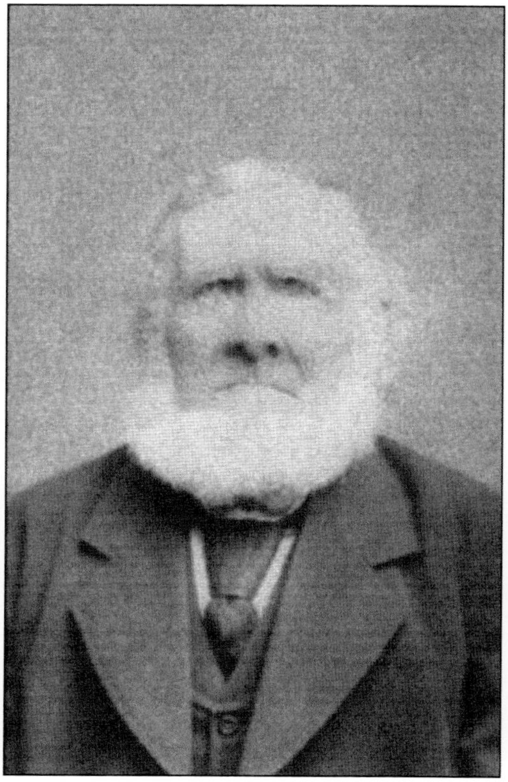

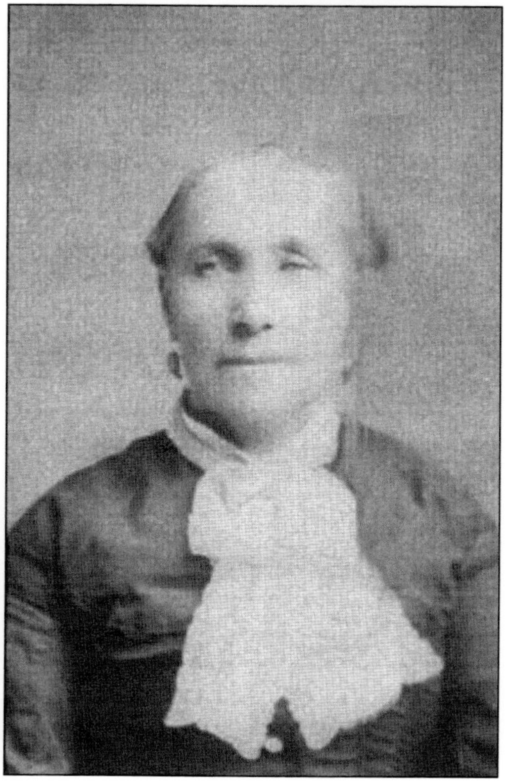

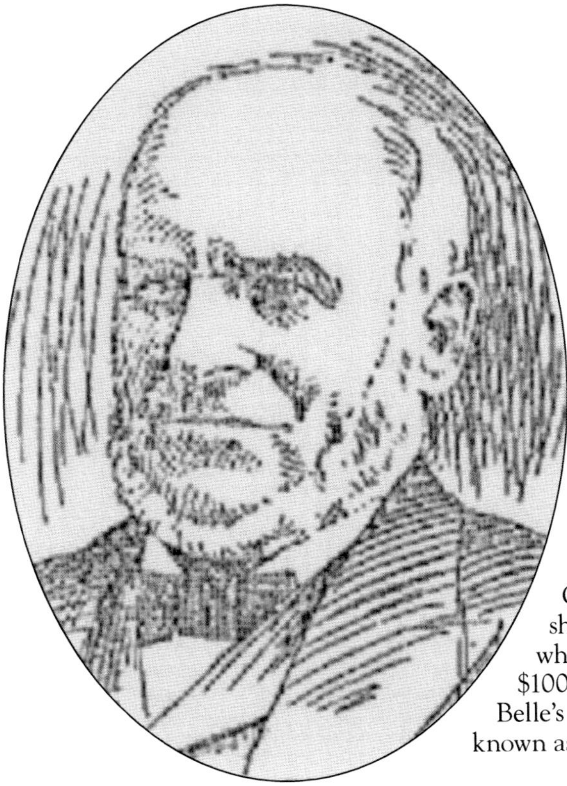

Daniel Corlett Jr. (1820–1899), a marine engineer who also worked as a boilermaker and farmer, came to America from Ballaugh, Isle of Man, in 1841 and settled in Newburgh. In 1845, he married Isabelle "Belle" Mollen (1821–1898) of Monaghan County, Ireland; they had six children. Daniel showed his friendship for the Mona Society, which he had helped to organize, by leaving $100 to begin a permanent endowment fund. Belle's brother Christopher Mollen became well known as Cleveland's first auctioneer. (Tim Davis.)

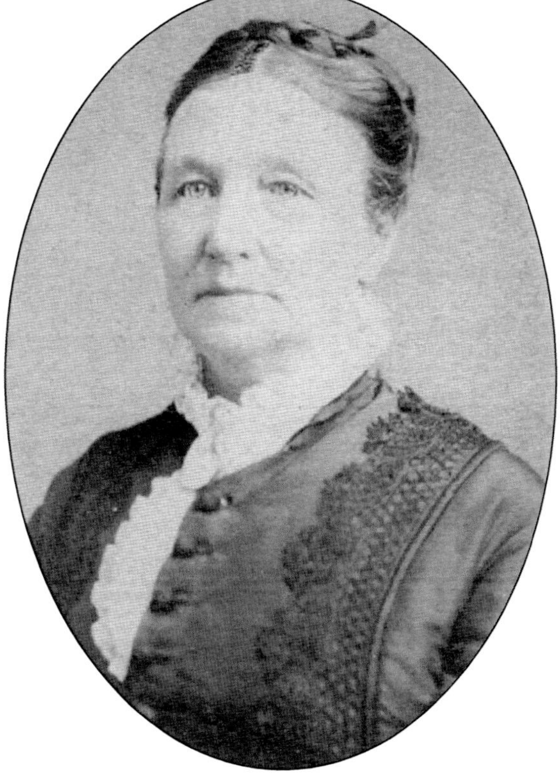

William Carl Dewald (1836–1910) from Baden, Germany, married Catharine "Katy" Klump and was the owner of W. Dewald Coal Yard, a retail coal business based on Woodland Avenue in Cleveland. William also worked as an iron molder and may have shared ownership of a saloon during the time he owned the coal yard. Carl and Katy had four children; one, Lillie, died young, but the other three, Charles, Frank, and Louisa, all reached adulthood. (Daryl Mallett and Barbara Biggs.)

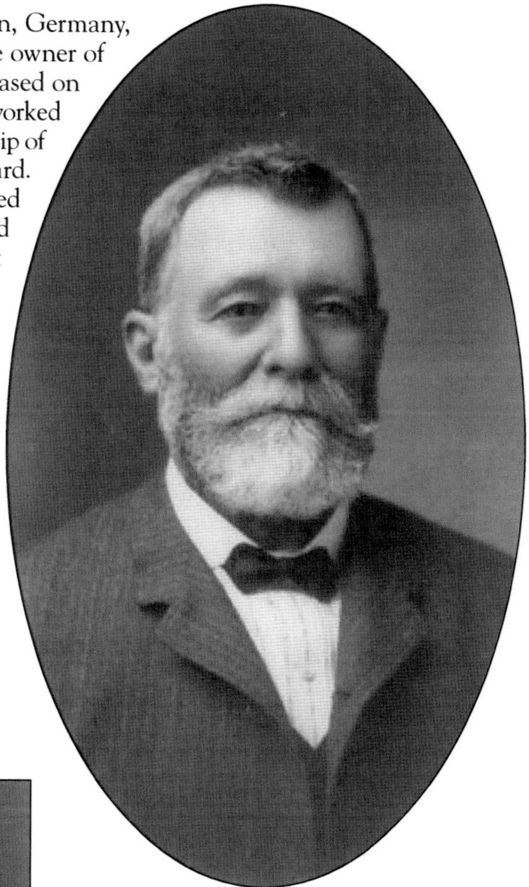

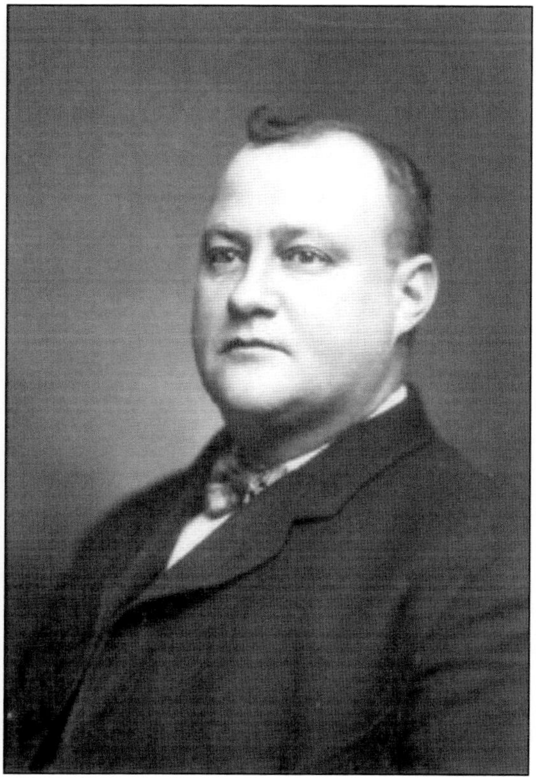

Charles H. "Carl" Dewald (1867–1904), born in Newark, New Jersey, became a professional baseball player in September 1890 at the age of 22. He pitched, left-handed, for the Cleveland Infants. The team disbanded after finishing that year with 55 wins and 75 losses. Carl married Nellie Gertrude Fiess (1880–1967) on July 11, 1900, when he was a bookkeeper and the superintendent of Woodland Cemetery. He died unexpectedly in 1904. (Daryl Mallett and Barbara Biggs.)

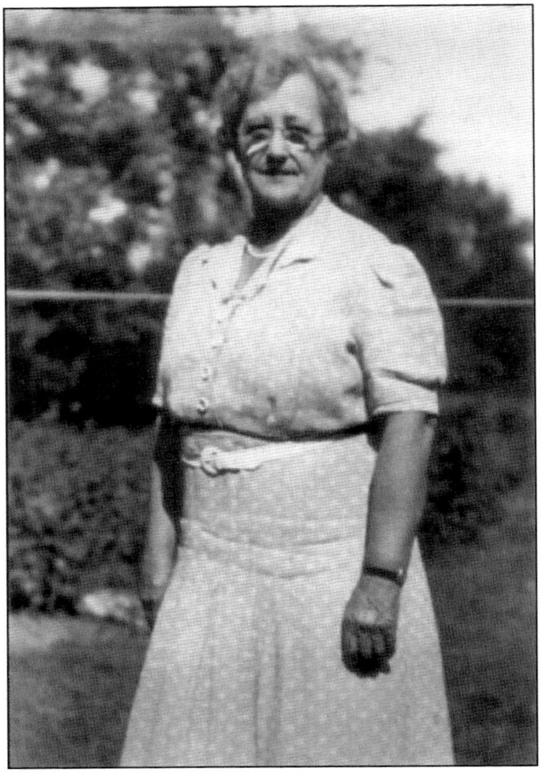

Louise Emily "Bill" Dewald (1877–1954) was the highest-ranking woman employee of the City of Cleveland for many years. She was employed by the city in 1900, under Mayor Tom L. Johnson, and remained through seven administrations. She was the city commissioner of cemeteries for 19 years, and her office was located at Woodland. Dewald resigned in 1942. When she died at Highland View Hospital, she was the last surviving member of her family. (Daryl Mallett and Barbara Biggs.)

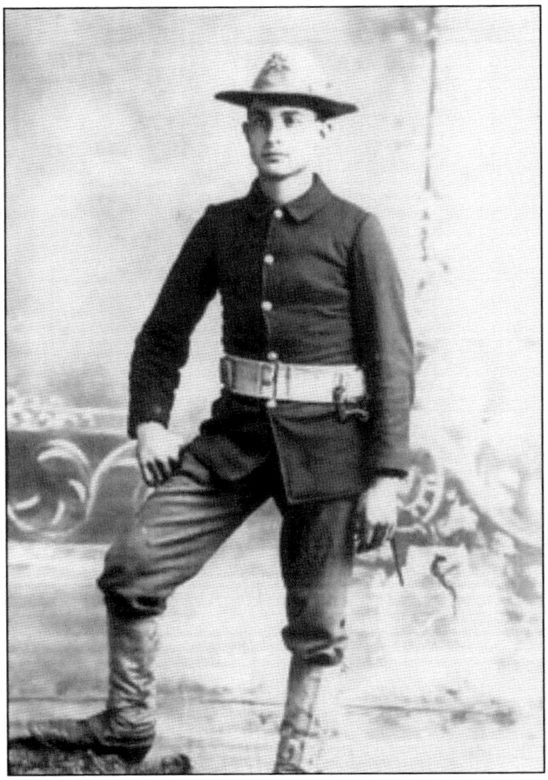

Frank Ernest Dewald (1875–1911), a private with the A 10th Ohio Voluntary Infantry Regiment, filed for his pension in 1902. Frank worked as the bookkeeper at his father's business, W. Dewald Coal Yard, as well as at other businesses in Cleveland. Frank and his wife, Elizabeth Mary "Bessie" Stutzman (1881–1965), had four children: William A., Luella Louise, and twins Erna Nellie and Ernest Leroy (born in 1907). (Daryl Mallett and Barbara Biggs.)

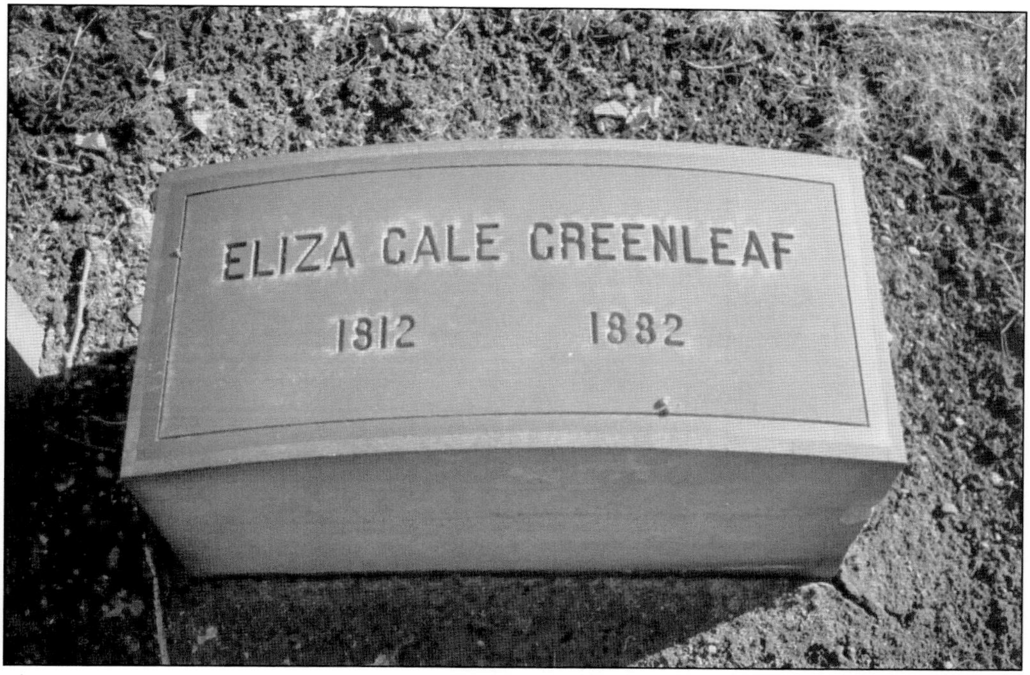

Eliza Gale Greenleaf (1812–1882), born in Cheshire County, New Hampshire, married Hiram Paige (1805–1835) in 1829; they had three children before he died and was buried in Vermont. Eliza then married Charles Ward Greenleaf (1805–1896) of Massachusetts, and they had one child. The 1880 census finds Eliza and Charles, a son named George, and a married daughter living in Rockport (now Rocky River). Charles, a farmer, died in 1896. (MAD.)

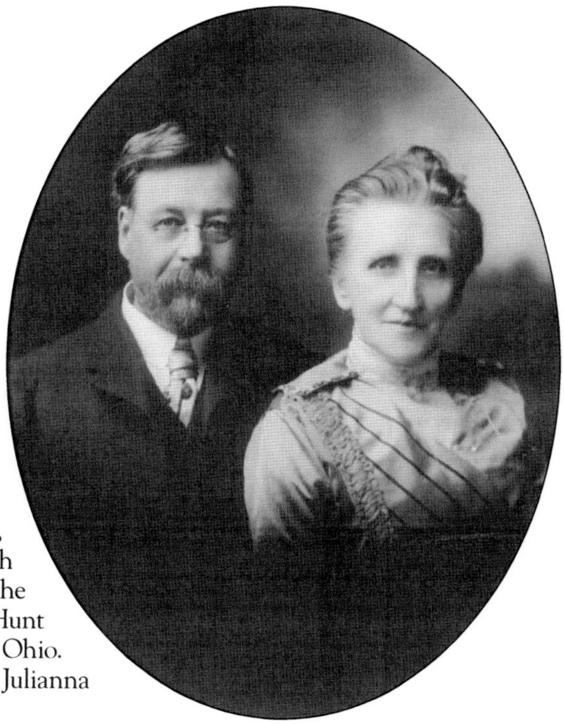

Alden Sidney Gulliford (1845–1922) married Julianna Stead (1845–1917) on November 27, 1871. Julianna came to America from England in 1859. During the Civil War, Alden served with several Pennsylvania regiments, including the 83rd, 58th, and 145th. In 1863, during his time with the 58th, the regiment was involved with the capture of the "dare devil confederate" John Hunt Morgan (of Morgan's Raiders) in Salineville, Ohio. Alden became a real estate agent, and he and Julianna had eight children. (Diana Devine.)

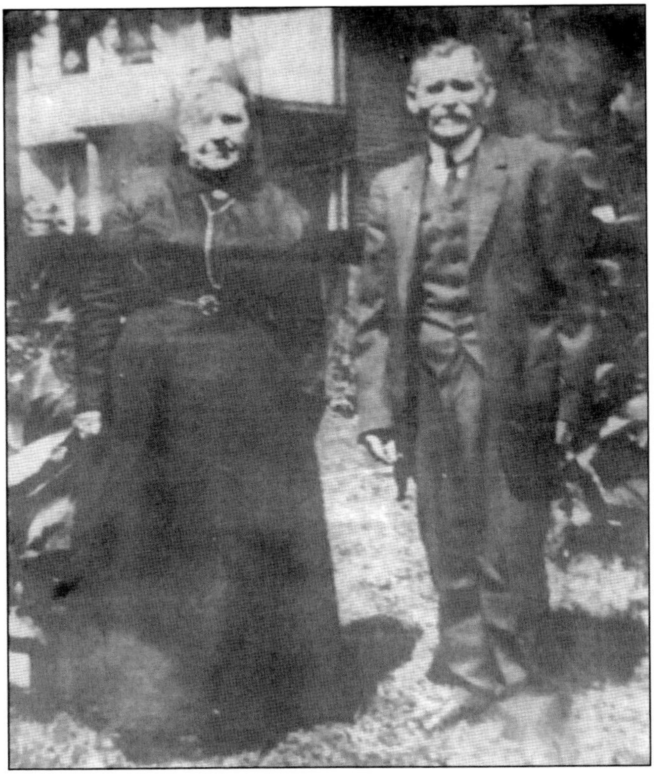

Frederick James Hickman (1850–1932) from London, England, worked at National Malleable and Steel Castings in Cleveland as an engineer and iron molder. He married Agnes Small (1852–1923) from Scotland on September 11, 1872, in Cleveland. Their five children were James R., Lillie, John, Samuel (killed in a 1913 motorcycle accident at Luna Pier), and Winifred. James loved growing and tending lilies and taking motor car trips. (Diane Oster.)

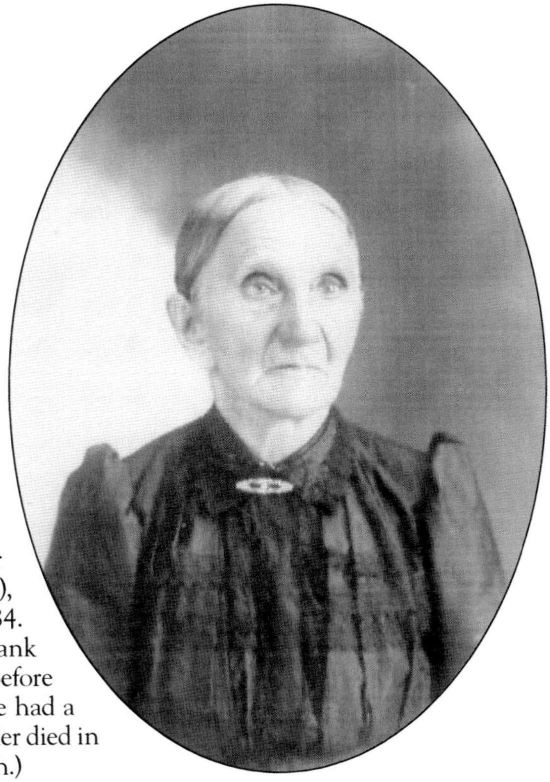

Johanna Langmeyer Kessler Hirkala (1842–1921), born in Bohemia, is buried with her second husband, George Hirkala (1857–1925), whom she married on December 1, 1884. Johanna had previously been married to Frank Kessler, with whom she had five children before they divorced in 1884. Johanna and George had a son, also named George, in 1887. Frank Kessler died in a railroad accident in 1909. (Cheryl Rudolph.)

Bozena "Bertha" Kliner (1865–1926) was born in Cleveland to John and Marie Kliner, who emigrated from Bohemia. Bertha, who never married, lived with her brother Edward (1872–1942), a machinist at White Sewing Machine Co. who also never married. Bertha was listed in the Cleveland City Directory from 1904 until 1920 as a dressmaker. She had two other brothers: Joseph, a cigar maker, and William, a brick mason. Bertha died at 66 years of age. (Diane Oster.)

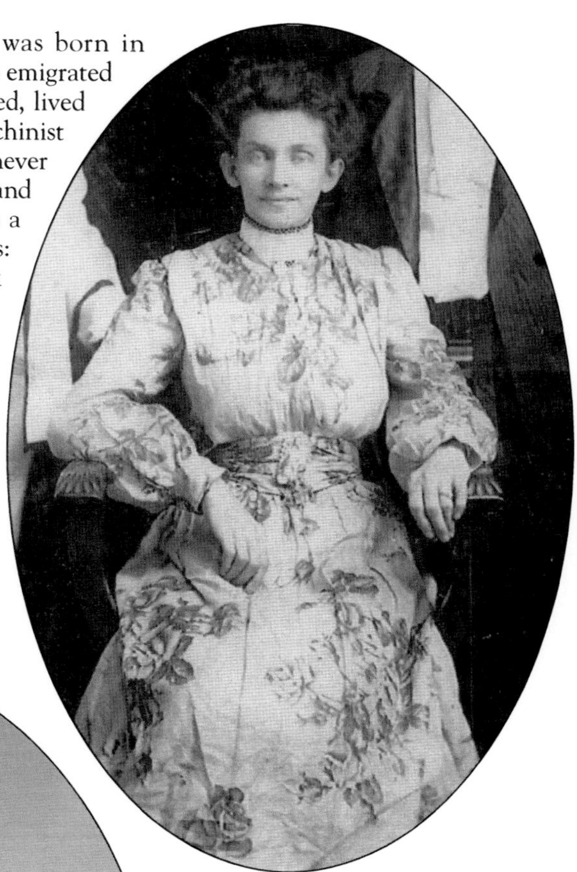

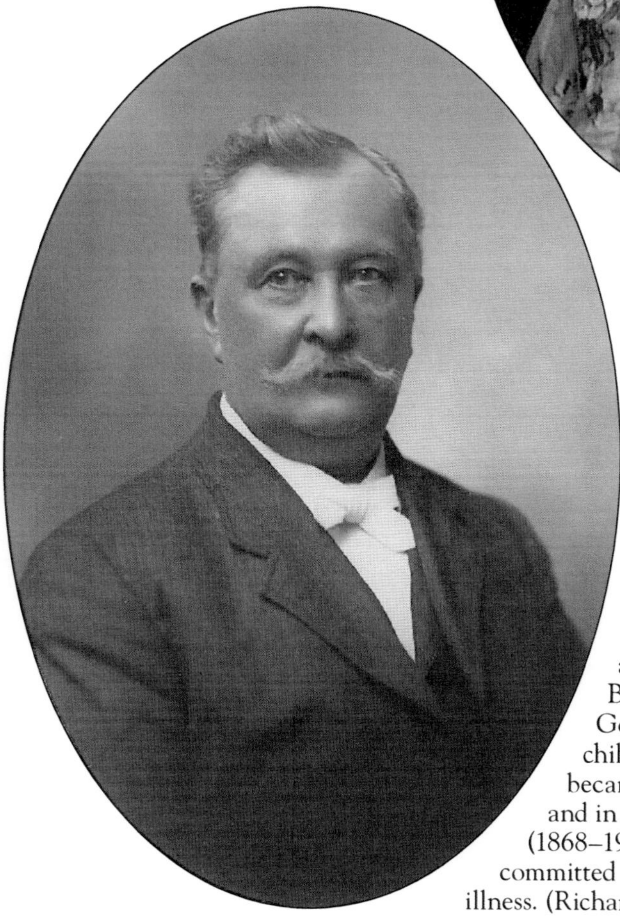

Eugene Leopold Lemmers (1845–1922) born in Antwerp, Belgium, was the owner of Lemmers Umbrella Co., a shop in the old Cleveland Arcade Building. Eugene married Adophine Goddaris (1844–1904) and had four children, three sons and a daughter. Eugene became a naturalized citizen before 1910, and in June 1911, he married Alma Frappier (1868–1941) from Quebec. In 1922, Eugene committed suicide after suffering an undisclosed illness. (Richard Lemmers.)

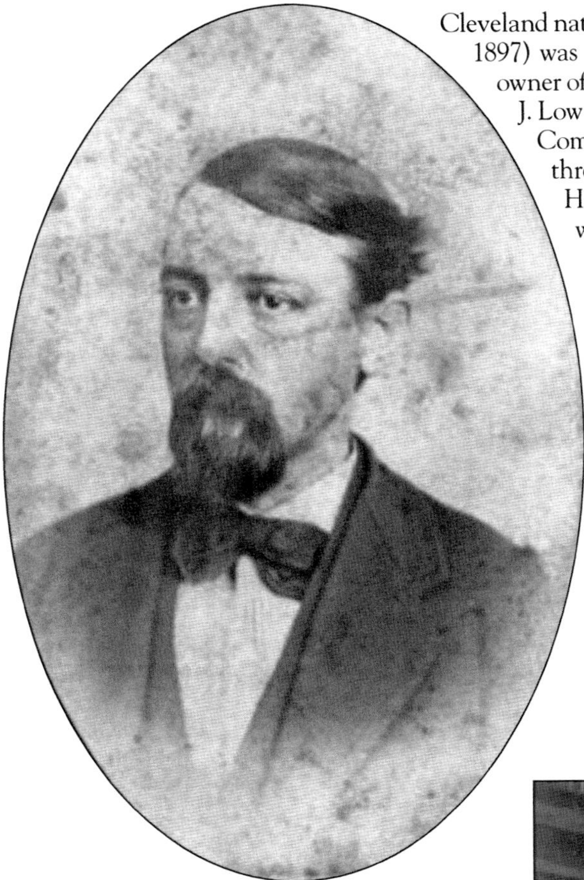

Cleveland native Mather Jacob "Matt" Lowman (1843–1897) was the seventh son born to Jacob Lowman, owner of a carriage manufacturing company called J. Lowman & Son. Matt served as a private with Company E, 84th Regiment Ohio Infantry for three months in 1862. In July 1865, he married Harriet E. McNary. He was a carriage builder with his father's company by 1880, having previously been the bookkeeper. (James McNary Bogart.)

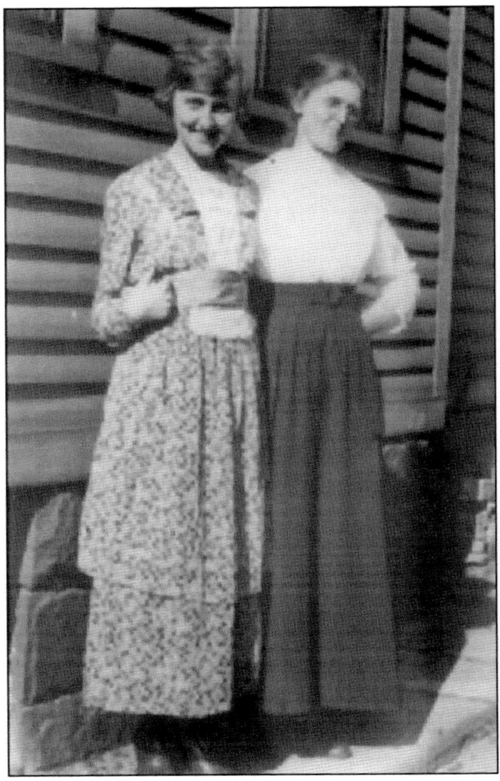

Pictured on the right in this photograph, Lulu Julia Simek Marsh (1873–1934), born in Cleveland to Frank and Mary Simek from Bohemia, married William J. Marsh (1871–1904), a Bohemian immigrant, on October 14, 1891. Pictured on the left in this photograph, Mildred Lucille Marsh Holz (1902–1943), Lulu's daughter, married and divorced. By 1930, Mildred and her two sons, Robert and Donald, were living with Lulu. Mildred's brother Frank Clarence Marsh had moved to California. (Robert W. Holz.)

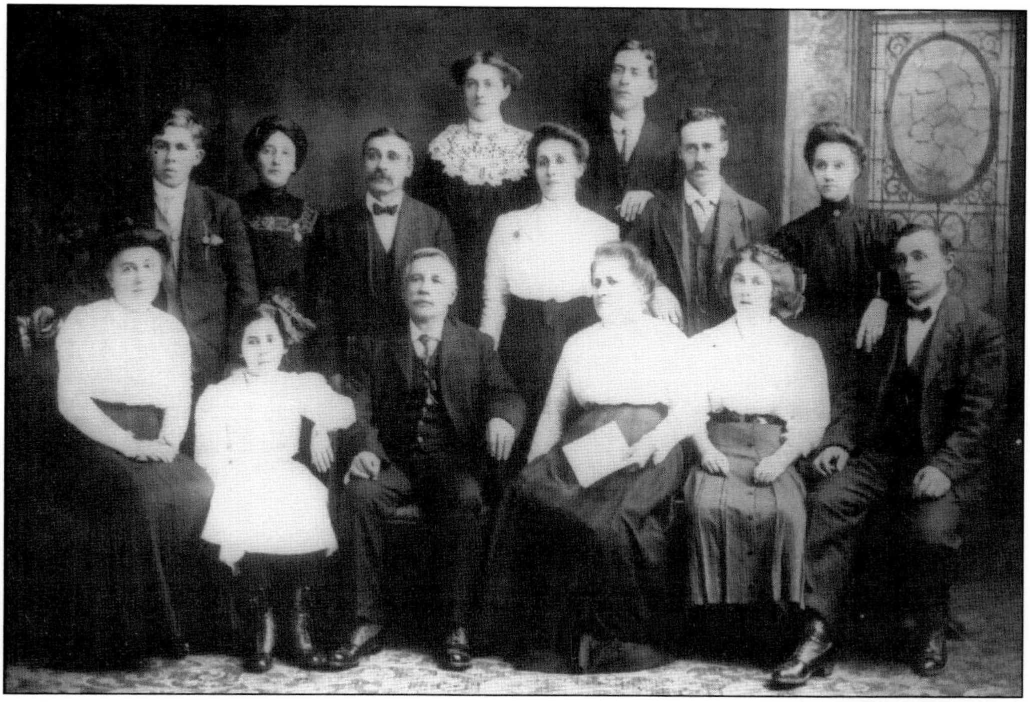

Fred Albert Sikes (1866–1950) married Alice Ella May Becker, one of five children born in Ashtabula to Jacob and Theora Corey Becker. Fred was a machinist when he married Alice; he later became an insurance agent. Fred and Alice had three children: John, Maude, and Ruth. Pictured in this family photograph are, from left to right, (first row, seated) Emma Louise Becker (sister of Alice), Ruth Sikes (daughter of Fred and Alice), Jacob Becker, Theora Corey Becker, and Maude Sikes (daughter of Fred and Alice); (second row, standing) John Sikes (son of Fred and Alice), three unidentified people, Alice Becker Sikes (wearing the white blouse), unidentified, Fred Sikes, and unidentified. (Minda Shun.)

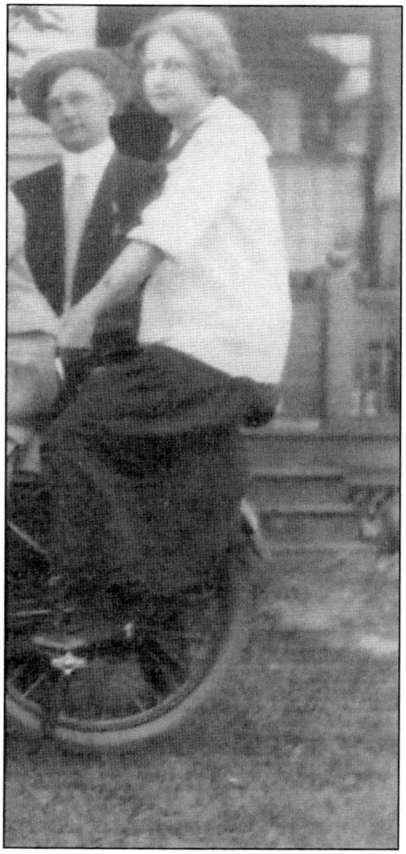

Lillian Kessler Cates Ney (1891–1919), the eldest of eight children born to Joseph and Josephine Dolezal Kessler, was born in Cleveland, Ohio, and married twice. Lillian's first marriage ended in divorce, and the two resulting children, Verna (1911–1916) and Fred (1913–1944), used the surname Kessler. On September 7, 1915, Lillian married William F. Ney, a motorman. They had a son, William Henry Ney, in 1916. Three years later, Lillian died in the influenza epidemic. (Cheryl Rudolph.)

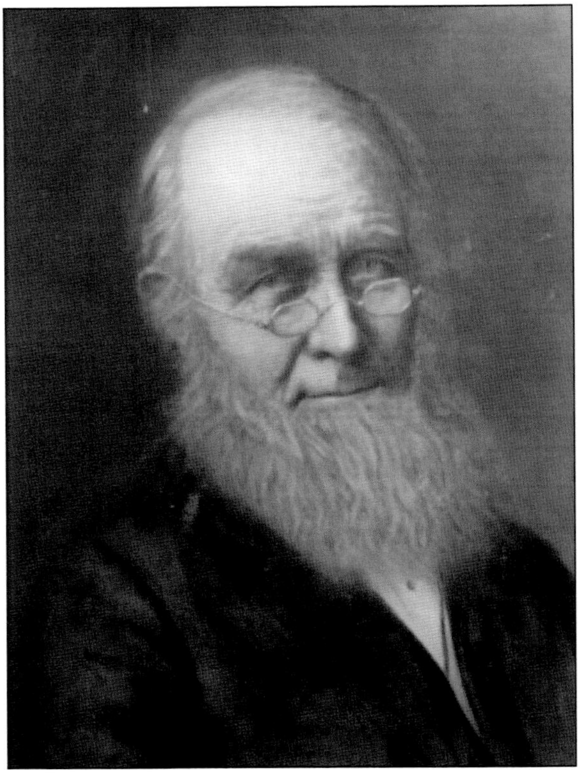

Samuel Russell (1816–1895), a sea captain's son, was born in England, where he apprenticed as a joiner and cabinetmaker. He married Ann Ransom Rushplumb, with whom he had 10 children. In 1868, Russell, Ann, eldest son Henry, daughter-in-law Hannah, and granddaughter Elizabeth embarked for America. Samuel's skills were welcomed in Cleveland, and he was soon in business as a builder. He constructed a large home in Cleveland and a cottage on Brady Lake. All of his other nine children followed him to Cleveland. (Sandra McGee and David Russell.)

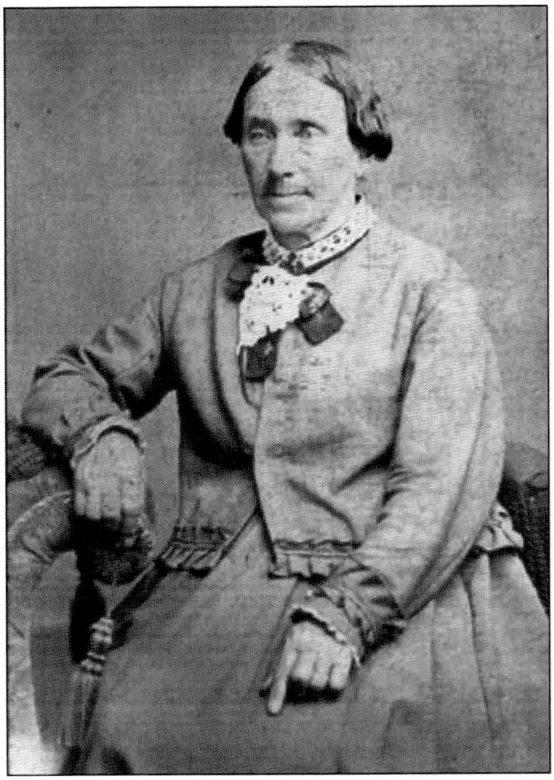

Ann Ransom Rushplumb Russell (1812–1875) was a young widow when she married Samuel Russell in 1839. They had 10 children while living in England, losing one infant, Ebenezer Armstrong, in 1853. Ann died just seven years after arriving in America and, according to family, had never really enjoyed the hurly-burly American life, which her husband had relished. (James Hollabaugh.)

Henry Russell (1840–1909) accompanied his parents to America, along with his wife, Hannah Wilson (1842–1914) whom he married in 1865. They had five children. Henry joined the Salvation Army Corps, working at the Cleveland Workhouse. He also led the singing and teaching in the prison Sunday school, as well as at the Rescue Home. He was a general contractor and owner of Russell & Son, which built various-sized factories and business blocks. (James Hollabaugh.)

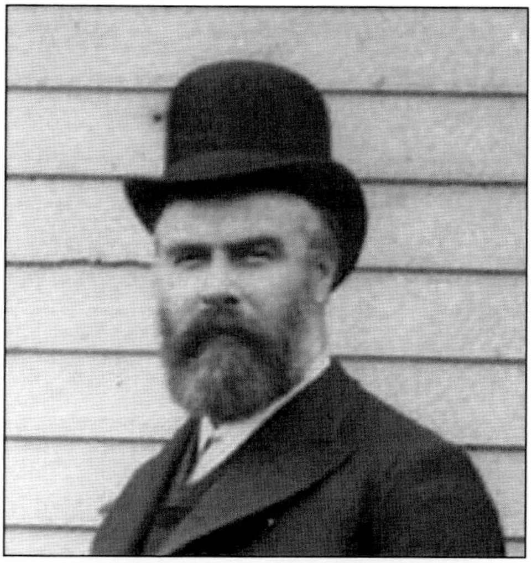

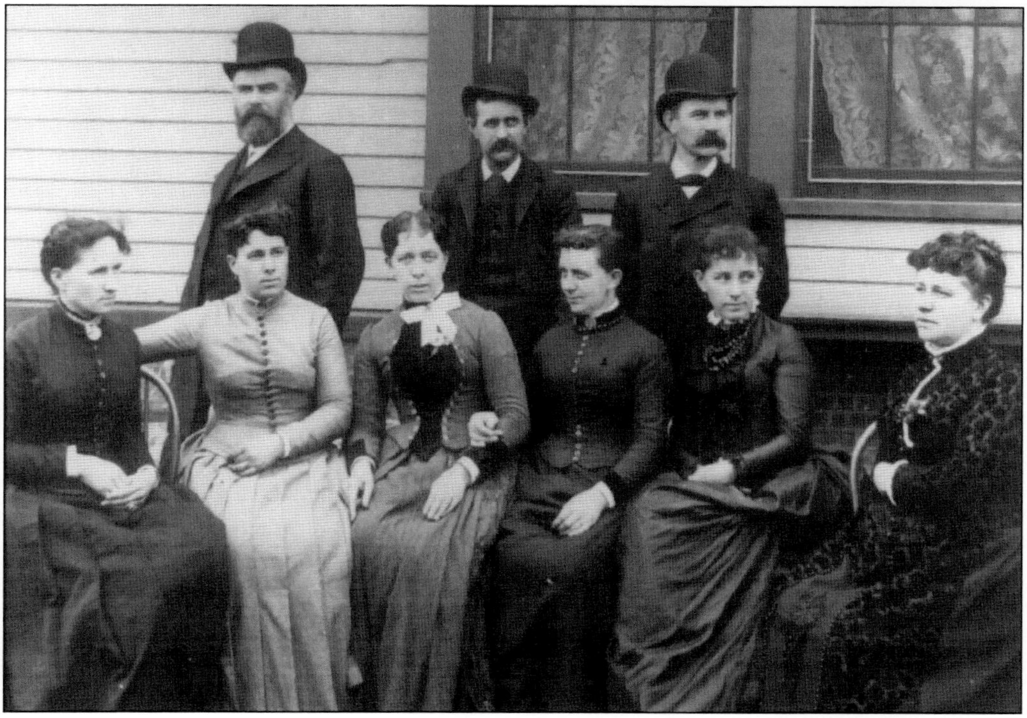

Pictured from left to right are (first row) Hannah Margaret Russell Jacobs (1854–1923), Ann Ranson Russell (1851–1924), Jane Russell Tate (1847–1932), Eleanor Russell Derby (1845–1908), Elizabeth Broom Russell Emerson (1844–1909), and Isabella Burlison Russell Pae (1842–1918); (second row) Henry Russell, Samuel Russell Jr. (1848–1908), and Ephraim Downs Russell (1850–1908). Samuel Jr. married Margaret E. Patterson, with whom he had one son and two daughters. Ephraim, a pattern maker, had two children with his first wife, Eliza Jane Duncan. Hannah married tinsmith Winfield Scott Jacobs in 1877 and had three sons. Jane, a dressmaker, married artist and photographer George Frederic Derby (1839–1889) in England in 1867, and together they had six sons and a daughter. In 1872, Elizabeth married pattern maker William Emerson in Ohio; the couple had one son, Edgar Russell Emerson. Isabella married carpenter Robert Pae, with whom she had one son, John William (1859–1910). (Sandra McGee and David Russell.)

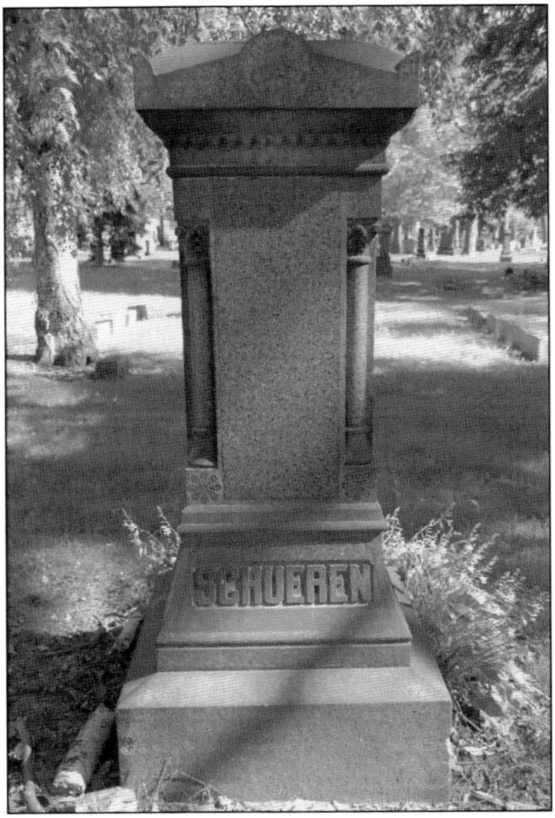

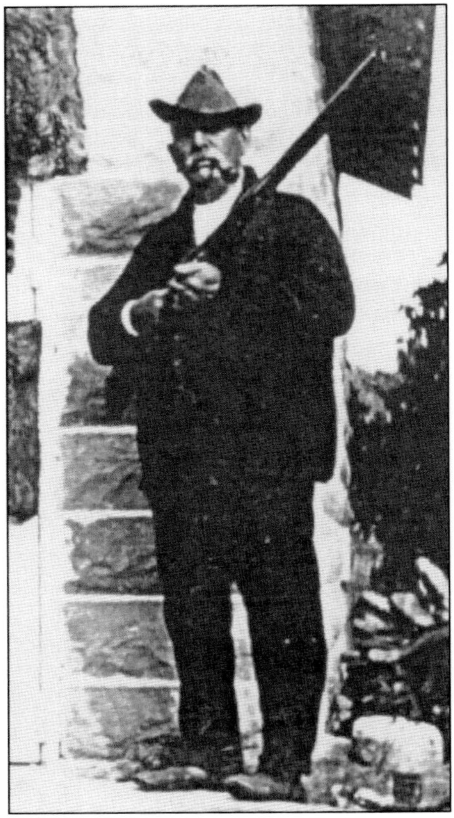

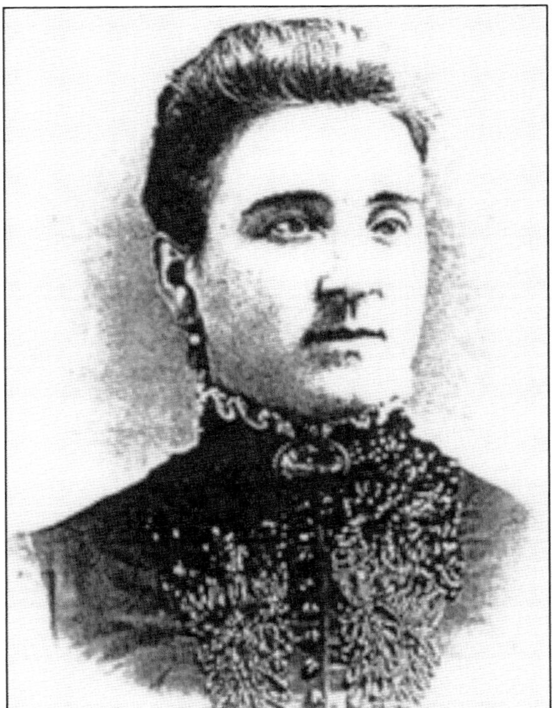

Casper Theodore Schueren (1854–1929) and Leonora Ganss (1860–1940) were married on July 10, 1883. They had two sons, Charles and Edwin. Theodore, who was born in Westphalia, Germany, became a naturalized citizen in 1876. He was the chief florist for Cleveland City Park and a propagator of flowers. Leonora's father, Jacob Ganss (1833–1900), had been a Cleveland policeman. As a widow, Leonora worked as a demonstrator of Singer Sewing Machines. (All photographs, Kathleen Glover.)

According to the 1870 census, Charles F. Thie (1851–1916), born in Prussia, worked as a brick mason and night watchman before becoming the owner of a successful wholesale liquor business, Thie Foreign & Domestic Wines & Liquors Import, at 198 Ontario Street. On November 1, 1873, he married Susan Klaus (1854–1908); the couple had two sons and a daughter. At the time of his death from a fractured skull in 1916, Charles had been living with his son Charles Jr. (James Heidenreich.)

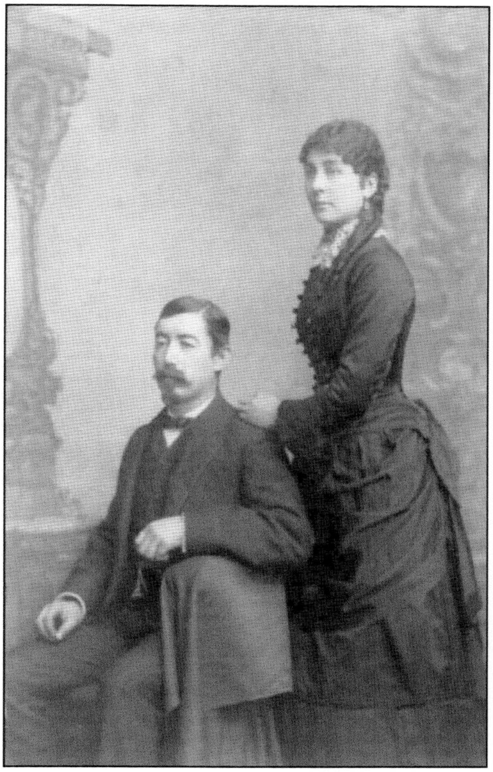

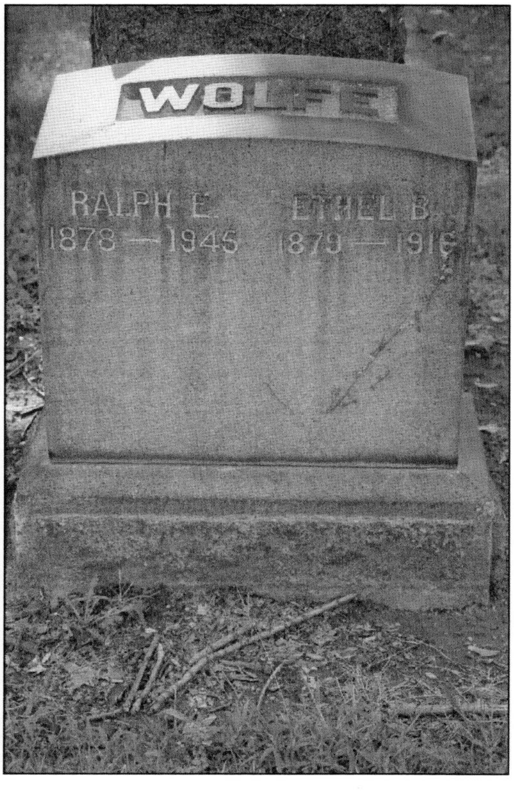

Ralph Edward Wolfe (1879–1945), from Illinois, made numerous acquaintances over his years in Cleveland as a barber; owner (1903–1913) of Haltnorth Gardens, a beer garden; and superintendent (for 25 years) of the Woodland Cemetery. In 1901, Ralph married Ethel Carroll (1880–1916), and they had three children. In 1918, he married Elizabeth Gore Webb (1884–1969) who had a son. Together they had a daughter, for a total of five children. (MAD.)

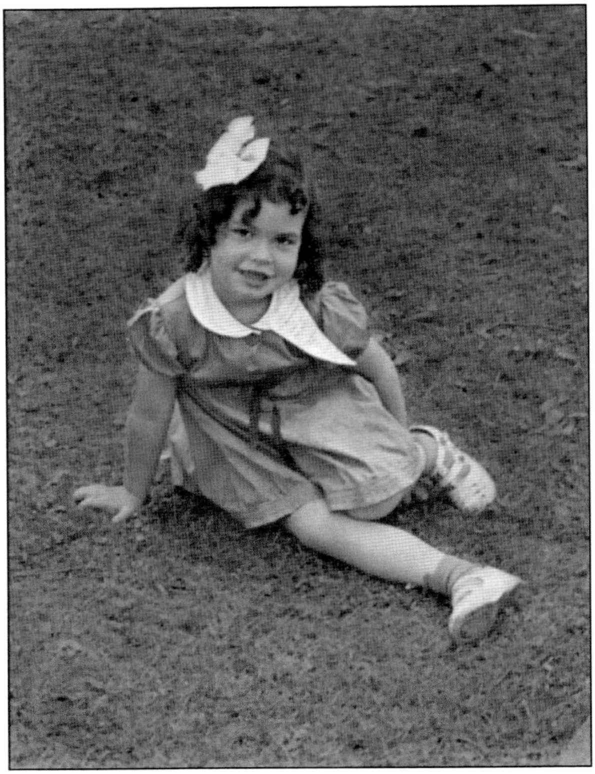

Phyllis Jean Verchio (1934–1939), the daughter of Pete and Eudora Runyan Verchio, had miraculously escaped death in June 1938 when she grabbed the fender of a moving automobile as it bore down on her, holding on until it stopped. She escaped with minor injuries, and the story was picked up by news agencies all over America. Phyllis Jean died six months later of cellulitis on January 29, 1939. (Elizabeth Crauswell Verchio.)

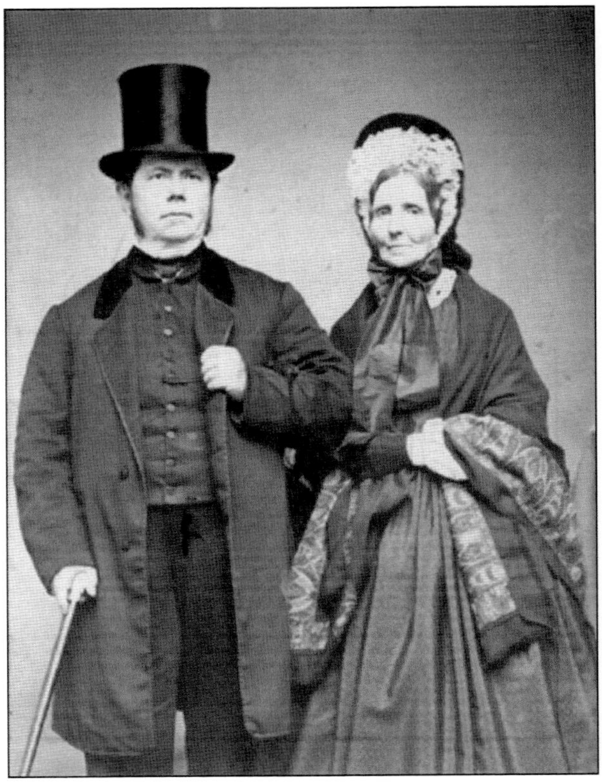

James Warr (1809–1874) from Tipton, Staffordshire, England, went to Boonton, New Jersey, when he heard they needed skilled ironworkers. In 1834, he married Lavina Bickley Hodgkins (1815–1896) and they began their family of 16 children; their youngest, Rufus, was born in 1855. James worked at Lake Shore Iron Works in Cleveland and, by 1868, owned a boardinghouse with a restaurant and saloon on Champlain Street. (Richard Anderson.)

George Michael Steinbrenner I (1825–1897) and his wife, Magdalena, came to Cleveland from Germany. His famous grandson, George Michael III, became the owner of the New York Yankees. George I worked as a carpenter. He and Magdalena had six children, none of whom are buried with their parents. However, additional relatives are buried with them. (MAD.)

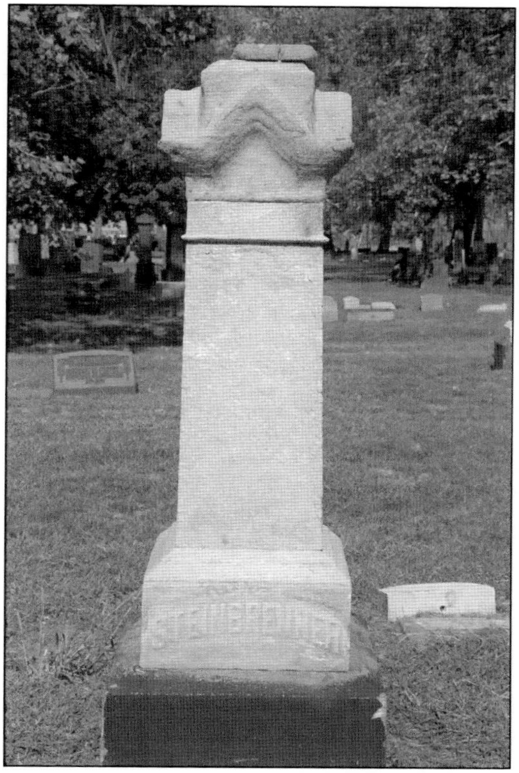

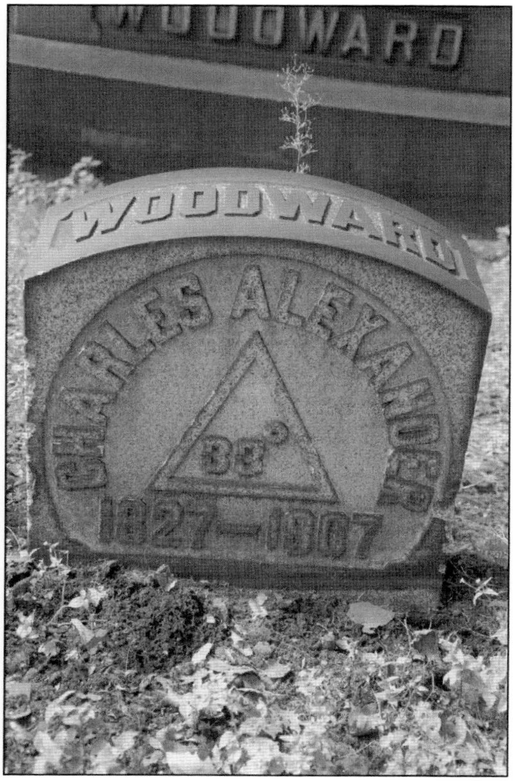

Charles A. Woodward (1827–1907) sold his interest in a wholesale grocery business and retired, with the objective to "get all the good out of life that there is in it." Woodward was one of the oldest and best-known Masons in Ohio when he died in 1907, having been the 29th Grand Master of Masons in Ohio from 1875 to 1877. He never married, and it saddened him to have no living relatives upon his death. (MAD.)

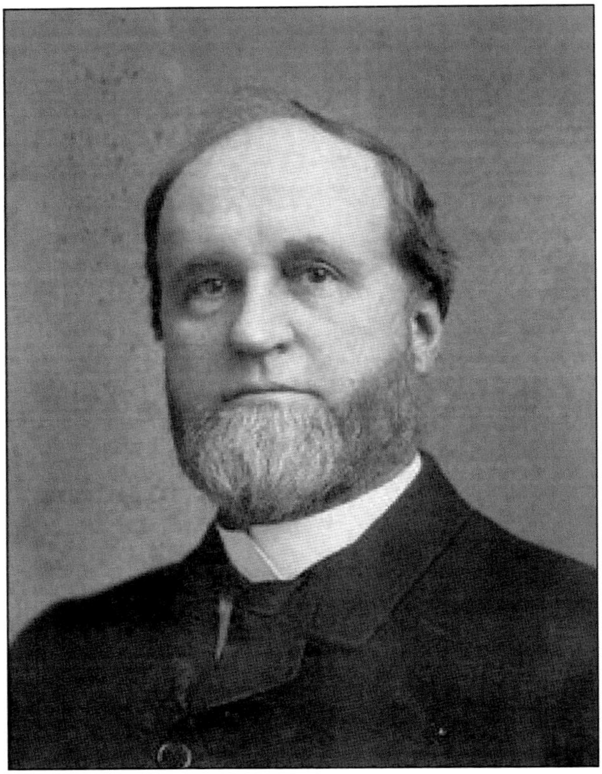

William Gustavis Yates (1830–1894) began working with the United States Express Company at a young age. He remained with them as the Cleveland agent until a month before he died of lung cancer. Yates was proud that he did not belong to any secret society, though he was a member and director of Expressmen's Mutual Benefit Association. His first wife, Marie Utley, died in 1858, and he was outlived by his second wife, Evaline E. Noble (1833–1903). (Sonia Cook.)

The Case of John Langmeyer.

Dr. Holliday who made a *post mortem* examination of the late John Langmeyer is of the opinion that the deceased came to his death from natural causes. At the Coroner's inquest held to-day in the Third Precinct Police Station Frank Langmeyer, an uncle of the dead man said that John before his death stated that Frank Kostohovic and Franz Matizka had assaulted him. Witness further said that on the day after the deed some girls came to his house and asked if John had been struck by a locomotive.

Dr. D. Hanson, who first attended Langmeyer, said that the wound seemed to be made by a train. He saw no marks of any assault.

Stephen Shada left Langmeyer at one o'clock on Sunday morning and saw him quarrel with some Bohemians on Saturday night.

James Pintara and Frank Blaha corroborated the testimony of the last witness. The Coroner then continued the hearing until the testimony of Julia and Barbara Pech can be obtained, these being the girls who inquired whether Frank had been hurt by a New York, Pennsylvania & Ohio train.

John Henry "Frank" Langmeyer (1862–1882), the only son of John (1838–1887) and Antonia Langmeyer from Czechoslovakia, was employed at the Cleveland Rolling Mill as a laborer. On the way home from attending a dance he was found injured. He told an uncle that he was attacked; yet it was suspected that he was actually hit by a train. He died of his injuries at the age of 20. (Cleveland Plain Dealer.)

Barbara Adin (1829–1875) married William Adin in 1858, bringing a daughter, Hattie McKay (1855–1875), to the marriage. William and Barbara began having some trouble in their marriage, which William blamed on his wife and stepdaughter. Hattie moved in with her friend Elizabeth Binley Benton (1845–1876) and Elizabeth's husband, George, who had a home behind their grocery store. On April 4, 1875, William went into a rage and, with an ax and a hammer, attacked and killed Barbara. He then drove to the Bentons' home and attacked and killed Hattie, attacking Elizabeth as well when she tried to help her friend. Elizabeth lingered until January 8, 1876, when she died of her head injuries. Her devastated husband died 4 years later. William Adin was executed by hanging on June 22, 1876; his was the last hanging on Public Square in Cleveland. (MAD/Ohio Historical Society/Louis Baus Collection.)

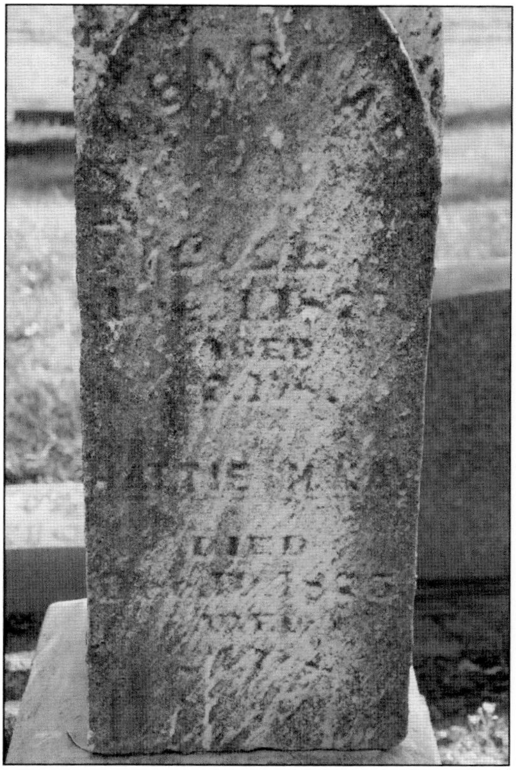

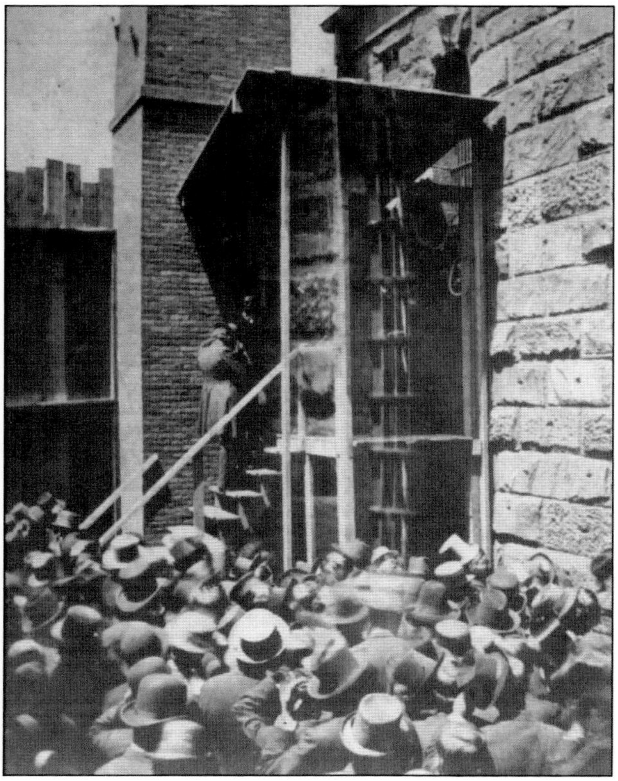

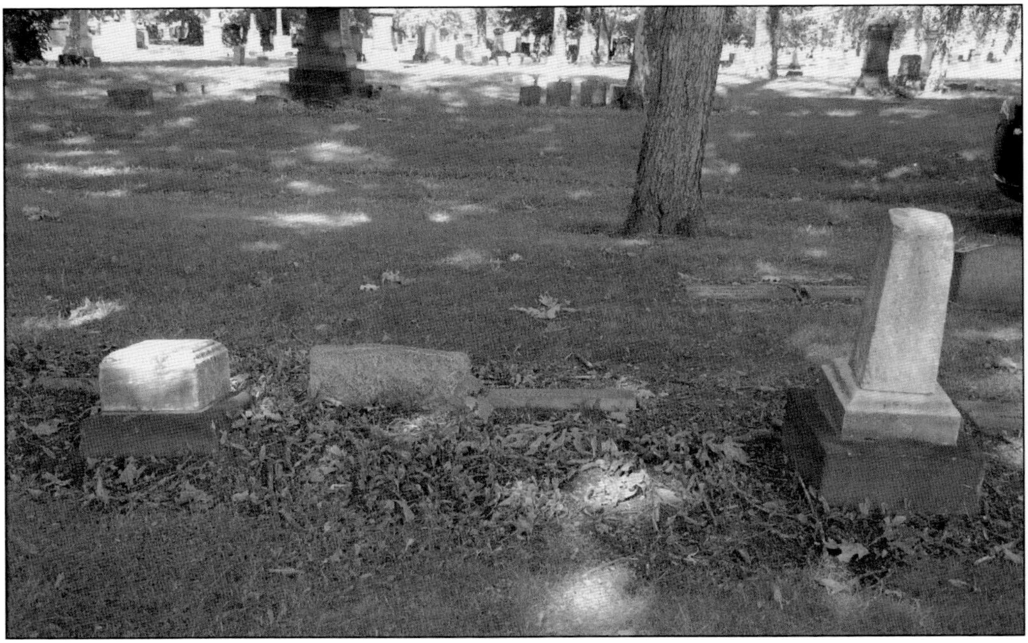

Buried in an unmarked grave, William Parquet (1839–1867) served as a private in Company F, 12th Regiment, Ohio Voluntary Infantry. He worked at Fenner's Tavern and was living with his sister, Sarah Victor, when, on February 3, 1867, he died of a strange ailment. When his body was exhumed a year later, arsenic was discovered. Sarah was found guilty of poisoning William for his life insurance and given a life sentence. Sarah was pardoned after serving 18 years. (MAD.)

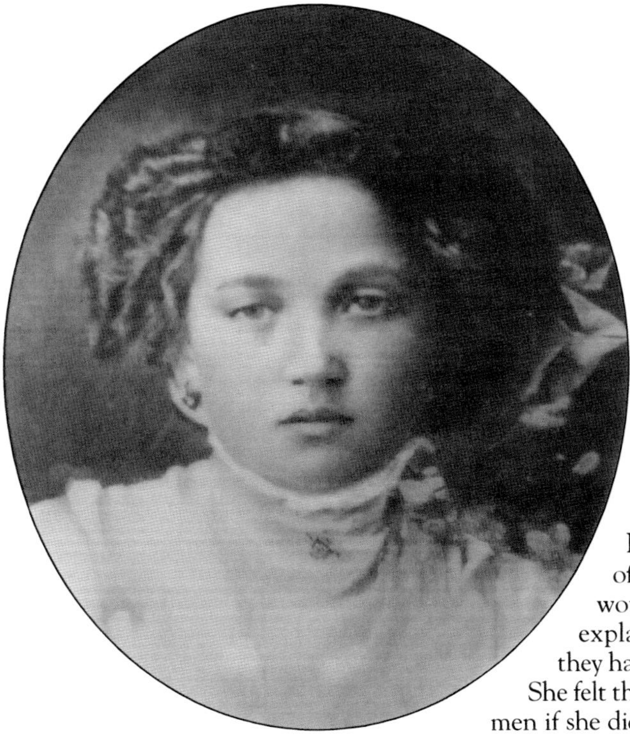

Elizabeth "Lizzie" Nemeth (1894–1911) was born in Hungary and came to America with her father, Marton Nemeth (1862–1946), and mother, Barbara. Tragically, Lizzie, at the age of 17, died of a self-inflicted gunshot wound. In a note to her parents, she explained she could not marry the man they had chosen for her, as she loved another. She felt there would be trouble between the two men if she did not die. (MAD.)

Elizabeth Metzger Buckstein (1888–1963) and three other policewomen were appointed in 1923 to the Cleveland Police Department. Buckstein carried a blackjack and wore a revolver but never had to fire her gun. During World War I, Elizabeth was a Red Cross nurse, and from 1933 to 1953, she worked as an industrial nurse for the Glidden Co. Elizabeth married Jacob Buckstein (1883–1943), a druggist from Warsaw, Poland, on April 25, 1925. (Cleveland Police Museum.)

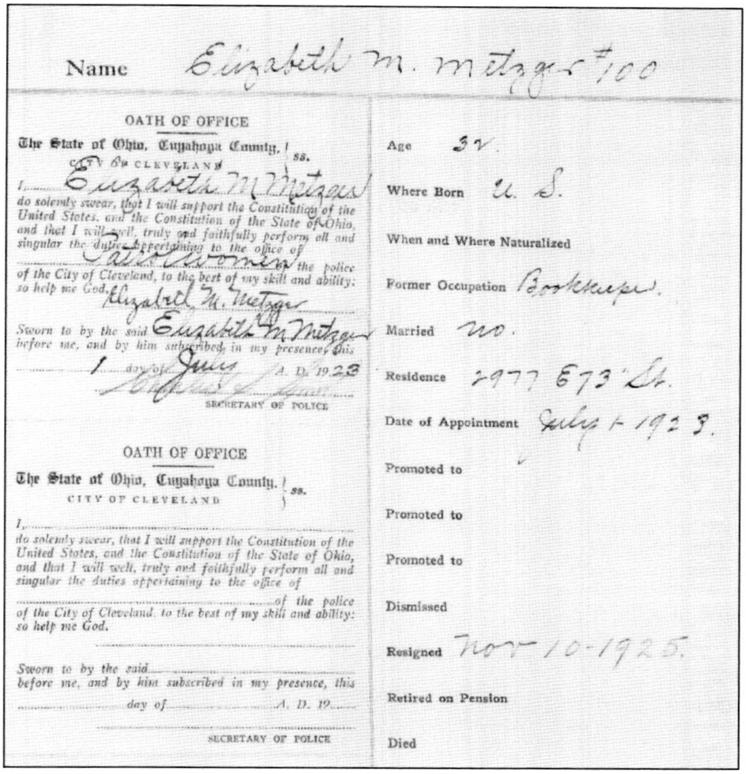

Name Elizabeth M. Metzger #100

OATH OF OFFICE

The State of Ohio, Cuyahoga County, } ss.
City of Cleveland

I, Elizabeth M Metzger
do solemnly swear, that I will support the Constitution of the United States, and the Constitution of the State of Ohio, and that I will well, truly and faithfully perform all and singular the duties appertaining to the office of Patrolwoman the police of the City of Cleveland, to the best of my skill and ability: so help me God. Elizabeth M. Metzger

Sworn to by the said Elizabeth M Metzger before me, and by him subscribed in my presence, this 1 day of July A. D. 1923

[illegible]
SECRETARY OF POLICE

OATH OF OFFICE

The State of Ohio, Cuyahoga County, } ss.
City of Cleveland

I, ...
do solemnly swear, that I will support the Constitution of the United States, and the Constitution of the State of Ohio, and that I will well, truly and faithfully perform all and singular the duties appertaining to the office of .... of the police of the City of Cleveland, to the best of my skill and ability: so help me God.

Sworn to by the said .... before me, and by him subscribed in my presence, this .... day of .... A. D. 19......

SECRETARY OF POLICE

Age 32
Where Born U. S.
When and Where Naturalized
Former Occupation Bookkeeper.
Married no.
Residence 2977 E73 St.
Date of Appointment July 1-1923.
Promoted to
Promoted to
Promoted to
Dismissed
Resigned Nov 10-1925.
Retired on Pension
Died

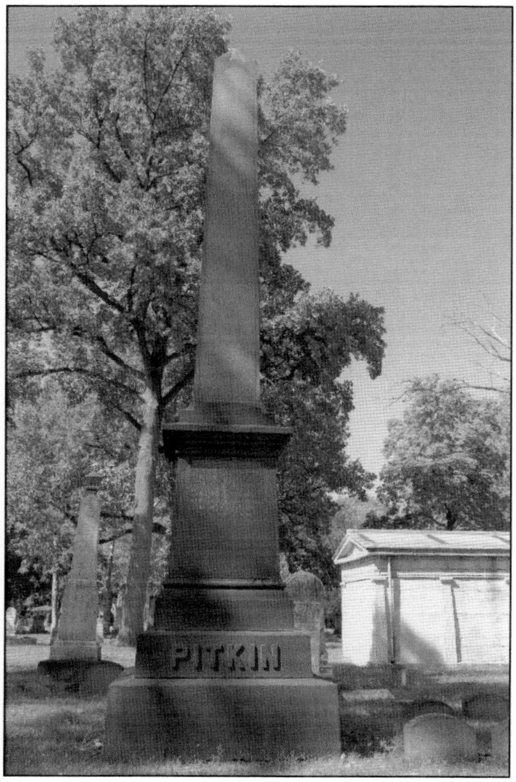

Dudley Pitkin (1799–1884) came from Marshfield, Vermont, to Cleveland in 1854 with his wife, Nancy Bachelder (1804–1865), whom he had married in 1824. Five children accompanied them, and five more were born after the move. Dudley had been an innkeeper in Vermont; in 1860, he was working as a butcher. By 1870, as a widower, he lived with a son and worked as a coal dealer. He died at the age of 85. (MAD.)

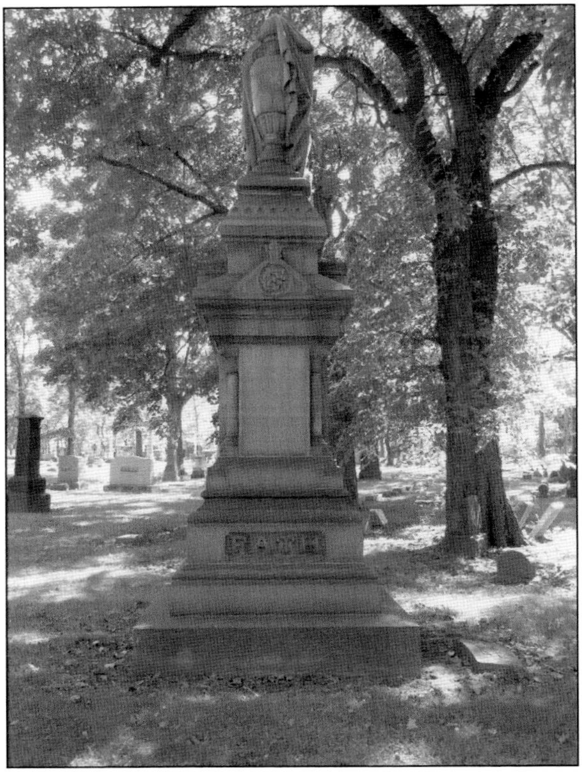

Caspar Heinrich Fath (1828–1907) owned a contracting business, C.H. Fath & Sons. He arrived in America in 1851 and became a naturalized citizen in November 1856. He and his wife, Christina, had four children together; one died as an infant; son William, who died of typhoid at 22; daughter Nettie, who married Dr. Thomas Ransom and died in childbirth; and son Charles, who inherited his father's business. (MAD.)

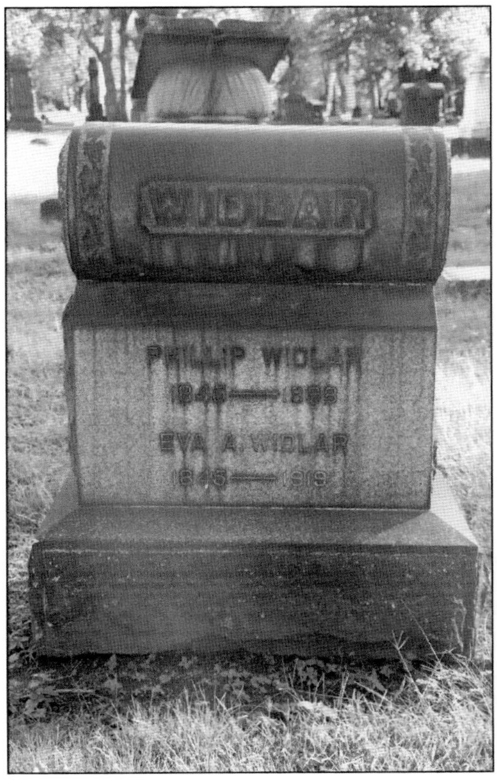

Phillip Widlar (1843–1888) was born in Cleveland, one of several children of Jacob Widlar (1813–1857) and Margaret Bilz (1816–1892). Phillip married Eva Fisher (1845–1919) in May 1867. In 1880, he was working as an iron molder and became a foreman for Cleveland Co-Operative Stove Co. on Quincy Avenue. Phillip was the superintendent of Woodland Cemetery when he died at the age of 45. He and Eva had no children. (MAD.)

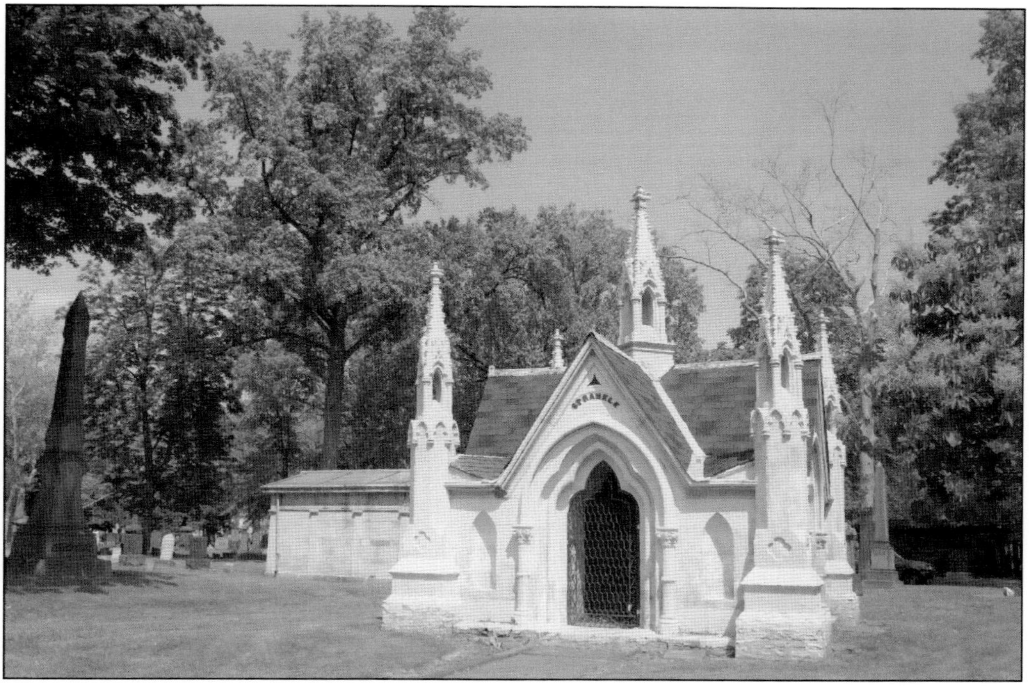

James Rudolph Sprankle (1817–1898), in the 1900 census, described his occupation as "capitalist." He was "a man of resolute purpose" and was "interested in everything related to Cleveland's progress and improvement." He and his father, Rudolph, were produce commission merchants involved in grain and seeds and owned several flour mills. James was a successful businessman in a variety of endeavors. He married twice; a son, James R. Jr., lived to adulthood. (Carolyn Vigneulle.)

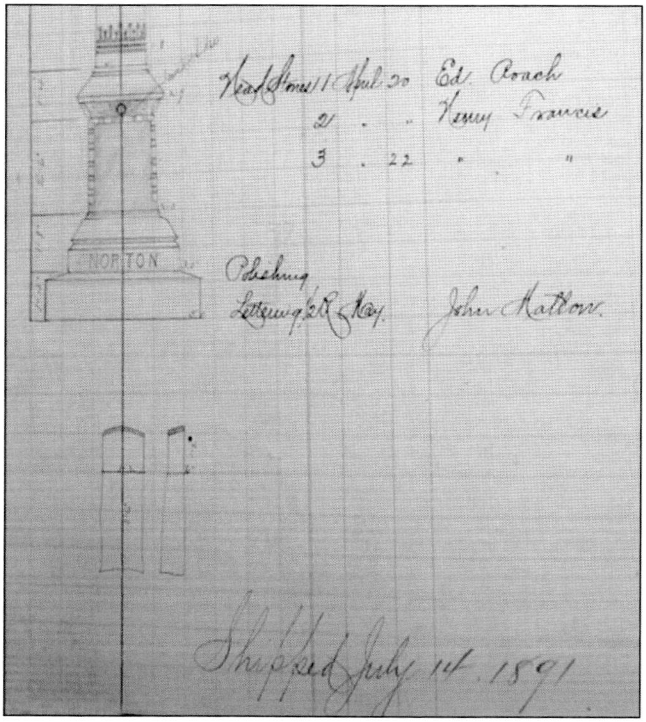

Charles Norton (1805–1881) was born in New York and worked as a merchant and gentleman farmer in Cleveland, living on Woodland Avenue for most of his life. In 1880, the value of his farm was $100,000, and his personal wealth amounted to $10,000. Charles and his wife, Caroline Brayton Cornell, had three sons who were all successful. Sidney became a physician; Frank, an architect; and Charles Edward, the vice president of Cleveland Providence Co. The family monument was built by Smith Granite. (Smith Babcock House Museum and the Smith Granite Company.)

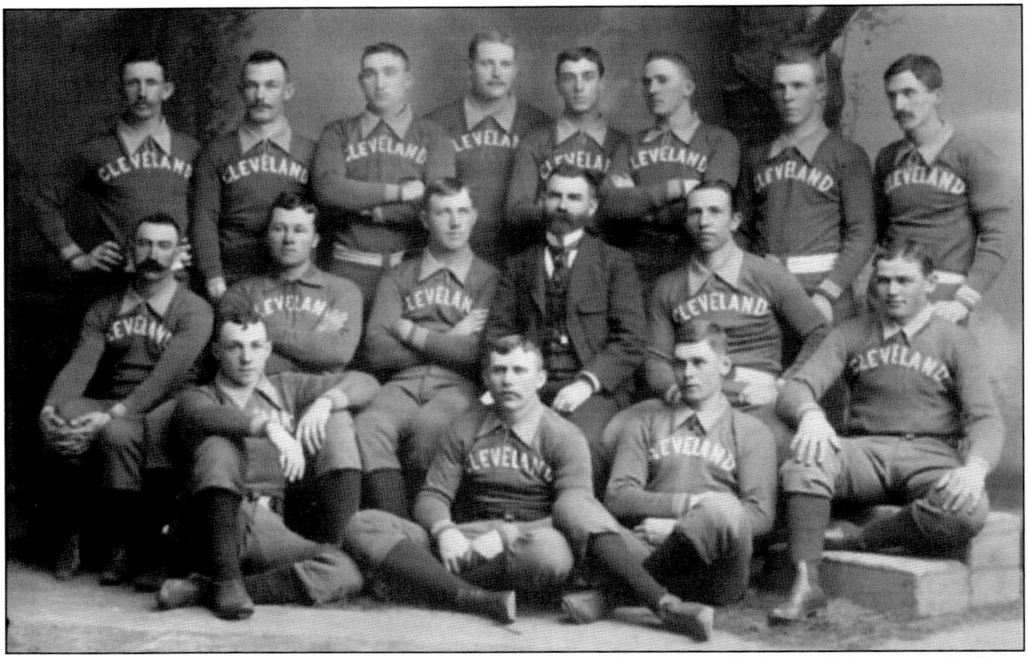

Joseph Ardner (1858–1935) was born in Knox County, Ohio, to Nicholas and Susanna Ardner. Joseph married Ada Trappe in 1884 and had a daughter, Jesse, in 1885. In May 1884, Joseph was signed to play professional baseball for the Cleveland Blues, and then with the Cleveland Spiders, until August 1890. In the baseball arena, he was known as "Old Hoss." He later worked as a machinist for a theater in Cleveland. (Baseball Hall of Fame, Cooperstown, New York.)

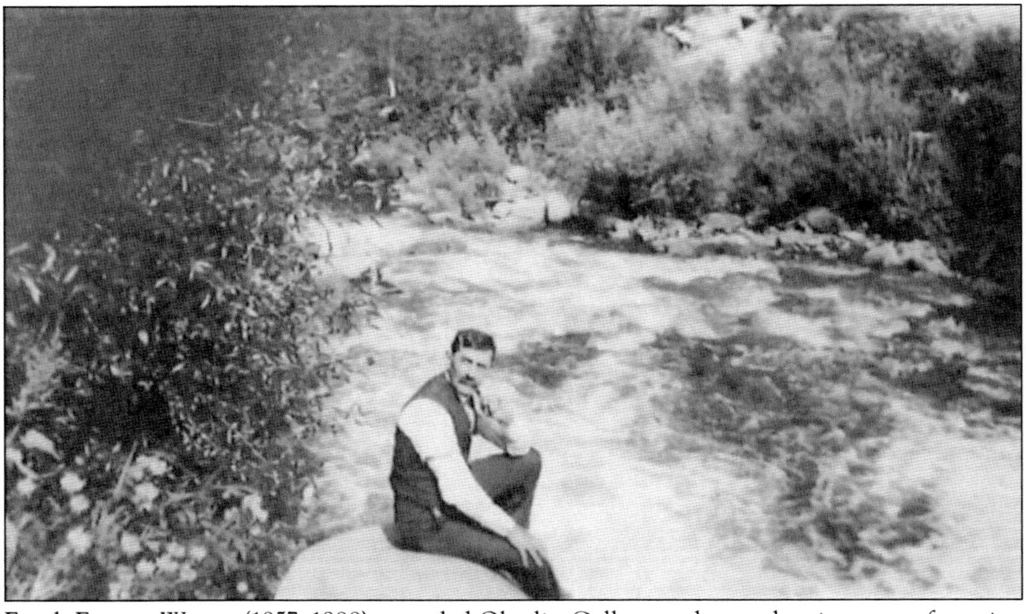

Frank Eugene Waters (1857–1888) attended Oberlin College and owned a cigar manufacturing business, F.E. Waters & Co., at 148 Champlain Street. His father, Medway N. Waters (1827–1911), a printer, was also involved in cigar making with his son. Frank married Ida Dale Ingersoll (1866–1944) in April 1884, and they had a daughter, Keosha, the following year. Three years later, Frank died at the age of 31. (Barb Woodbeck.)

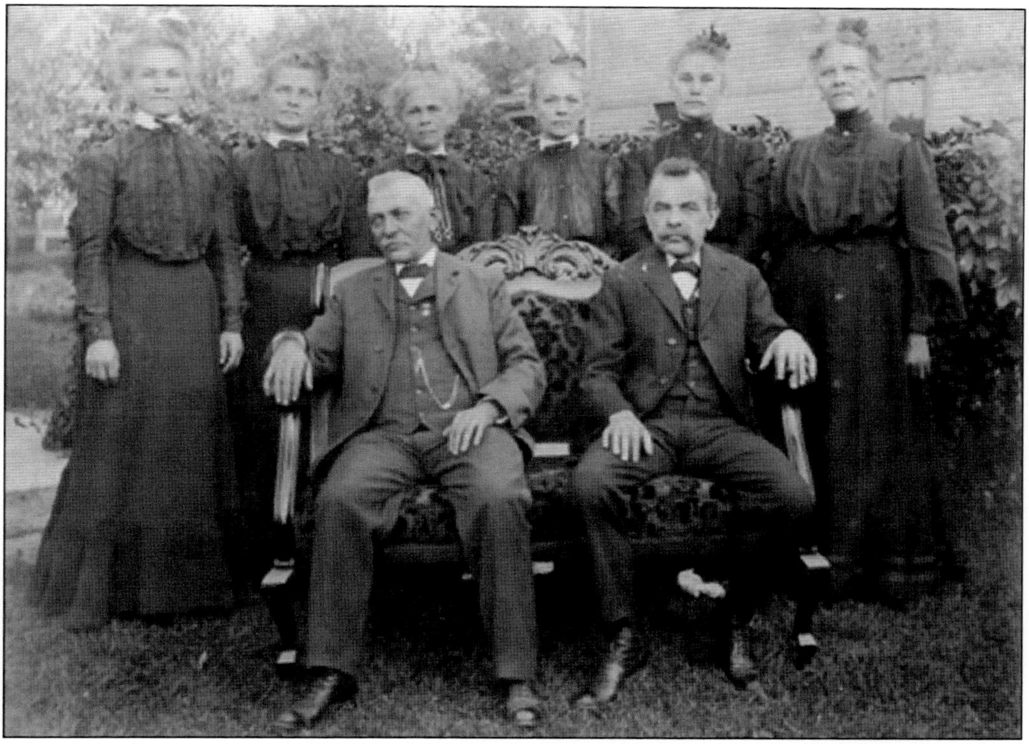

Ludwig "Louis" Regenauer (1849–1926) arrived in America from Rheinland-Pflaz, Germany, with his six siblings and his parents in August 1871. A brother, Joseph, had gone to Cleveland in 1865 to prepare their home. Louis married Pauline Bender in January 1882; they had one son, Joseph Louis (1887–1942). This photograph was taken in 1893 at the funeral of Louis's mother, Barbara Eva Schotthefer Regenauer (1822–1893), the wife of George Michael Regenauer (1818–1895). George Michael (left, seated) is next to his son Louis. Standing behind them are, from left to right, Helena Ellen (1863–193?), Anna Maria (1861–1936), Gertrude (1859–1933), Johanna (1855–1933), Franciscka (1853–1929), and Margret (1862–1939). They all died in Cleveland except for Franciscka, who had moved to Kansas. (Dale Taddie.)

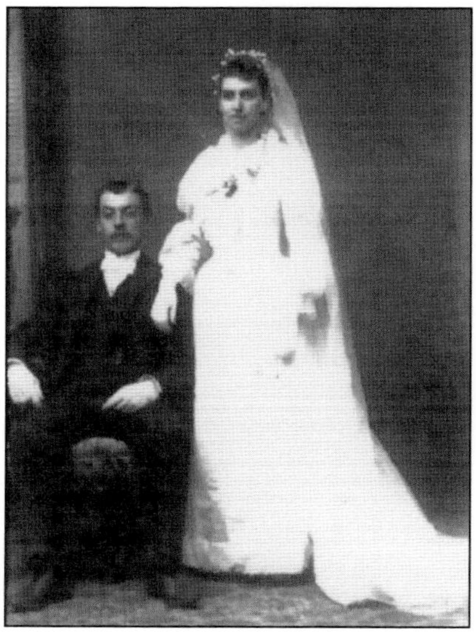

Carl Axel Rosequist (1869–1933) arrived from Sweden in 1886. In November 1891, Carl married Hilma Josephina Johnson (1870–1903), with whom he had four children. Carl, an artistic man, was a fresco painter, a musician, and vocal teacher with a studio in the arcade. He sang in a well-known quartet in Cleveland. After Josephina died, he married Catherine Fennell Kiely, also from Sweden. He is buried with Josephina. (Sonia Cook.)

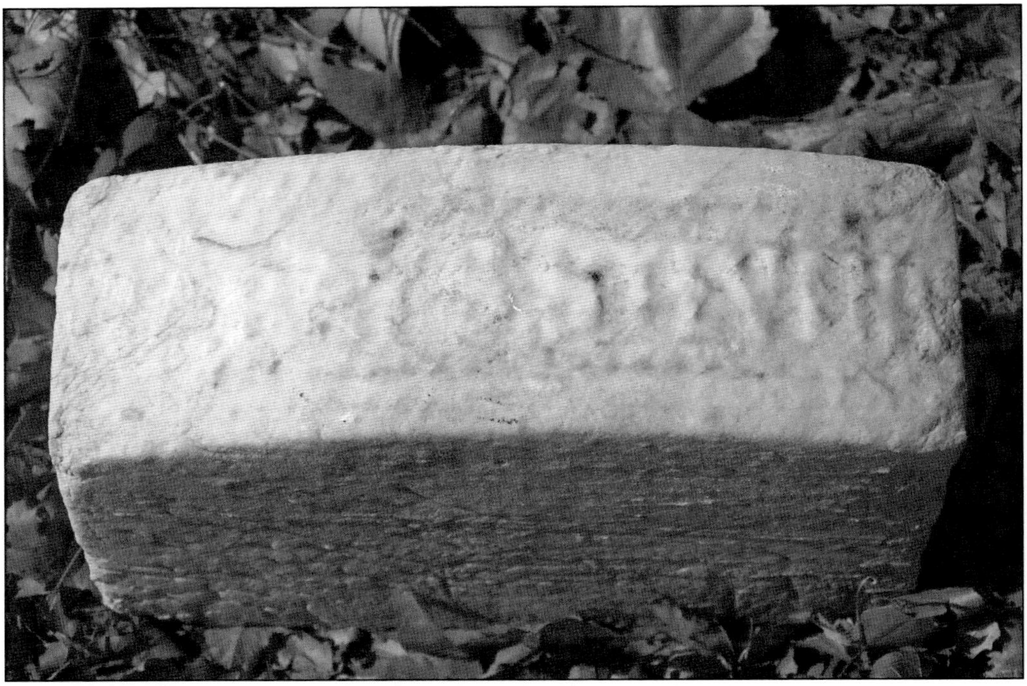

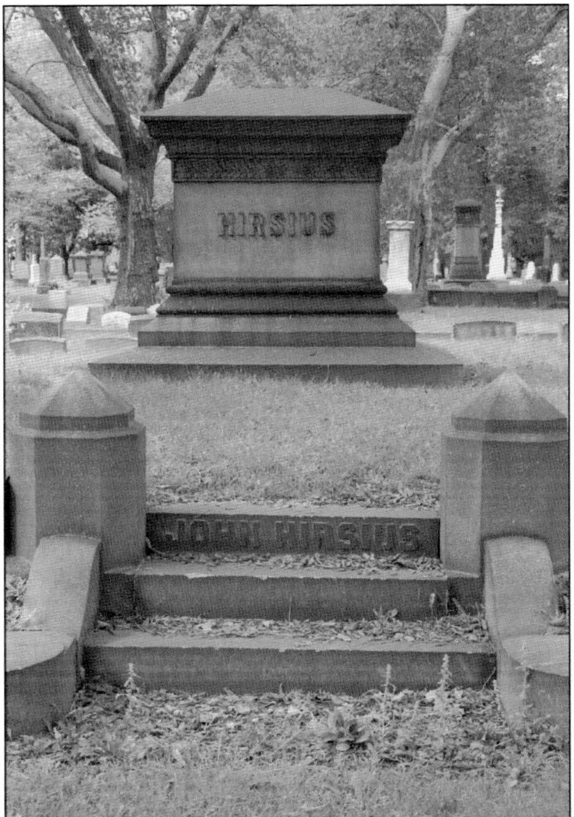

Henry Shipley "Harry" Stevens (1855–1898), a Cleveland native and stockbroker, married Helen Elizabeth Deming (1864–1918) on April 21, 1890. Harry became interested in purchasing stock in the gold mines of Cripple Creek, Colorado, and made several trips there. He was very well known, and it was a shock to many when, on August 27, 1898, during a short-term illness, he shot and killed himself. He left a wife, a son, and a daughter. (MAD.)

John Hirsius (1843–1913), born in Essenheim, Germany, immigrated to America in April 1855. He became a successful businessman who served as director at various banks and at the Cleveland Brewing Co. and also became the founder and director of Canfield Oil Co. When he died in 1913, he was the oldest cooper (a maker of wooden casks) in Cleveland. John married Carolina Muhl (1866–1924) on October 30, 1892. The couple reared six children. (MAD.)

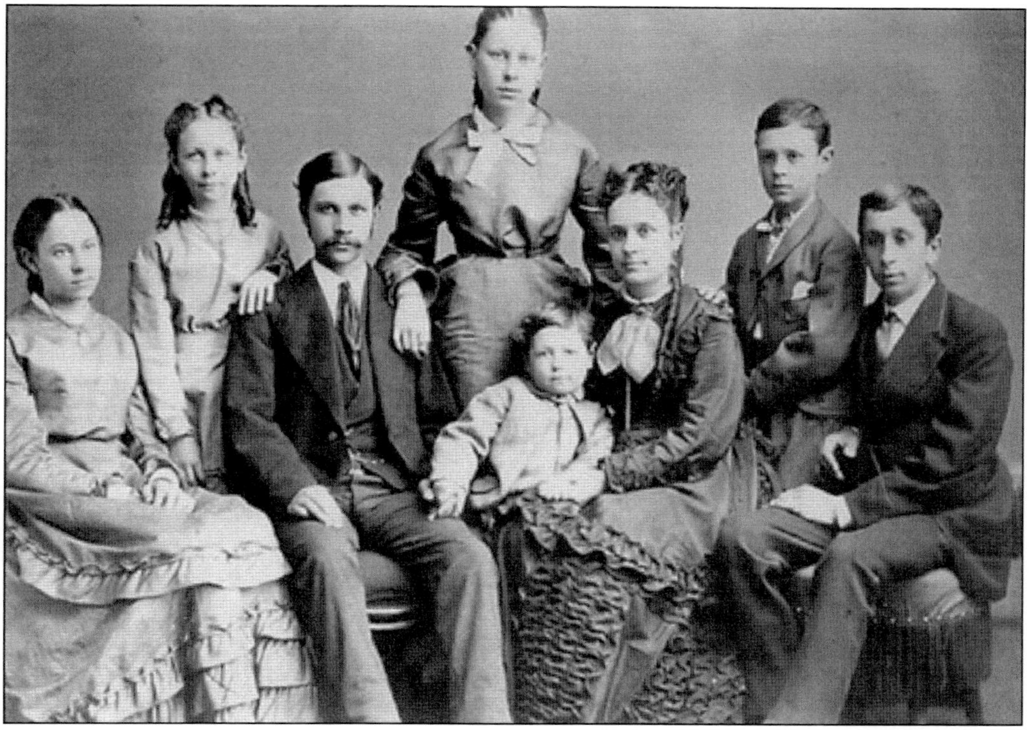

William K. Corlett (1820–1907) was a highly respected pioneer contractor in the Cleveland community. In 1887, he purchased a livery, which became Corlett & Son (Charles Edward being the son). William founded and owned Cleveland Spring Co., which made steel springs for locomotives, cars, wagons, and carriages. William came to Cleveland in 1837 from the Isle of Man and was a founder of Mona's Relief Society. He married Mary Ann Rayburn in March 1848. (Judy Wersted Kelley.)

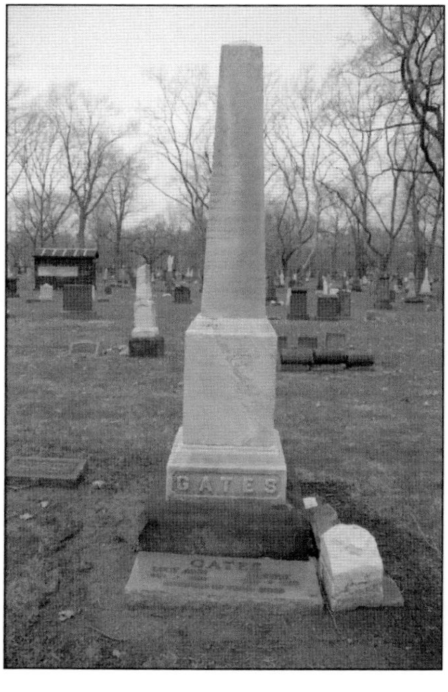

Holsey (1799–1865) and Lucy Ann Bradley Gates (1803–1875) married in New York on July 21, 1826, before moving to Ohio. They were early settlers in the Western Reserve and became the namesakes of the village of Gates Mills. Holsey purchased 130 acres of Chagrin River land to secure a good supply of water for a sawmill. He designed and built some 18 structures in the area. The couple had nine children. (MAD.)

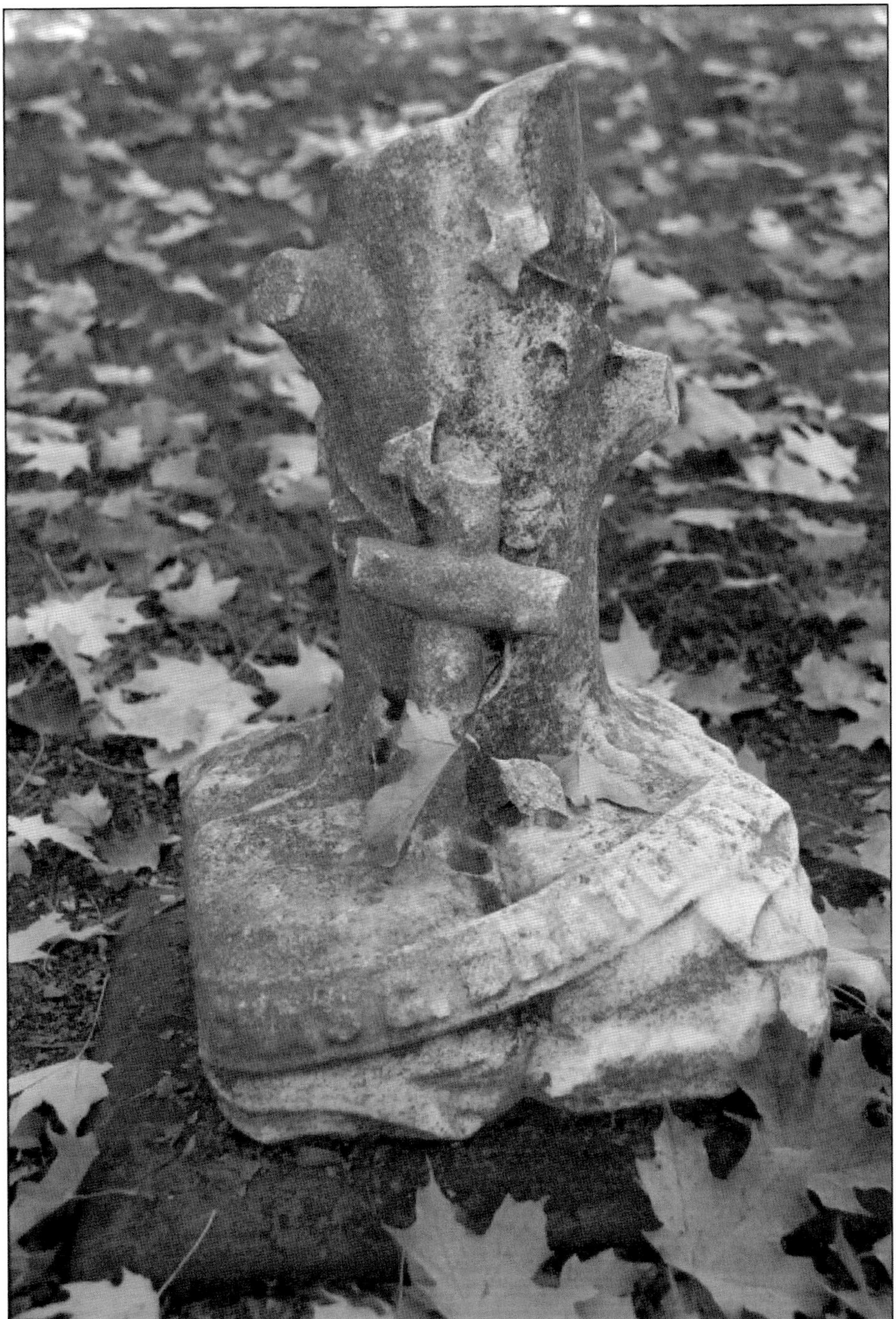

Charles George Bratenahl (1817–1870) immigrated to Cleveland with his brother Louis in 1846. By 1850, they owned a wholesale-retail leather dealership. Charles invested in real estate and devised ways to assist other businessmen. He married Mary Grant Fitch in June 1861 and died nine years later, leaving two sons. Carl George Fitch Bratenahl became a clergyman who was honored with the deanship of the Washington National Cathedral, while his brother Gustav Weber Bratenahl became a successful physician. (MAD.)

Three

Lots Owned by Social and Fraternal Organizations

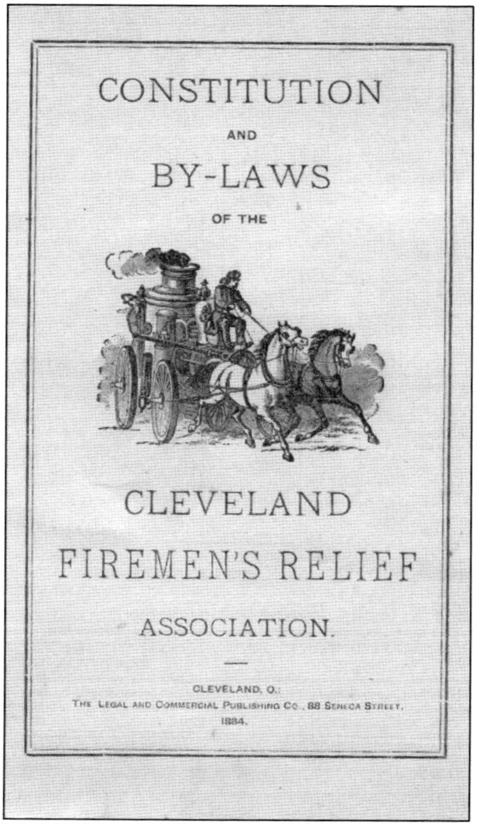
CONSTITUTION

AND

BY-LAWS

OF THE

CLEVELAND

FIREMEN'S RELIEF

ASSOCIATION.

CLEVELAND, O.:
THE LEGAL AND COMMERCIAL PUBLISHING CO., 88 SENECA STREET.
1884.

A Volunteer Firemen's Relief Association was established in 1845 under an act of the state legislature. It took the name Firemen's General Association Fund, which was created to provide assistance to any fireman injured or disabled while on duty in the city of Cleveland. It remained in effect until 1863 when the Volunteer Fire Department disbanded and the remaining funds were distributed amongst its members. Members of the department, now being paid, formed a mutual benefit organization known as the Cleveland Firemen's Relief Association in February 1868. Sixty members of the department signed the constitution as participants and elected Fire Chief James Hill as president. The intent of the association was to provide proper protection for firemen and establish a fund for pensions and sick needs. It was to pay $10 per week if the member was unable to work and $100 upon his death. If sufficient funds existed, assistance would be provided for burial expenses and to the widow and any children. Funds to maintain the new program were provided by monthly dues, an initiation fee, and voluntary contributions from any source. (Western Reserve Fire Museum & Education Center.)

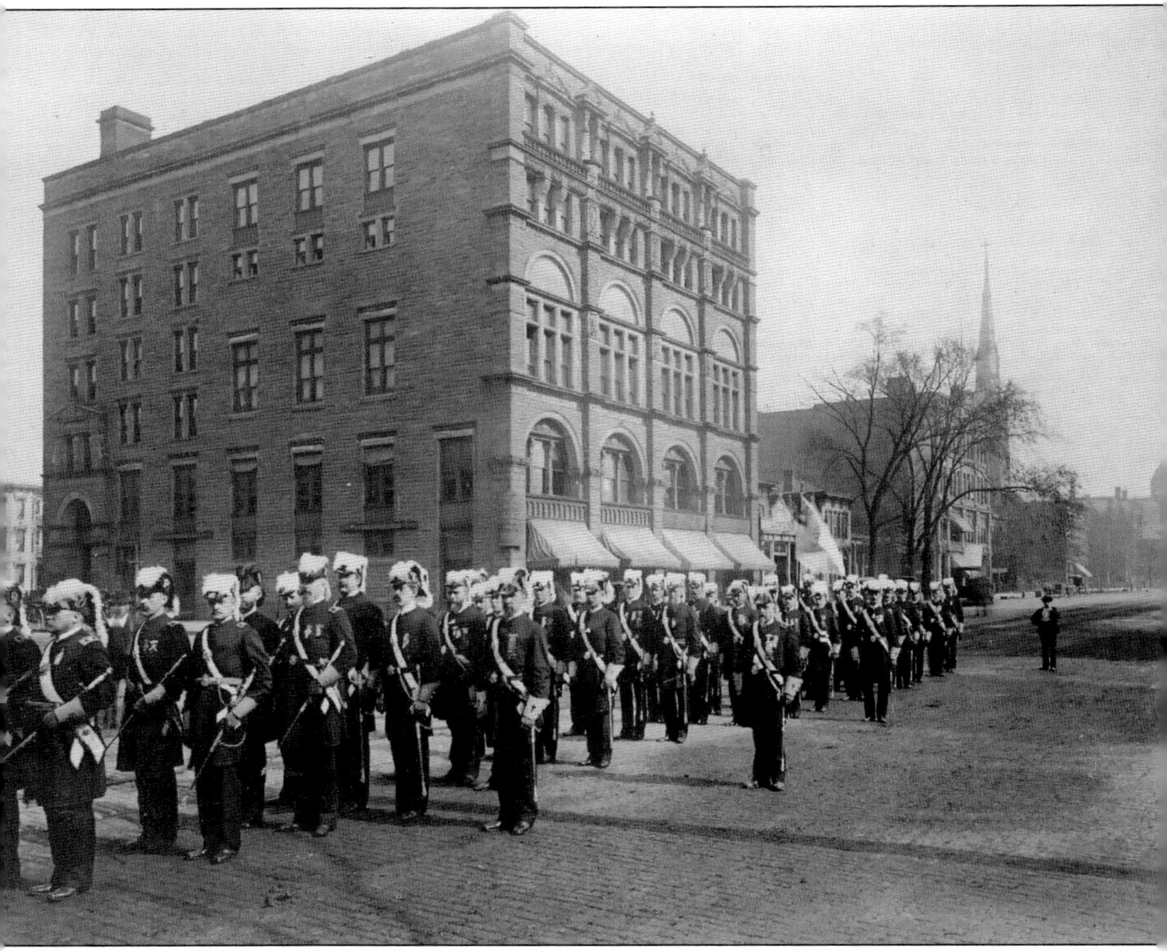

The well-known fraternal organization of Freemasonry began its history in Cleveland with Concord Lodge No. 15. In 1830, its charter lapsed. In 1836, Webb chapter No. 14 was organized, and Cleveland City Lodge No. 15, or "Old Fifteen," was reformed in September 1841. The first Masonic temple was built in 1883 and was used by Webb Chapter No. 14, Iris Lodge No. 229, the Cleveland Council, and the Oriental Commandery. (Ohio Historical Society/Louis Baus Photograph Collection.)

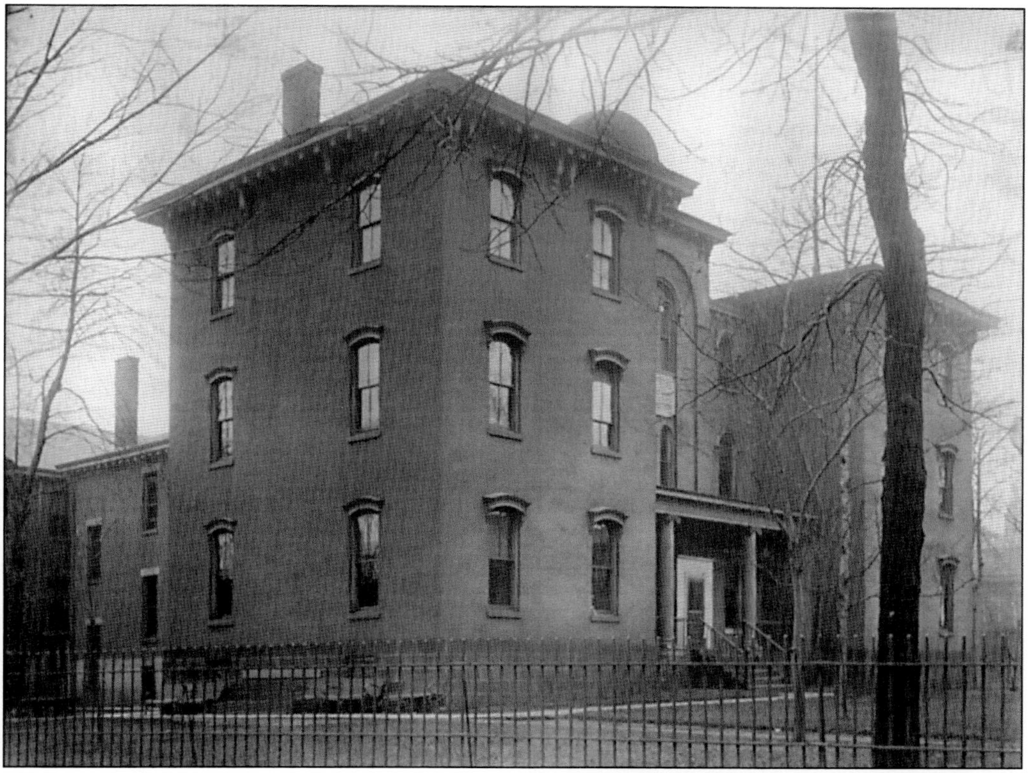

On January 22, 1852, the ladies of the Martha Washington Society gathered downtown at the Stone Church to address the problem of children who were left alone and homeless because of a cholera epidemic. These women laid the groundwork for the Cleveland Orphan Asylum, a place that could shelter the city's "orphaned and destitute children." The institution eventually became the Cleveland Protestant Orphan Asylum; it later became known as Beech Brook. (Beech Brook.)

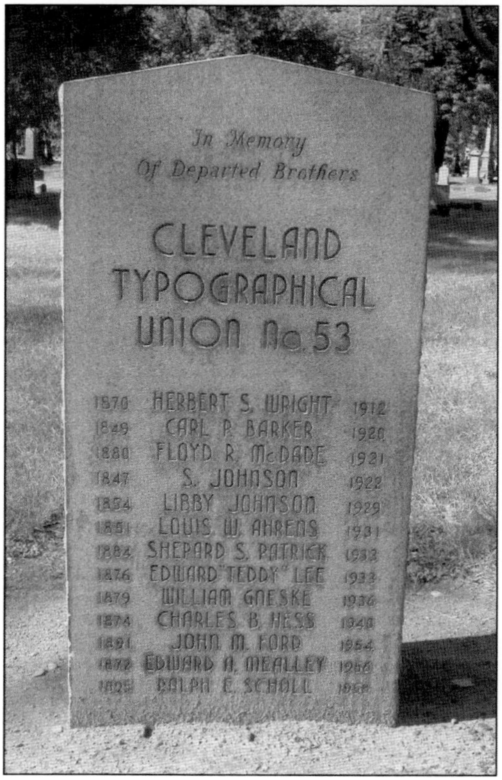

Cleveland Typographical Workers Union Local No. 53 was chartered in July 1860 as part of the International Typographical Union (ITU) formed for the printing industry in 1852. Its members, because of the popularity of newspapers, represented many aspects of the printing trade. A mortuary benefit allowed 34 members to be interred in Woodland. The ITU ceased to exist on December 31, 1986, when it merged with the Communication Workers of America. (MAD.)

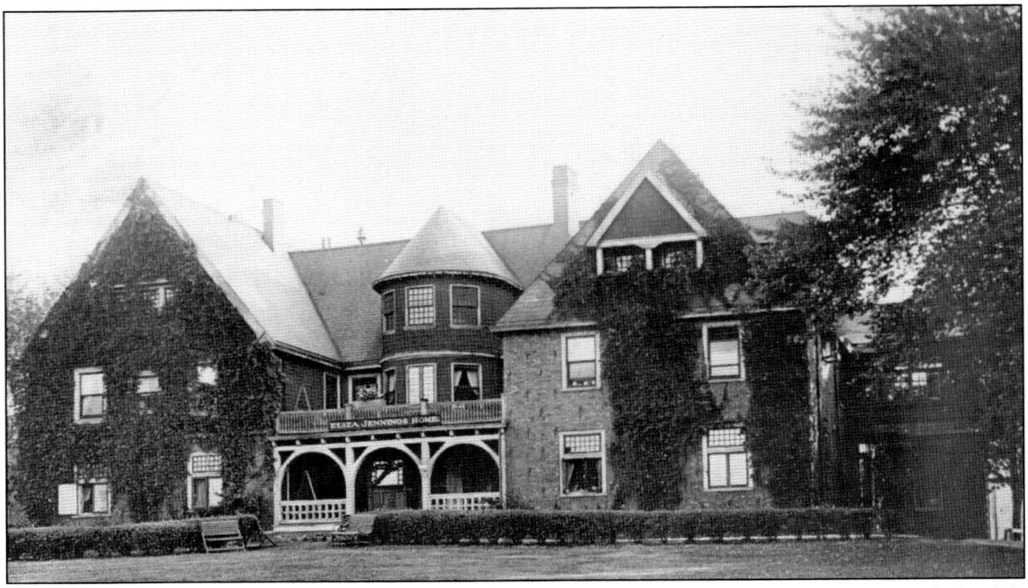

Eliza Wallace Jennings donated the land and funds for a haven for needy women with health concerns. Her inspiration in this endeavor was her elderly friend, Mary Love, who was homeless, indigent, and incurably ill. The home, named in honor of Jennings, opened in October 1888, a year after her death. The organization, now known as the Eliza Jennings Senior Care Network, owns a plot in Woodland Cemetery. (CPLPC.)

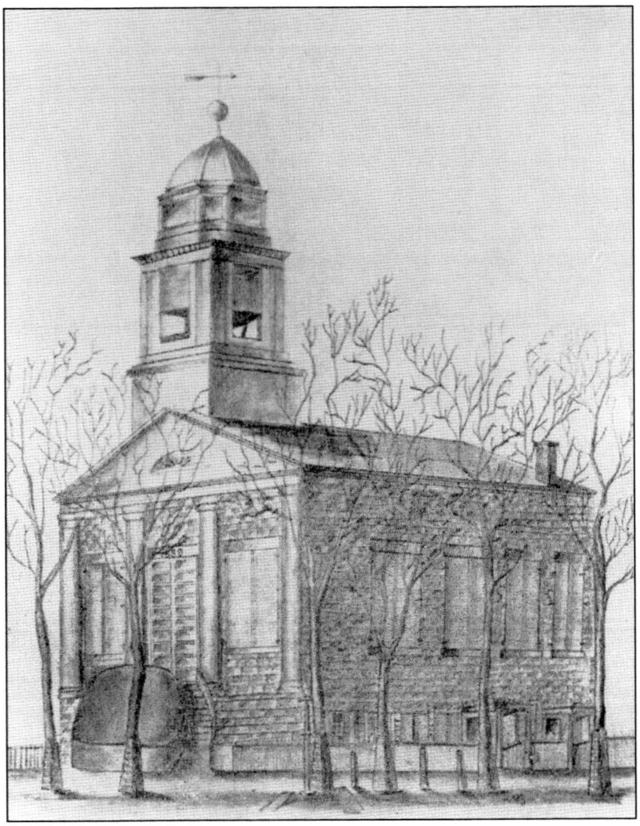

The First Presbyterian Church, which owns several lots in Woodland Cemetery, was incorporated in 1827 after a charter had established the congregation in 1820. In 1834, their first church was built from gray sandstone, causing it to be known as "the Stone Church." This church stood until 1853, when it was demolished to make room for the new Romanesque Revival church, which was also made of local sandstone and was dedicated in 1855. (CPLPC.)

The first, failed attempt at organizing a Presbyterian church occurred in 1832. In 1844, 58 dedicated members made a second, successful attempt. The first Second Presbyterian Church on Public Square was destroyed by fire in October 1876, and a new building was dedicated by October 1878. The present building, completed in October 1904 in the Norman style of architecture, with cream-colored stone, was described as "massive, dignified and beautiful." (CPLPC.)

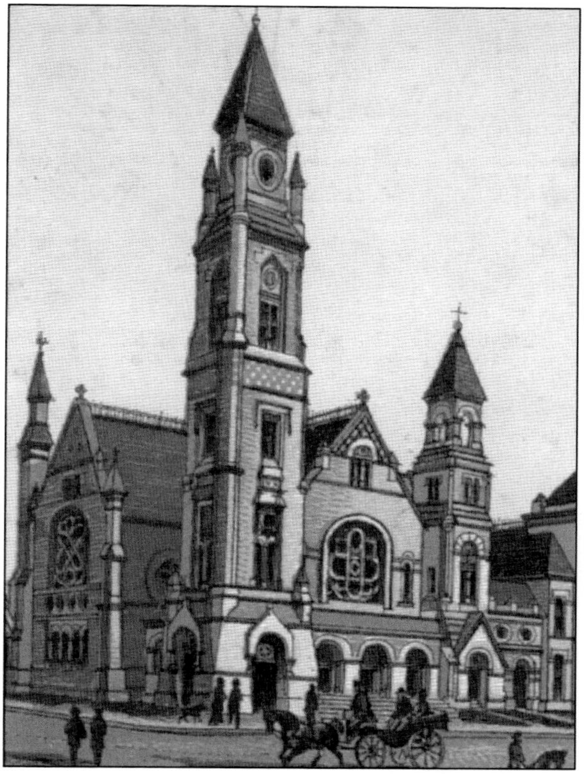

In March 1856, Rev. James A. Bolles organized a charity at Trinity Parish (established in November 1816) to provide a home to those who were sick and alone in the world. In June 1859, the Trinity Church trustees for the Home for the Sick and Friendless asked the City of Cleveland for a lot in the Woodland Cemetery to bury those without friends or family. (CPLPC.)

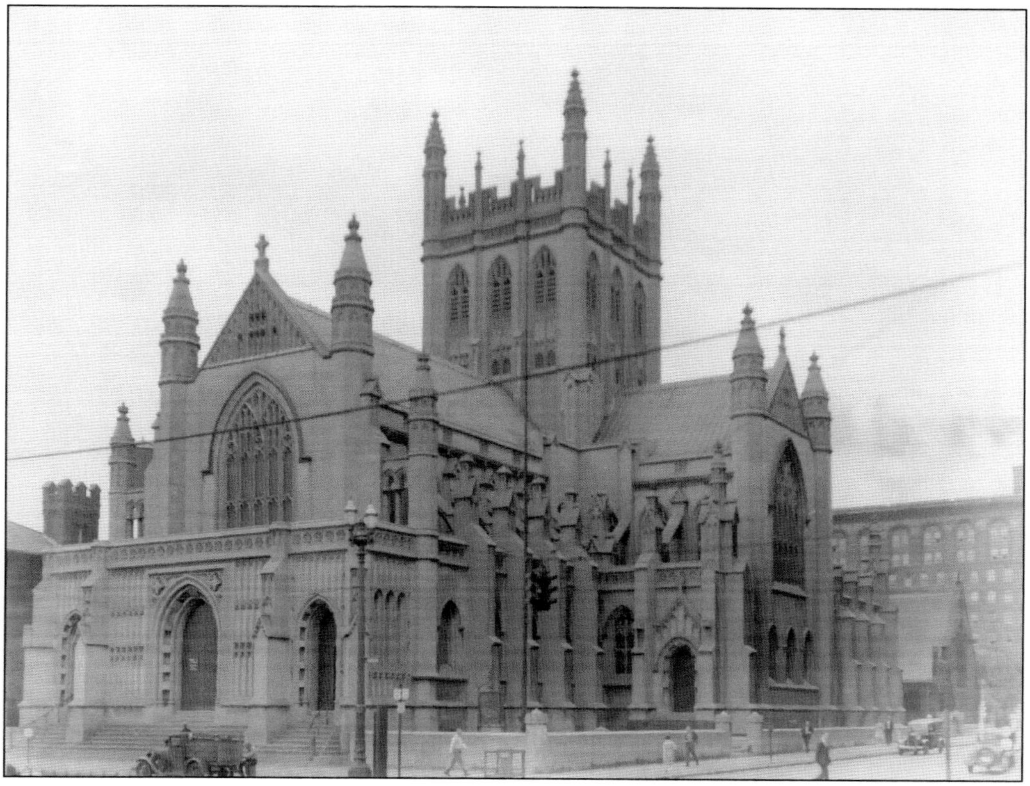

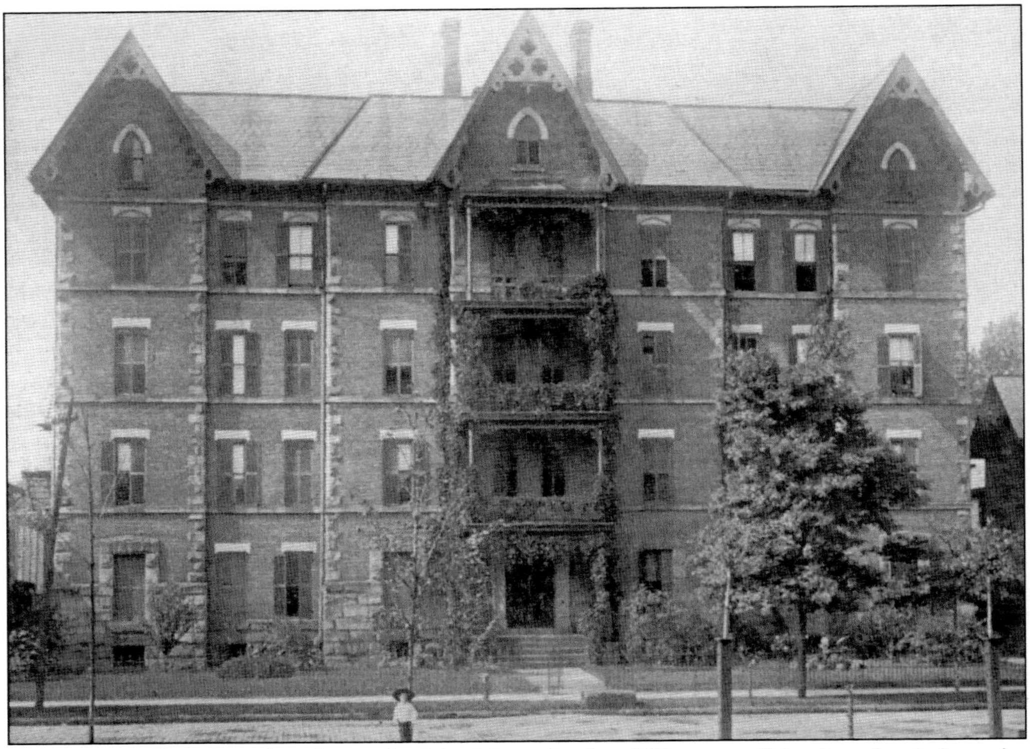

An 1885 headline describes the work of the Home for Aged Women as "clearing clouds from the evening of lives whose sun would otherwise set in gloom." The home, owned by the Women's Christian Association, held sales to earn monies to support itself, accepted donations of foodstuffs and clothing, and encouraged visits to gladden the hearts of its aged inmates. (CPLPC.)

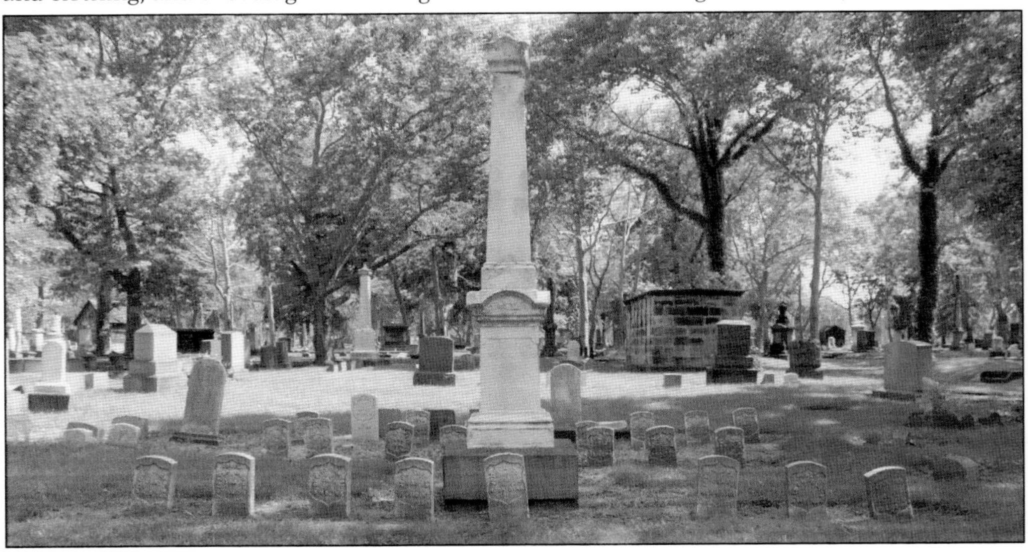

The Army and Navy Post No. 187 was organized on November 12, 1892, with 104 members installed and another 39 waiting to muster. On May 4, 1909, Post 187 purchased Lot 45, Section 21 in Woodland Cemetery for use as a soldier plot. The first burial occurred in November 1909, and the last soldier was buried in 1912. The most notable burial in this plot is Medal of Honor recipient Cpl. Theodore Mitchell. (MAD.)

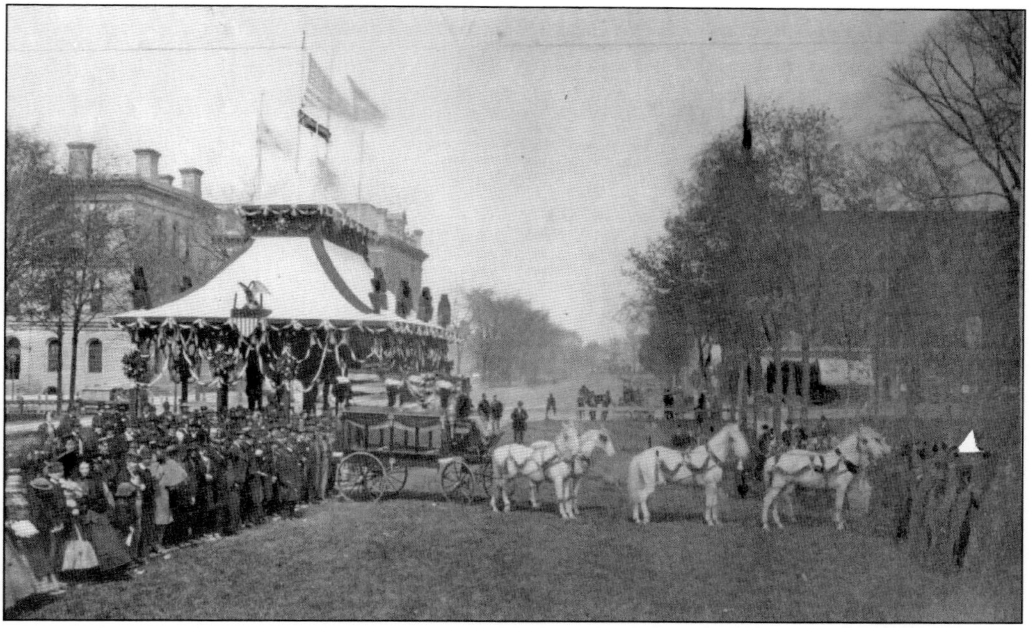

In 1862, the Grand United Order of Odd Fellows (GUOOF), an African American fraternal secret society that was established in 1843, bought two lots in Woodland Cemetery. Odd Fellows adhered to a strict code of moral conduct, provided financial and fraternal assistance to members at times of illness (and, when needed, for burial), and offered the diversion of regalia, ritual, and parades. This society carried a banner on which was inscribed the following: "We mourn for Abraham Lincoln, the True Friend of Liberty." The Colored Equal Rights League followed. (CSUSC.)

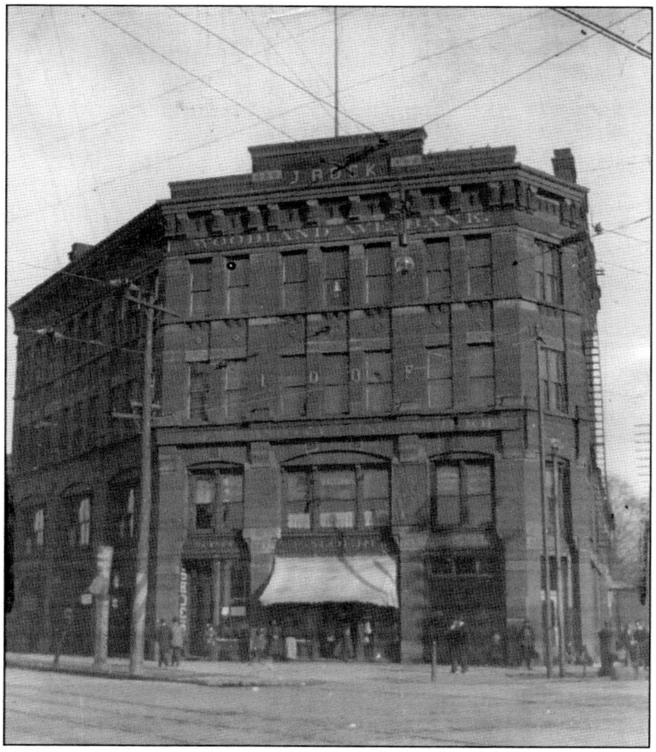

The Mayflower Lodge, No. 679, International Order of Odd Fellows (IOOF), was organized June 16, 1879. They owned a plot partly because of the command of the IOOF to "visit the sick, relieve the distressed, bury the dead, and educate the orphan." Cleveland's oldest IOOF lodge originated in 1842. (CSUSC.)

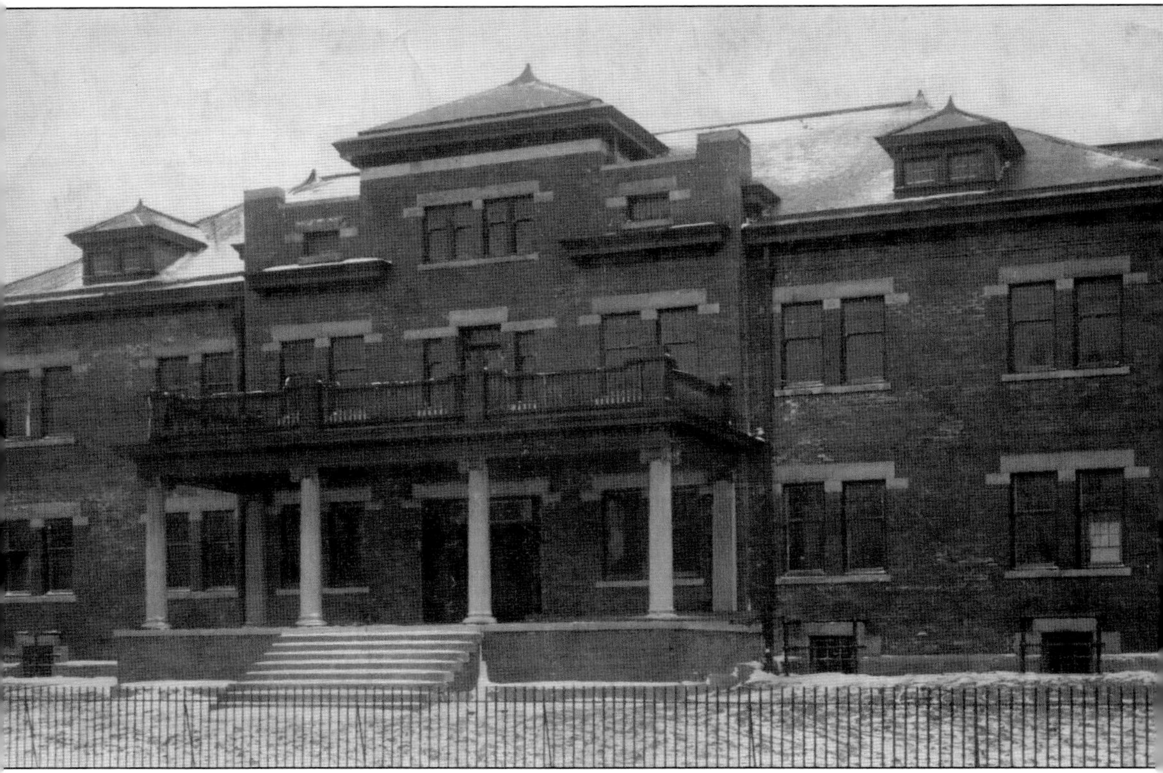

The Dorcas Home was operated by the Dorcas Society, a charitable organization formed in 1867 by 14 women and led by two women who were philanthropists. The home was founded in December 1884 (and incorporated in 1885) as a haven for sick and destitute women and later served as a residence for elderly women from 1917 until 1967 when the doors closed and the property was transferred to the Eliza Bryant Village. Several cemetery lots were purchased in 1882 and 1885; 67 women are interred in Lots 27, 34, 35, 42, and 43 N 2/3 of Section 45. (CPLPC.)

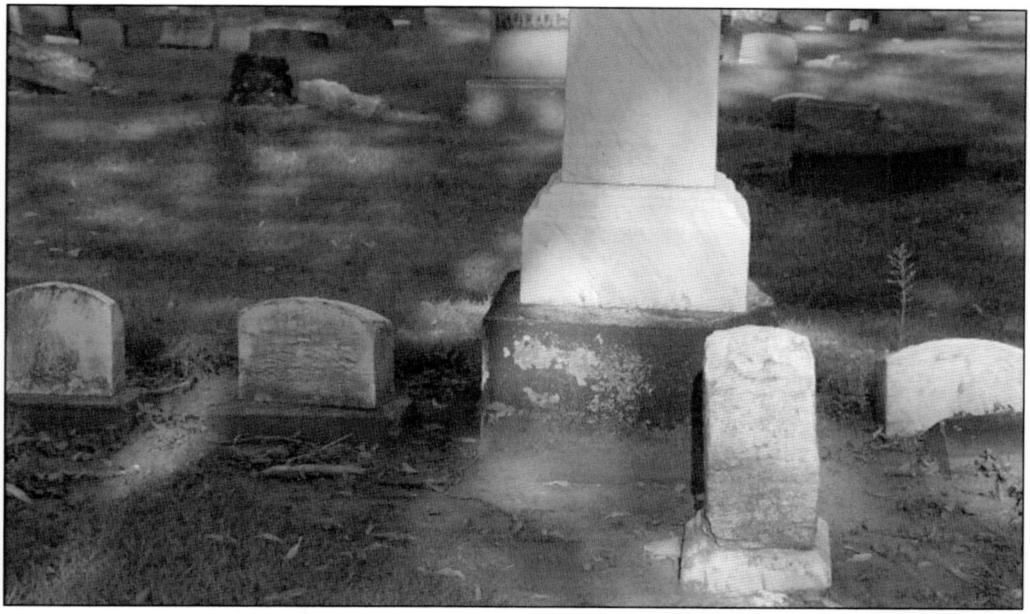

The Railroad and Telegraphers Aid Society lot holds the remains of three known telegraph operators and two men who may have worked for the railroad. One man died at the age of 23 from smallpox. Also interred here is 19-year-old Alice Wright, an English entertainer with the Harrison Troupe managed by W. Hanley. After obtaining approval from the society for the burial, Hanley planned a beautiful funeral at Trinity Church. (MAD.)

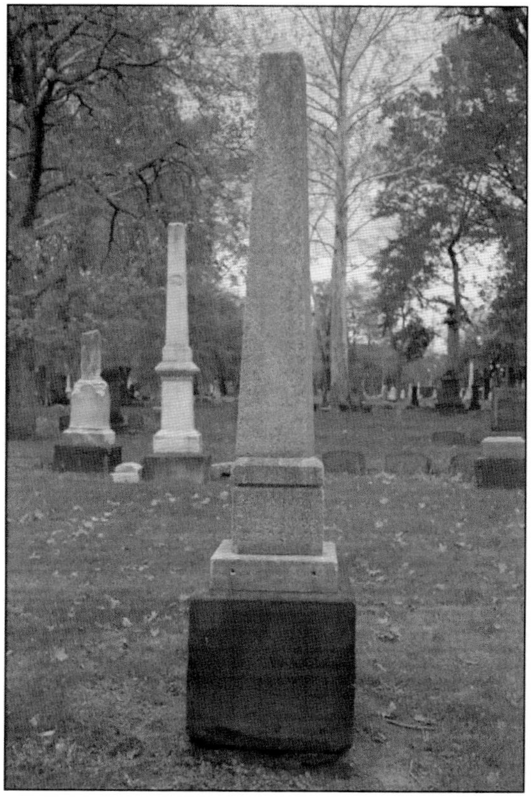

The Improved Benevolent Protective Order of the Elks of the World (IBPOEW) is the largest African American fraternal organization in the world. The organization works to stay current to the concerns of African American and black Elks worldwide. When the IBPOEW Cuyahoga Lodge No. 95 was active in Cuyahoga County, they purchased a plot in Woodland Cemetery that holds 80 of its members. (MAD.)

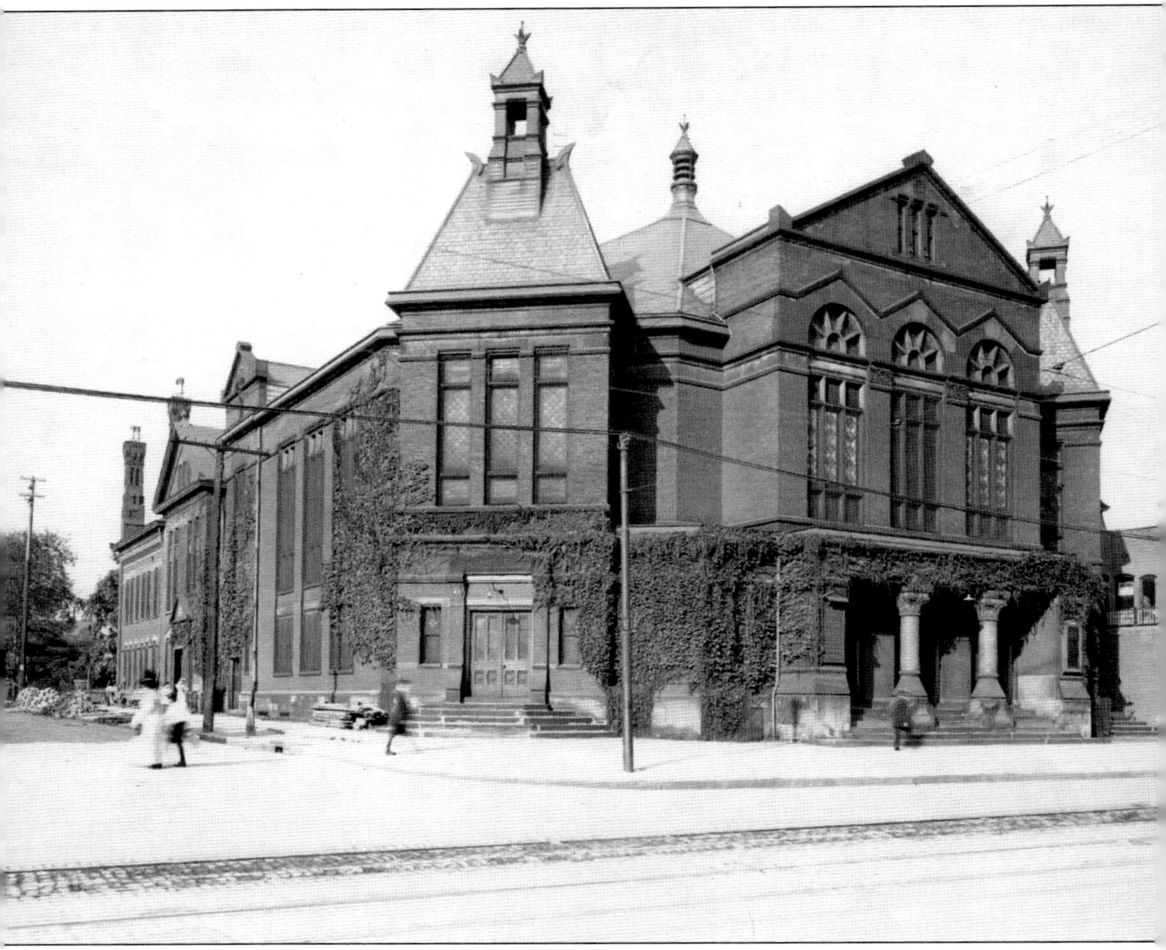

Woodland Avenue Presbyterian Church began in 1853 as the Mayflower Sunday School. By 1855, the school was adopted as a mission of the Second Presbyterian Church. A building was erected on a donated lot, with a lower room ready for occupancy by April 1872; the chapel was finished in time for a May dedication. The church, organized with 54 members, had a seating capacity for about 1,200 persons when finished. (CPLPC.)

Four

They Honorably Served

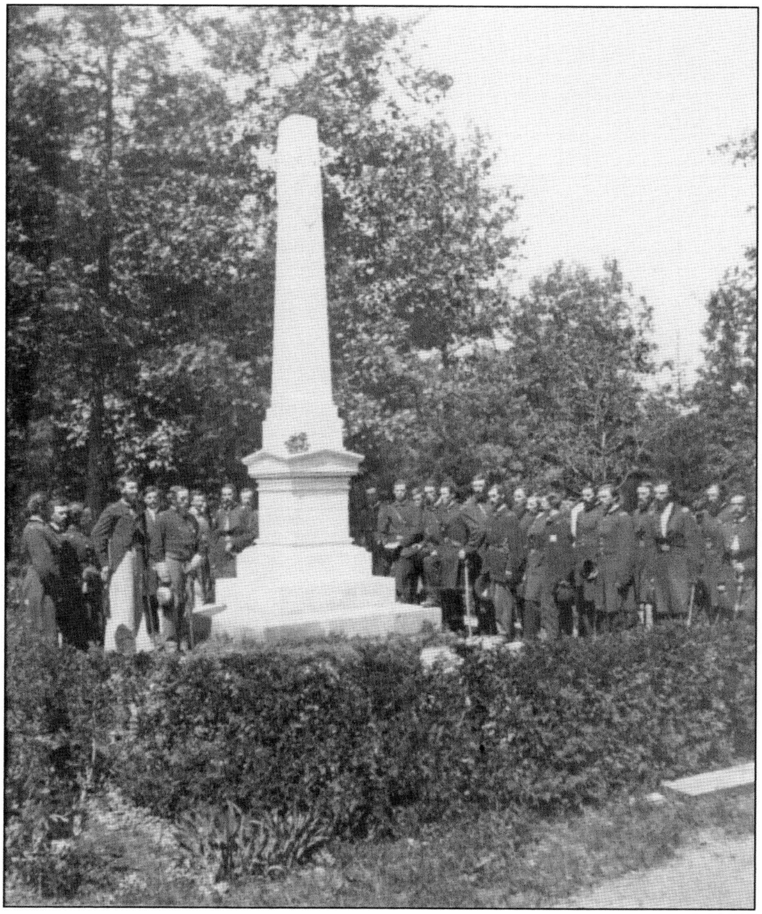

On July 26, 1865, the 23rd Ohio was mustered out of service. On that very day, its officers gathered at the cemetery around the monument that had previously been erected in honor of the regiment following its service at Antietam, Maryland, in 1862. It is thought to be the first regimental monument erected in the United States and marks the rise to prominence of two future American presidents from the 23rd Regiment, namely, Brig. Gen. Rutherford B. Hayes and Maj. William McKinley. (United States Army Military History Institute.)

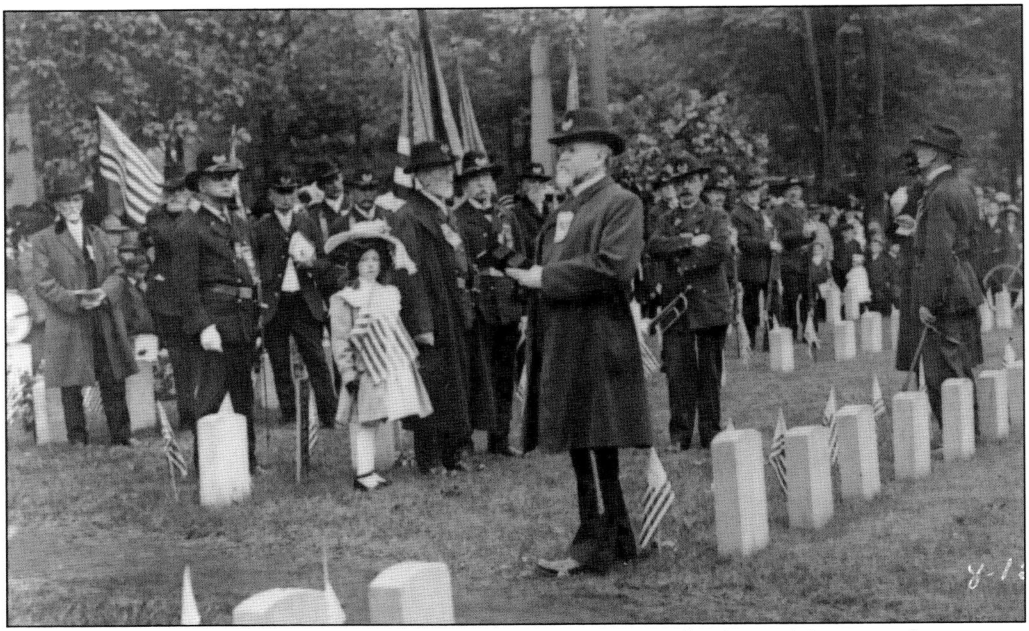

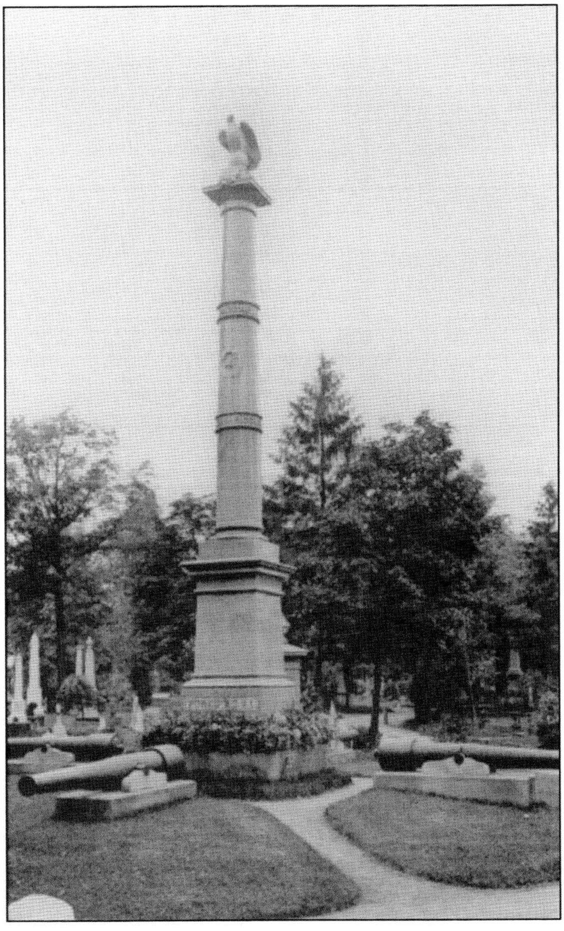

During the first celebration of Decoration Day, May 20, 1868, Gen. James Garfield gave a speech at Arlington National Cemetery, after which 5,000 participants helped to decorate the graves of the more than 20,000 Union and Confederate soldiers buried there. In 1882, the name was changed to Memorial Day to honor all comrades who died in the defense of their country. Memorial Day became a national holiday in 1971. (CPLPC.)

The 7th Ohio Volunteer Infantry monument is the second of two regimental monuments located at the front entrance to the cemetery. The City of Cleveland donated the site to the memory of the fallen soldiers. At the first reunion of the regiment on September 10, 1866, it was resolved to erect a monument upon that location, which was dedicated in May 1872. The four cannons, from an 1861 patent, were installed later. (CPLPC.)

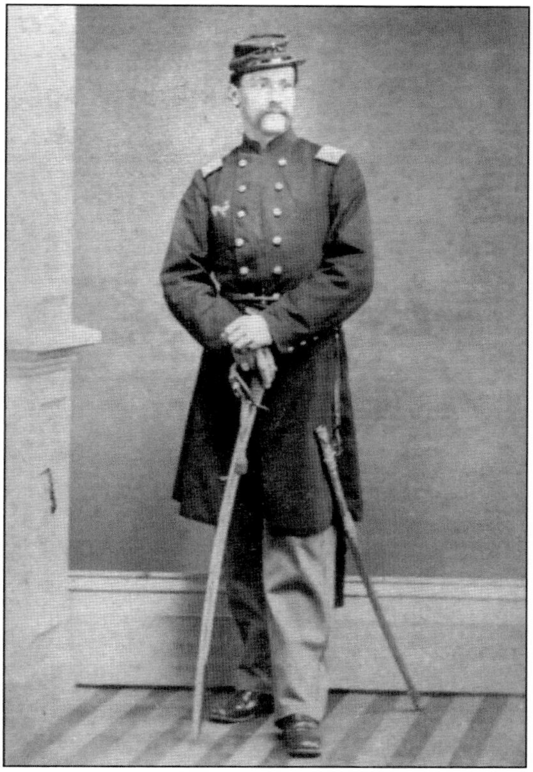

Col. William R. Creighton, 27, and Lt. Col. Orrin J. Crane, 35, of the 7th Ohio Volunteer Infantry, were both killed at the Battle of Ringgold, Georgia, on November 27, 1863. Crane was killed at the top of Taylor's Ridge; Creighton was shot in a failed attempt to retrieve his friend's body. The two were accompanied back to Cleveland as heroes and were laid in state for two days at city hall. Thousands lined the streets for the funeral, which included the firing of minute guns, the tolling of bells, and the bands dirges. In July 1864, they were buried side by side in Woodland Cemetery. Creighton left a wife, while Crane left a wife and two children. (United States Army Military History Institute.)

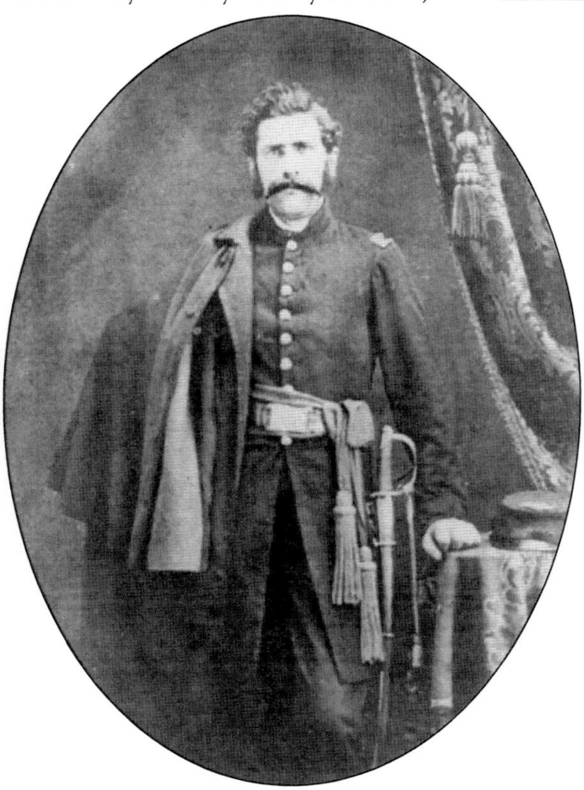

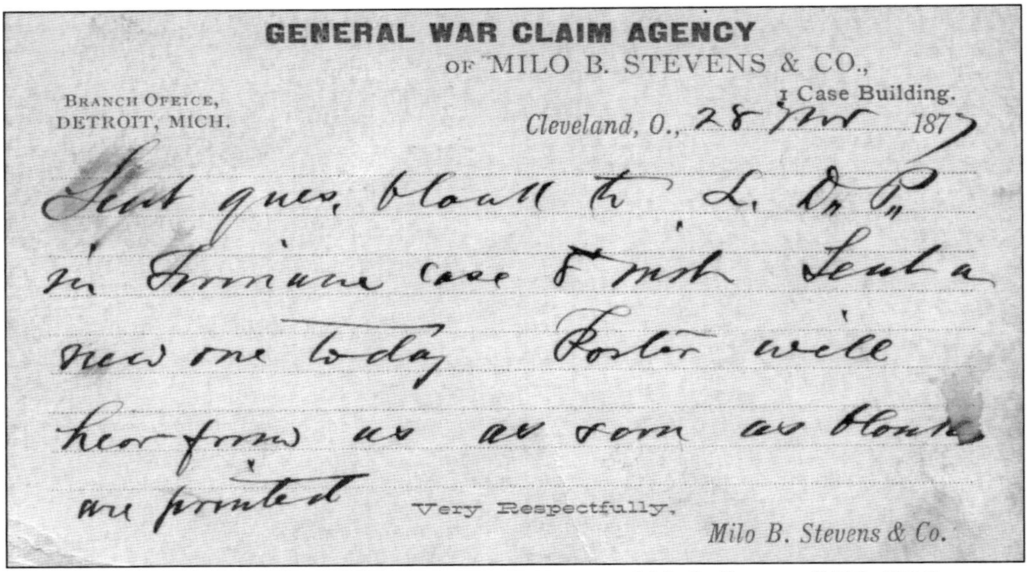

GENERAL WAR CLAIM AGENCY

OF MILO B. STEVENS & CO.,

1 Case Building.

Branch Office,
DETROIT, MICH.

Cleveland, O., 28 Nov 1877

Sent ques. blank to L. Dr. P. in [illegible] case 8 inst. Sent a new one today. Foster will hear from us as soon as blanks are printed

Very Respectfully,

Milo B. Stevens & Co.

Milo B. Stevens (1838–1896), one of the best-known pension claim attorneys in the United States, established offices in Cleveland; Detroit; Chicago; and Washington, DC. He served as a soldier in Company B, Ohio 17th Infantry from 1861 to 1864. Later, as a lawyer, he became interested in the pension claim process. He married twice and had three children. A son, Eugene, inherited the business but lost it due to mismanagement. (MAD.)

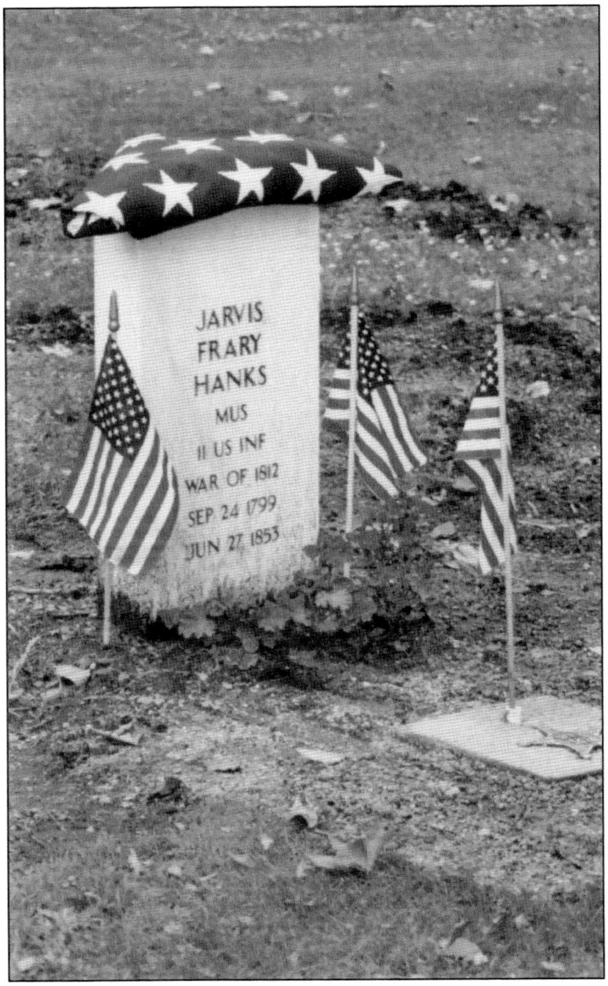

Jarvis Frary Hanks (1790–1853) wrote a memoir after serving as a 14-year-old drummer boy during the War of 1812. He became well known as a portrait painter and, being an accomplished musician, taught voice, violin, and additional instruments while introducing the concept of music education to Cleveland Schools. In 1850, he was appointed music director of the Cleveland Mendelssohn Society. Hanks became the sixth person to be buried in Woodland on June 30, 1853. (MAD.)

Henry May (1845–1922), born in Germany, enlisted in May 1861 as a private in Company B, 21st Regiment and also served with Company B, 39th Regiment, New Jersey Volunteers. He was wounded in the left thigh during the Battle of Fredericksburg, Virginia, and was a prisoner of war for a short time. (Rene Holz.)

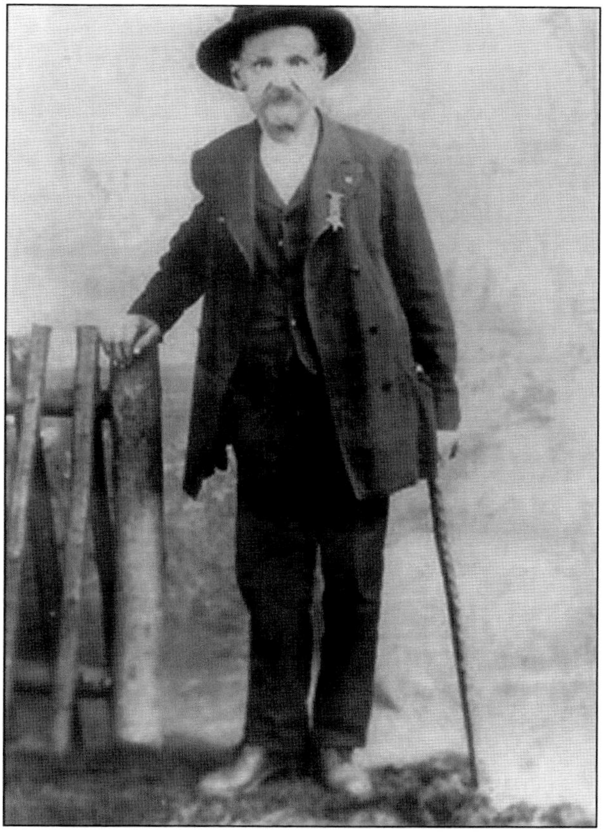

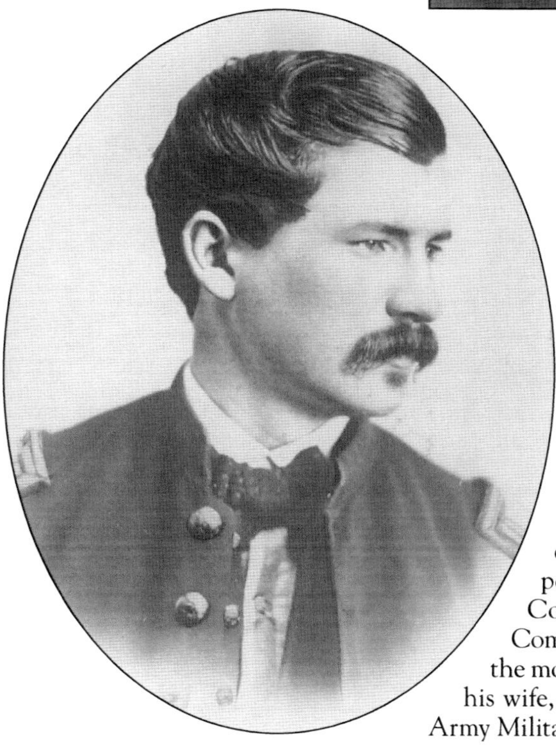

Joseph B. Molyneaux (1840–1925) was a volunteer Civil War officer who captured a sword from a Confederate officer during a hand-to-hand fight at Antietam. He returned to his printing business, served as deputy Cuyahoga County recorder, assistant postmaster, and secretary of the Cuyahoga County Soldiers' and Sailors' Monument Commission. He proudly served as custodian of the monument until his death. He was survived by his wife, Henrietta, and three sons. (United States Army Military History Institute.)

In 1861, Theodore Mitchell (1835–1910) enlisted in Company F, 61st Pennsylvania Volunteer Infantry for three years. He participated in all major campaigns in the eastern theater as he was assigned to the Army of the Potomac. After he mustered out on December 20, 1863, he reenlisted the very next day in Company F as a veteran volunteer. He was awarded the Medal of Honor for capturing the flag of the Tennessee Brigade. (MAD.)

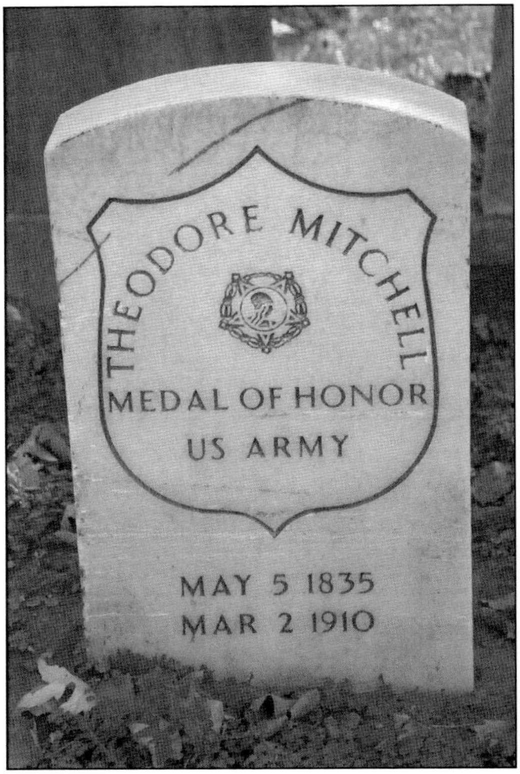

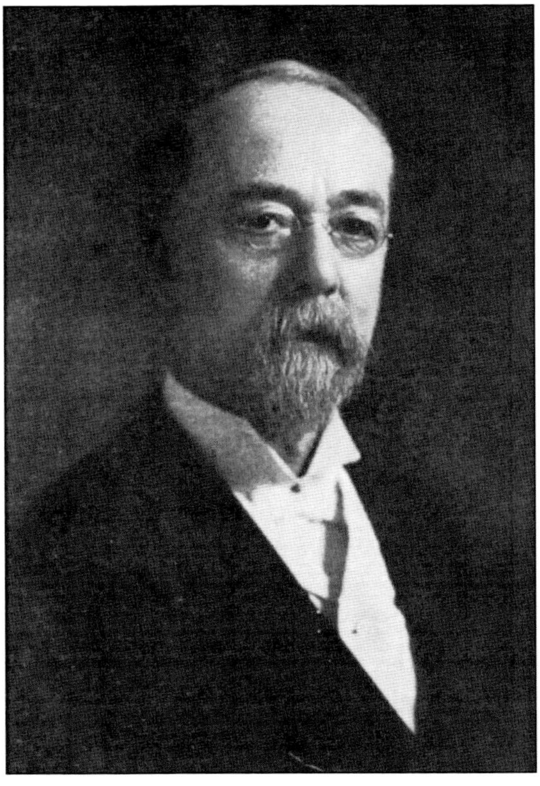

Henry Ebenezer Handerson, MD (1837–1918), was born in Orange, Ohio. He was adopted and was living in Tennessee when he enlisted with the Confederacy in 1861 with Company B, Louisiana 9th Infantry Regiment as a full second lieutenant. Henry attended Columbia University and became an allopathic physician in 1867. He and his first wife, Juliet A. Root (1841–1881), had four children; he married Clara Ann Corlett (1862–1955) in 1888 and had two sons. (Ann Handerson.)

Capt. Gershom Morse Barber (1823–1903) was a soldier, teacher, lawyer, and jurist. Having earned a degree, he taught at Baldwin Institute in Berea and then studied law until his admittance to the bar in 1857. Barber was the mayor of Berea and its postmaster before the Civil War. In 1862, he became captain of the 5th Independent Company of Ohio Volunteer Sharpshooters, serving until 1865. In that same year, Barber was elected to be president of the council for officer retention and became the person who reduced Gen. George Armstrong Custer to lieutenant colonel, the rank he held when he died at the Little Big Horn. He returned to Cleveland and served two terms as Ward 4 city councilman before being elected to the bench as judge of the superior court. In addition, he served two terms as State of Ohio commander. (United States Army Military History Institute.)

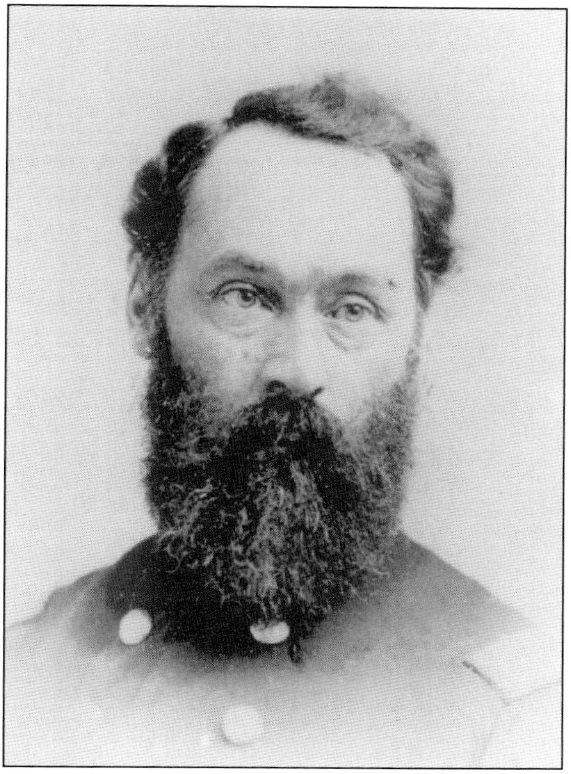

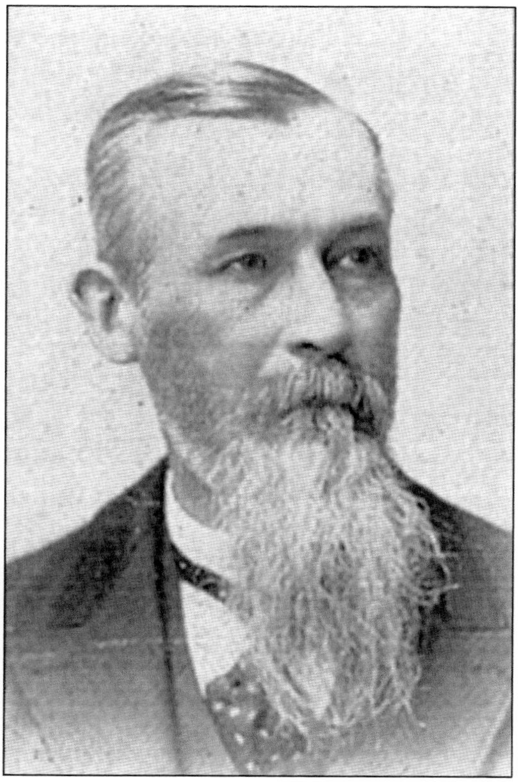

John Eaton Darby, MD (1835–1918), was a physician, professor of Latin and Greek, and demonstrator of anatomy at Western Reserve Medical College (1861–1862). He served as a physician in the Civil War from 1862 to 1866 with the 85th Regiment, Ohio Volunteer Infantry. He also served as the regimental surgeon of the 5th United States Colored Troops. In Cleveland, he taught continuously from 1866 until his retirement in 1906, when he was honored as Professor Emeritus of Therapeutics. Once, while making his rounds as a physician, he was held up by a thief who demanded the doctor's wallet, his watch, and the bag he was carrying. When the thief realized he had a medical bag, he promptly returned it to Dr. Darby, keeping the wallet and watch. Dr. Darby was also well known as a naturalist and instituted special studies in natural history.

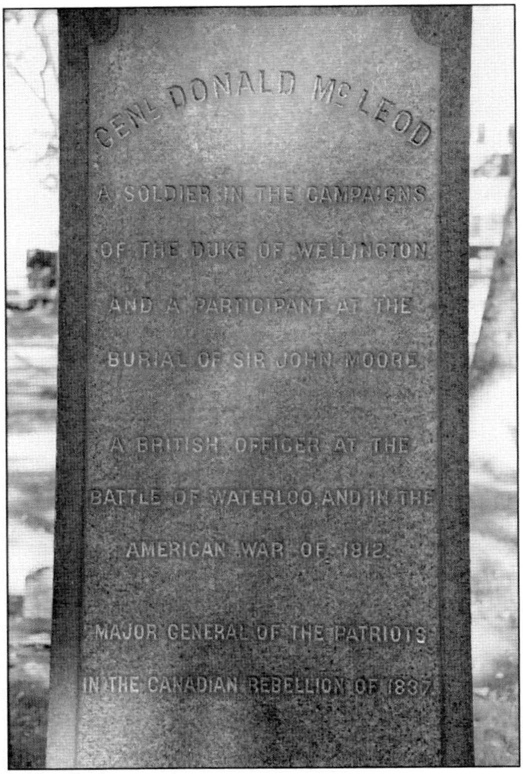

Gen. Donald McLeod (1779–1879) entered the British Navy in 1803, and the Army in 1808. He served in Canada during the War of 1812; fought at the Battle of Waterloo; and returned to Canada in 1816, where he opened a classical school. He took part in the Rebellion of 1837 as a major general in the insurgent army, fleeing to Detroit where he was arrested, tried, and acquitted. He retired to Cleveland, where he lived to be 100. (MAD.)

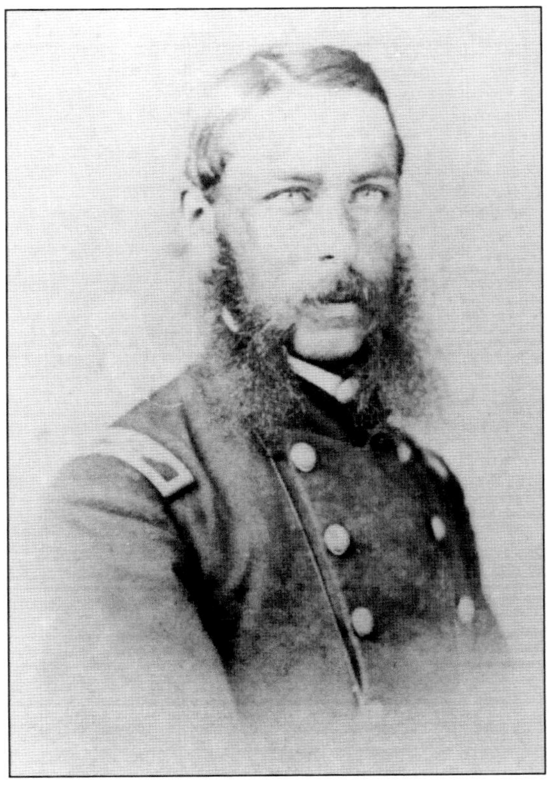

Maj. Alexander Doull (1836–1865) was with the Royal British Artillery when he married Elizabeth Maria King and left for America. As a major, Doull enlisted with 2nd New York Heavy Artillery in October 1861; he resigned in August 1863. He was returning to New York to his wife and four children when he died. To obtain his pension, after being denied several times, Elizabeth was able to prove to Congress that her husband died from a disease he contracted during the war. (United States Army Military History Institute.)

Edward H. Bohm (1838–1906) was a Civil War officer, newspaper publisher, and popular public official. After the war, Bohm prosecuted soldiers' claims against the federal government, served on the school board, founded a German daily newspaper, and served as county recorder. In 1885, he was elected justice of the peace, a position he held for the next 18 years. From 1896 to 1906, he was a member of the Soldiers' and Sailors' Monument Commission. (United States Army Military History Institute.)

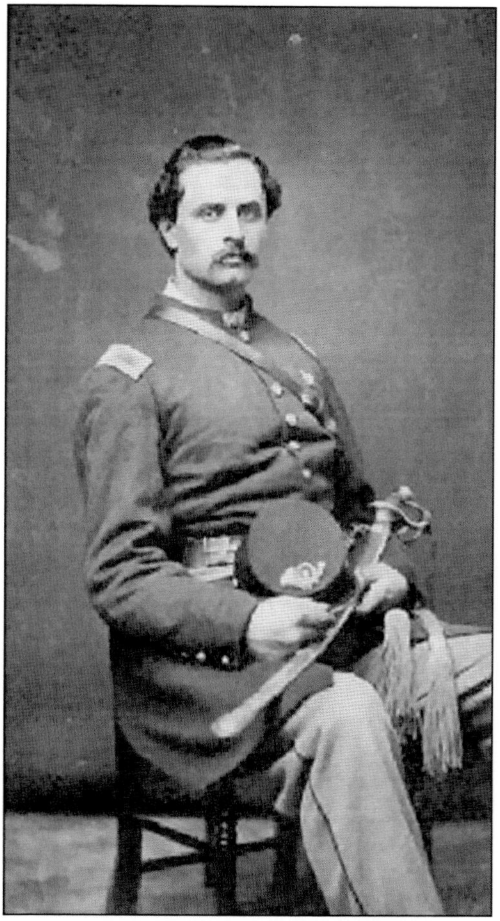

William H. Kneale (1845–1922), a Civil War veteran, enlisted in the 6th Cavalry in October 1861 and received five promotions, ending with full first lieutenant in May 1865. He mustered out of Company I, 6th Cavalry Regiment Ohio in August 1865. The war sword he carried throughout his three years (including at the Battle of Gettysburg, July 1–July 3, 1863) has become a valued family heirloom. (John Ganster.)

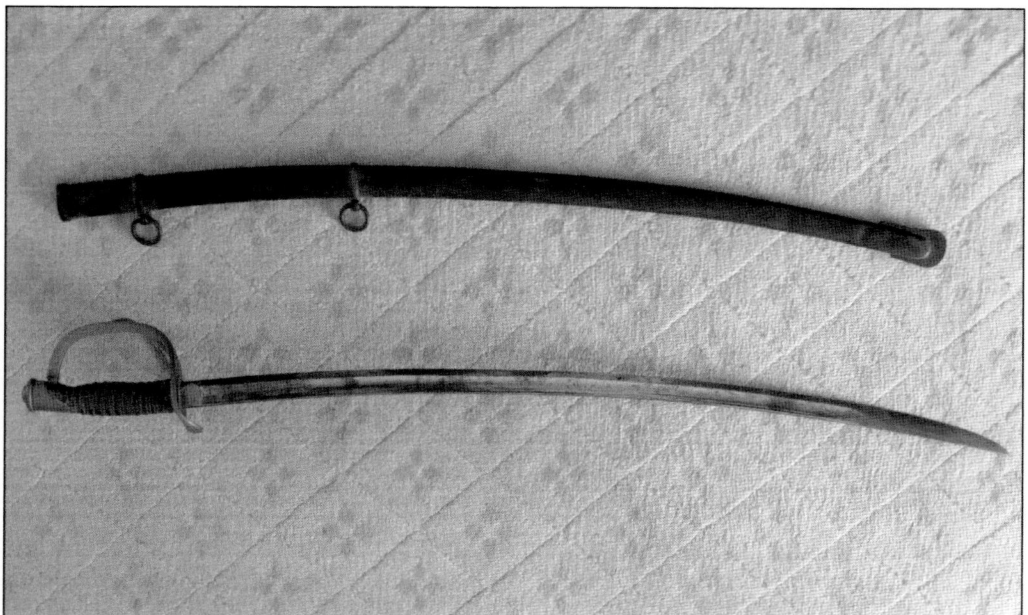

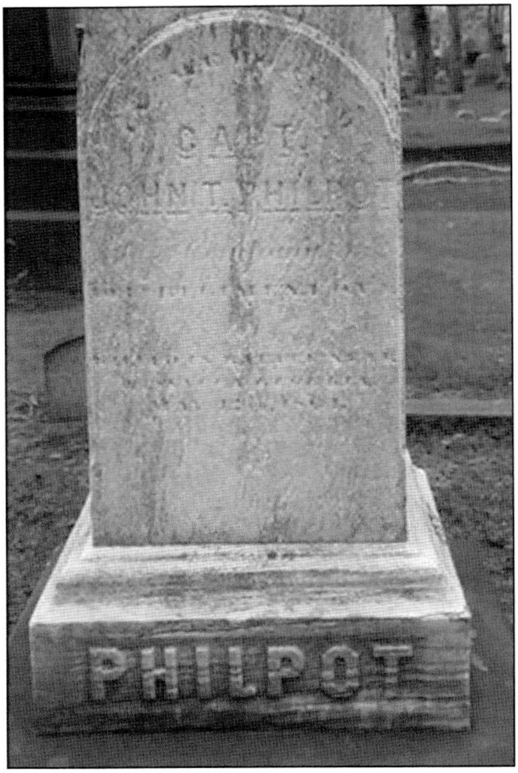

John T. Philpot (1832–1864) was born in Eaton, New York, to George and Mary Toke Philpot. The captain of Company D, 103rd Ohio Volunteer Infantry Regiment was killed in action in Resaca, Gordon County, Georgia, on May 14, 1864. One account of his death states that he was nearly severed in two by a round of solid artillery as the regiment in his command advanced. Philpot, who never married, had been a practicing attorney when he enlisted on August 15, 1862. His name is engraved on Panel 13 of the Cuyahoga Soldiers' and Sailors' Monument in Public Square. (William Stark.)

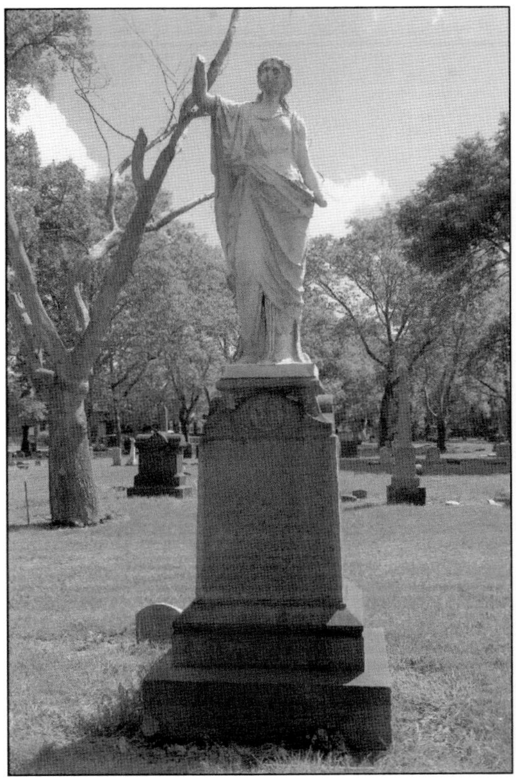

Martha L. Carpenter Carey Mowrie Lacey (1832–1917), born in Summit County to Aaron and Tirzah Drake Carpenter, was a Civil War nurse attached to the 15th Volunteer Regiment of Pennsylvania. Martha brought her five-year-old son, Thomas J. (1881–1925), to her third marriage when she wed William Lacey (1817–1896) on September 6, 1886. In September 1916, Martha applied for her pension, which was not accepted before she died. (MAD.)

John J. Elwell (1820–1900) was a doctor, an attorney, and a brigadier general in the Civil War. He wrote a text, *Medical Jurisprudence*; edited the *Western Law Monthly*; and served as a college professor and member of the Ohio Legislature. He raised and equipped the 2nd and 3rd Ohio Cavalry and Sherman's Brigade. Elwell obtained permission for the construction of the Soldiers' and Sailors' Monument, which he had pursued for years. (John T. Griffith.)

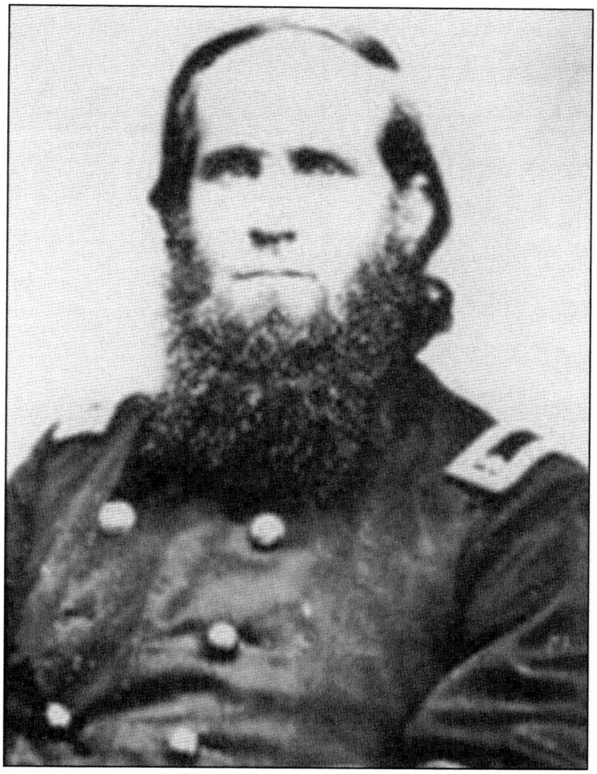

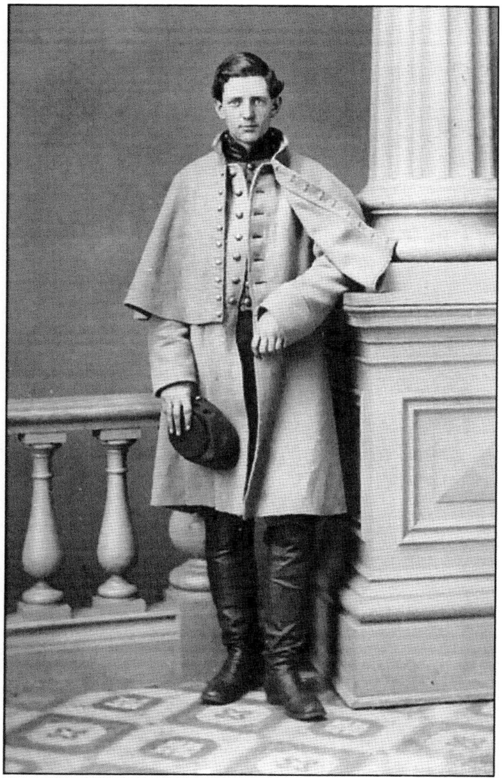

Samuel Jones "Sammie" Pickands (1843–1862), a loyal member of Phoenix Fire Engine Company No. 4, enlisted as a private on February 1, 1862, with 1st Battery Ohio Light Artillery Company K. About a month later, on March 5, 1862, Sammie died of disease in Parkersburg, West Virginia. His brother, James, also a fireman with Phoenix, brought his body home to Cleveland. James and another brother both rejoined the Army. (Ron Coddington Collection.)

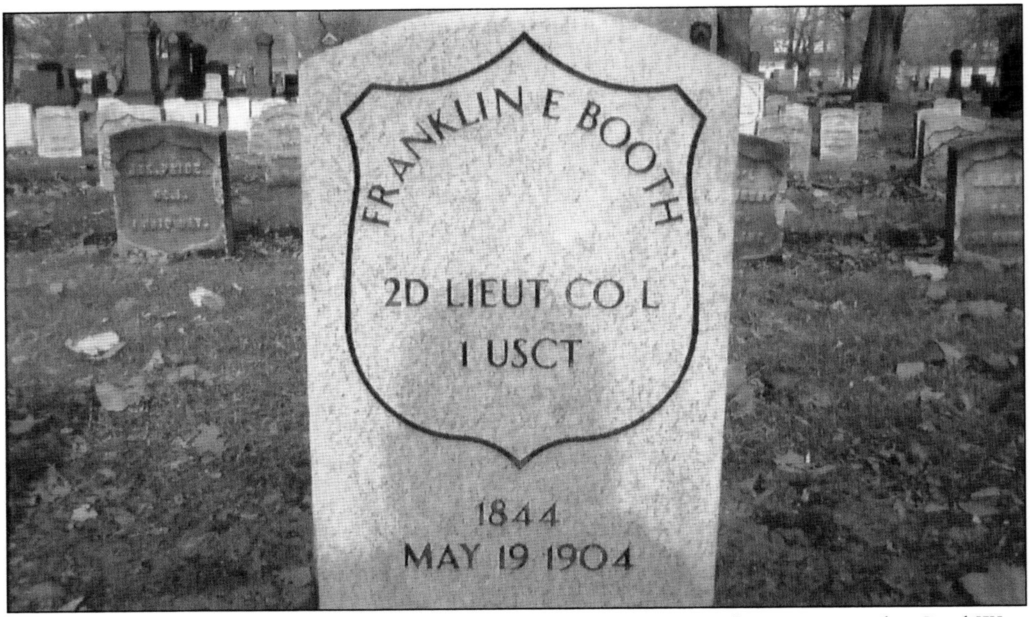

Frank E. Booth (1844–1904) of New Jersey enlisted in August 1862 for service in the Civil War, Company I, 103rd Regiment, Ohio Voluntary Infantry in Medina County; he was discharged in September 1864 to accept a promotion as second lieutenant in the 1st US Colored Heavy Artillery. He married Maria Louisa Houghton in April 1865 and began working as a clerk and a bookkeeper for the railroad. They had one son, Frank. (William Stark.)

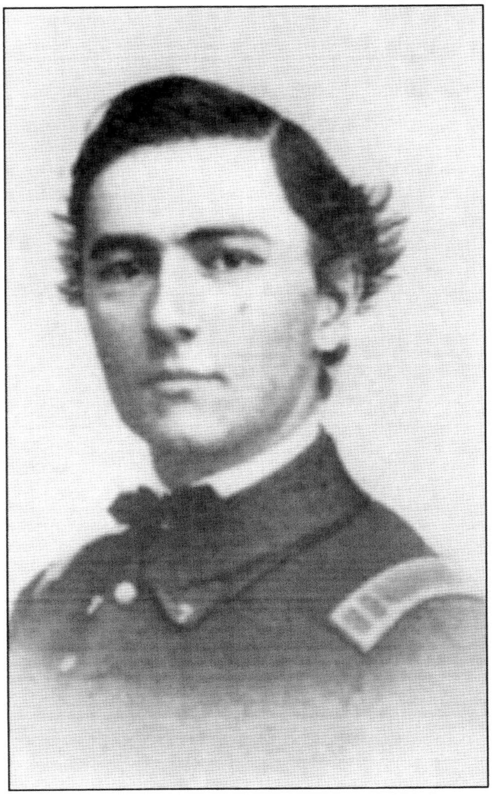

Lt. Col. Mervin Clark (1843–1864), born in Cleveland to Mervin and Caroline Guptil Clark, was killed in action at Franklin, Tennessee on November 20, 1864, the very same day he was commissioned as lieutenant colonel. The brave 21-year-old had seized the colors when his regiment, the 183rd, began to retreat. They returned to find Mervin dead. His body was recovered from the battlefield and returned to Cleveland. (Itinerary of the 7th Ohio Volunteer Infantry.)

Nathaniel Fairfax (1845–1899) was born in Damascus, Mahoning County, Ohio, to Leeds and Jane Fairfax of Virginia. Nathaniel enlisted as a private first class in Company A, 4th Infantry Regiment, United States Colored Troops. In 1870, he was living in Portage County. In 1888, he applied for an invalid pension but was denied. He died in Cleveland on October 16, 1899. (William Stark.)

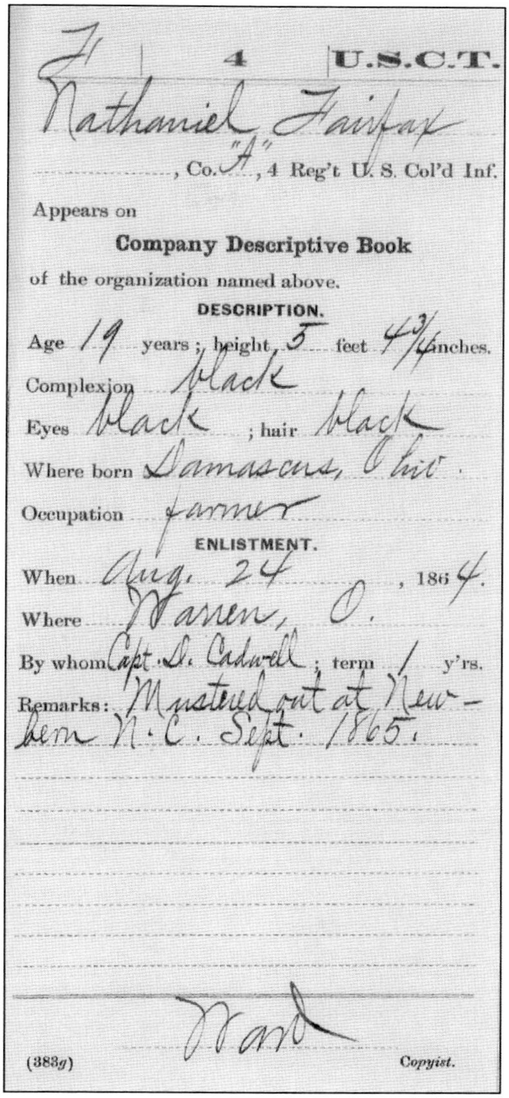

F | 4 | U.S.C.T.

Nathaniel Fairfax

, Co. "A", 4 Reg't U. S. Col'd Inf.

Appears on

Company Descriptive Book

of the organization named above.

DESCRIPTION.

Age 19 years; height 5 feet 4 3/4 inches.

Complexion black

Eyes black ; hair black

Where born Damascus, Ohio.

Occupation farmer

ENLISTMENT.

When Aug. 24, 1864.

Where Warren, O.

By whom Capt. D. Cadwell ; term 1 y'rs.

Remarks: Mustered out at New-bern N.C. Sept. 1865.

Ward

(383g) Copyist.

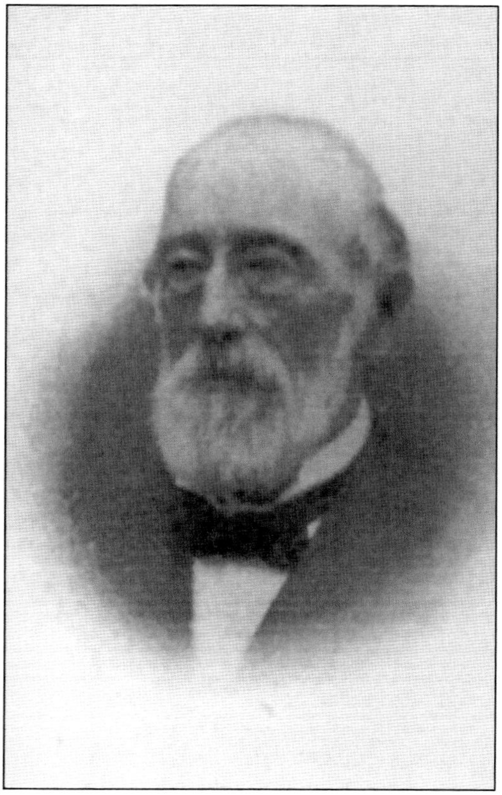

William Henry Hayward (1822–1904) came to Cleveland in 1825 from Connecticut. He helped organize the Cleveland Grays, a private militia company, in 1837 and was one of the first Clevelanders to volunteer for Civil War service. In April 1861, he enlisted with Company E, 1st Ohio Volunteer Infantry (Cleveland Grays) and later served in Company A with the 103rd and 150th Ohio Volunteer Infantries. He remained active in veterans' activities during the postwar period. (William Stark.)

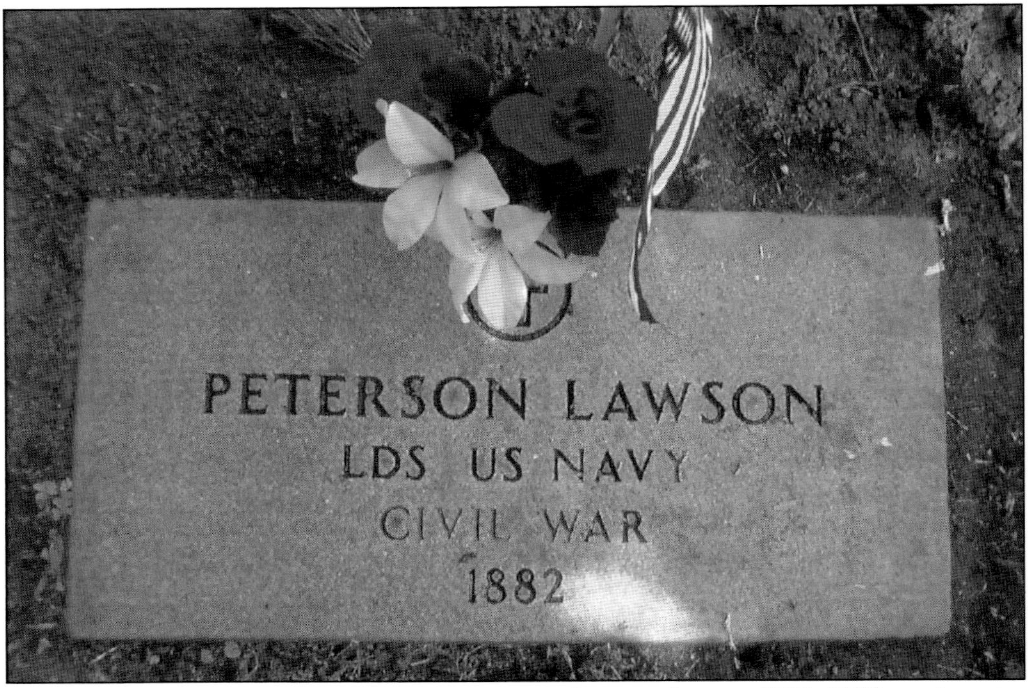

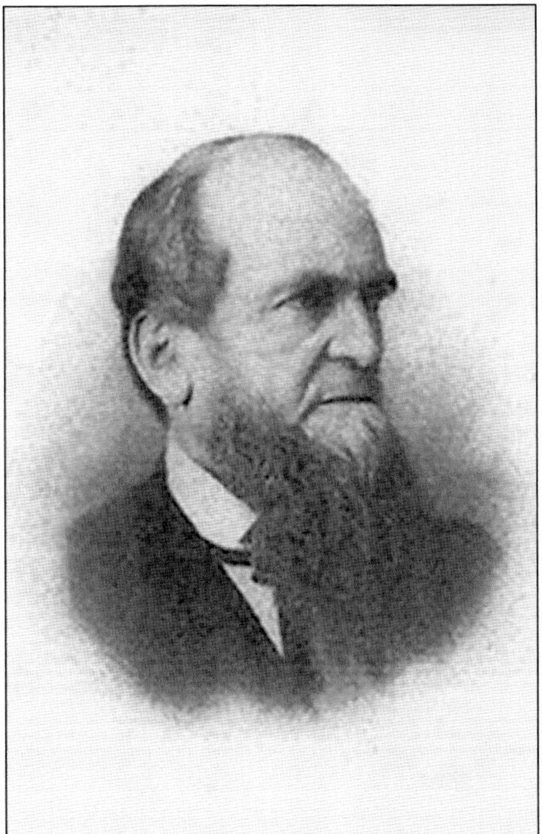

Peterson Lawson (1833–1882) was born in Virginia and married Catherine Hayes, of Kentucky. The couple had nine children, including two sons who were born in Ontario, Canada. Peterson served in the US Navy aboard the *North Carolina* during the Civil War, earning the rank of landsman. His application for a pension was accepted. At the time of the 1900 census, eight of their children were still living with Catherine. (William Stark.)

Thomas S. Paddock (1814–1891), from Herkimer County, New York, commanded the Cleveland Grays from the very beginning of the Civil War until August 1864. As captain of Company A, 150th Ohio Volunteer Infantry, his regiment helped thwart the Confederate advance on Washington, DC, in July 1864. At home in Cleveland, he was a fur merchant, then owner of T.S. Paddock & Son, which dealt with "hats, caps and fur" at 221 Superior Avenue. Thomas married twice; he had five children with his first wife, Mary Ann Barnett, and a son, Thomas, with his second wife, Jane DeWolfe. (William Stark.)

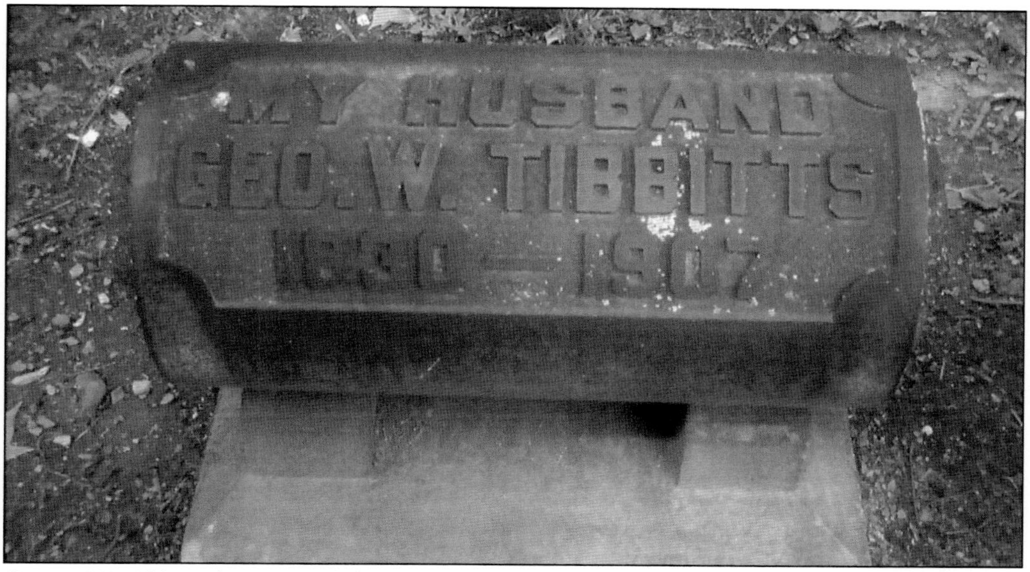

George W. Tibbitts (1835–1907), born in New York, came to Cleveland with his parents in 1833. George served in Company E, 1st Regiment, Ohio Volunteer Infantry (Cleveland Grays) and served as captain with Company E, 103rd Ohio Volunteer Infantry and as a second lieutenant in Company A, 150th Ohio Volunteer Infantry. George married twice and had two sons; he was also a patent attorney and a wood engraver and carver. (William Stark.)

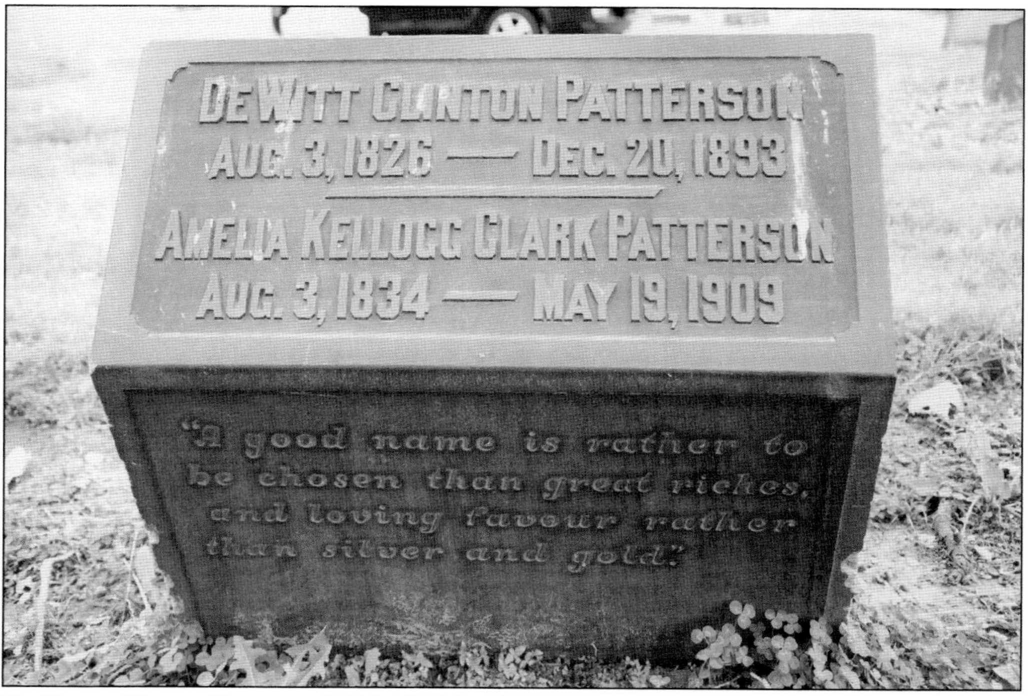

Dr. Dewitt Clinton Patterson (1826–1893) lived in Lorain, Ohio, and earned his medical degree from Western Reserve in 1857. He married Amelia Clark in 1852. In 1862, he enlisted as a surgeon and coroner with the 124th Ohio Infantry; became an officer, and was assigned to Washington, DC. On July 3, 1881, Dr. Patterson was summoned as a consulting physician for Pres. James A. Garfield, who had been shot the previous day. (MAD.)

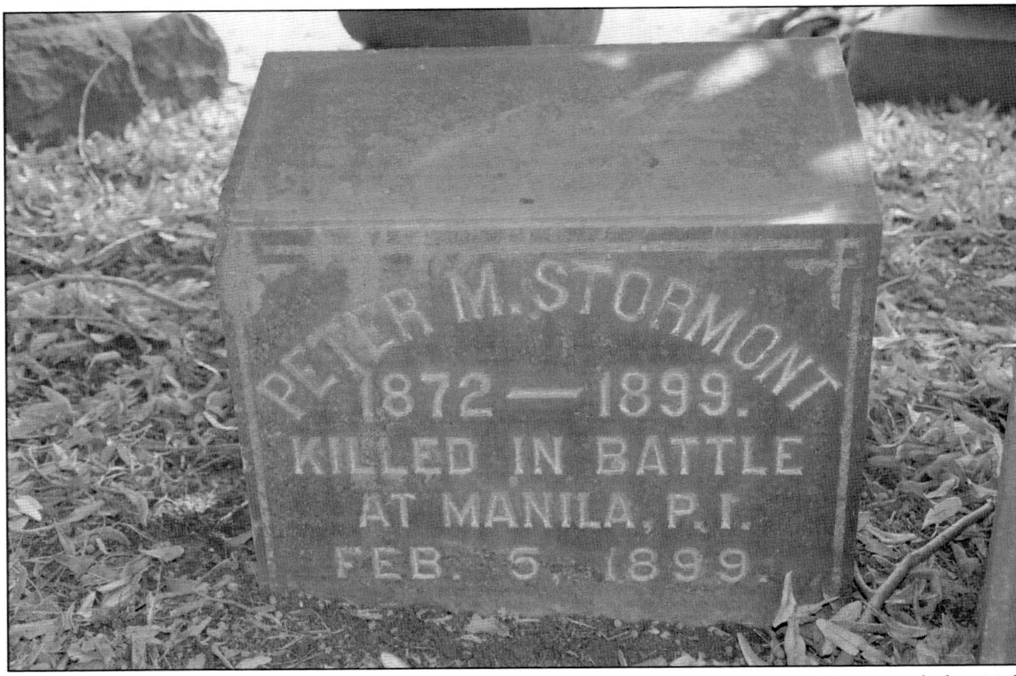

Peter M. Stormont (1862–1899) was born in England to James Stormont. He joined the 14th Infantry and was killed in action on February 5, 1899, in a charge on the military blockhouse in Manila, Philippines. A year later, on February 21, 1900, his remains were met in Cleveland by his brother George, who had arranged for his burial. The Cleveland Scottish Honor Guard and some of Peter's regiment escorted his body to the grave. (MAD.)

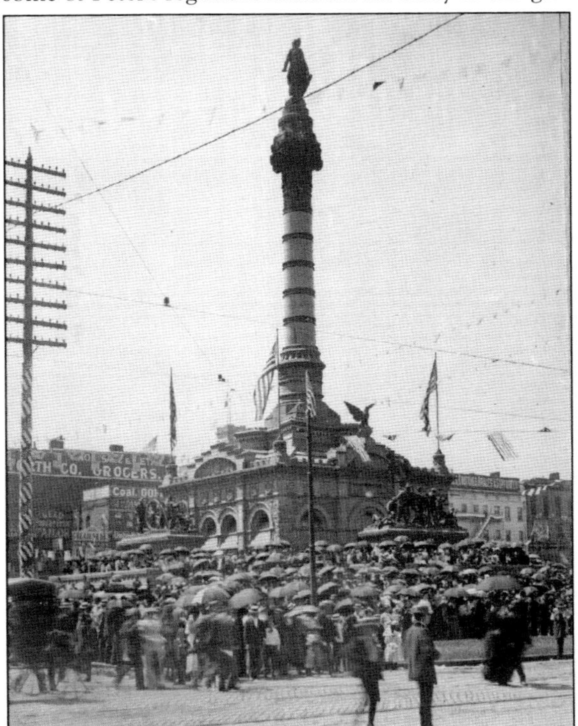

The Soldiers' and Sailors' Monument was built in tribute to Civil War soldiers and sailors from Cuyahoga County and is prominently located on Public Square in downtown Cleveland. The monument, designed by architect and sculptor Levi Scofield (1842–1917), opened July 4, 1894, and was restored in 2010. It was recently referred to as "the best example of statuary anywhere." Over 8,800 names are etched in the marble tablets; over 550 of those names represent individuals buried in Woodland Cemetery. (Ohio Historical Society/Louis Baus Collection.)

Five

The Preservation of History Continues

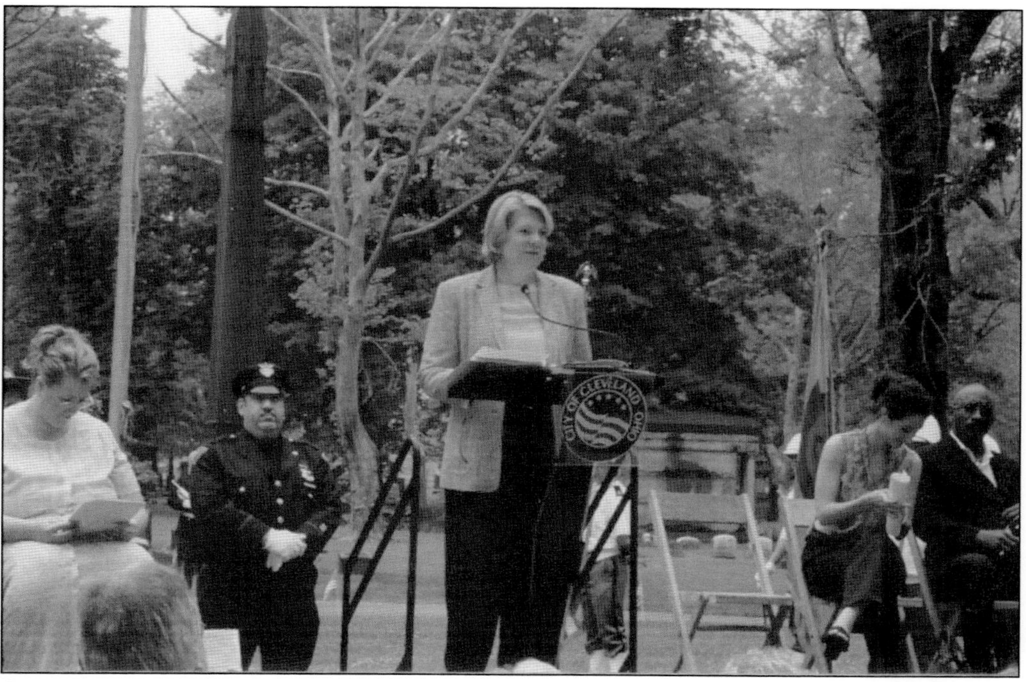

On June 14, 2003, Mayor Jane L. Campbell addressed the crowd of about 500 persons gathered to celebrate Woodland Cemetery's Sesquicentennial Anniversary. The goals first expressed in 1853, which included the cemetery being created as a public, nonracial, and nonreligious cemetery, were rededicated. The first burial occurred on June 23, 1853, for 15-month-old Fanny Langshaw; 150 years later, in 2003, more than 87,000 burials had taken place. (City of Cleveland.)

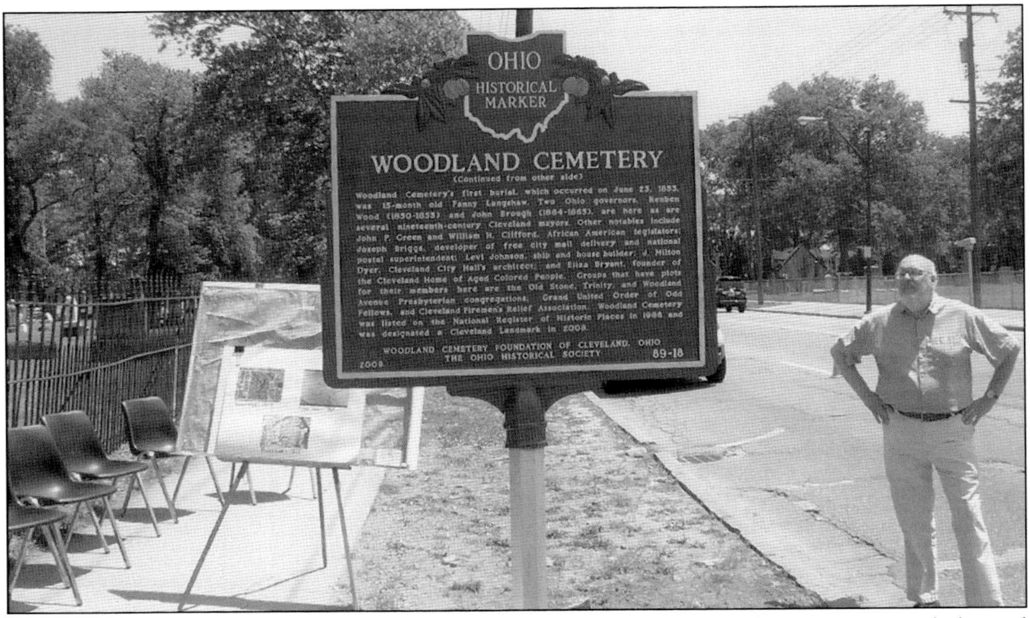

The Ohio Historical Marker located outside the entrance to Woodland Cemetery, was dedicated on June 14, 2009, in a ceremony that also marked the 156th anniversary of Woodland Cemetery's existence. One side of the marker describes the rich history of the cemetery and its mission for generations of Clevelanders, while the other side describes some of the more prominent residents and groups that owned plots. (Katharine Ott.)

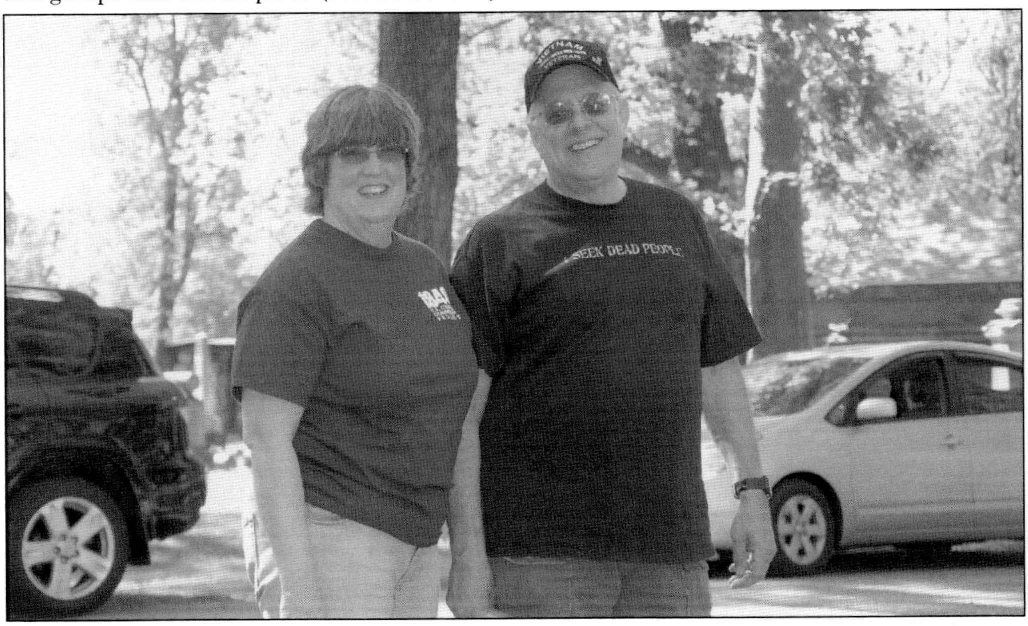

The weekend before the actual Memorial Day holiday weekend has become an annual event in which volunteers spend time (sometimes an hour or two, sometimes all day) to pay their respects and honor our service men and women. Volunteers, such as Terry and Marcia Hart, help to decorate the veterans' graves with a flag, often for members of their own family or for a particular section. There are over 2,100 veterans buried in the cemetery from the War of 1812 to the present. (MAD.)

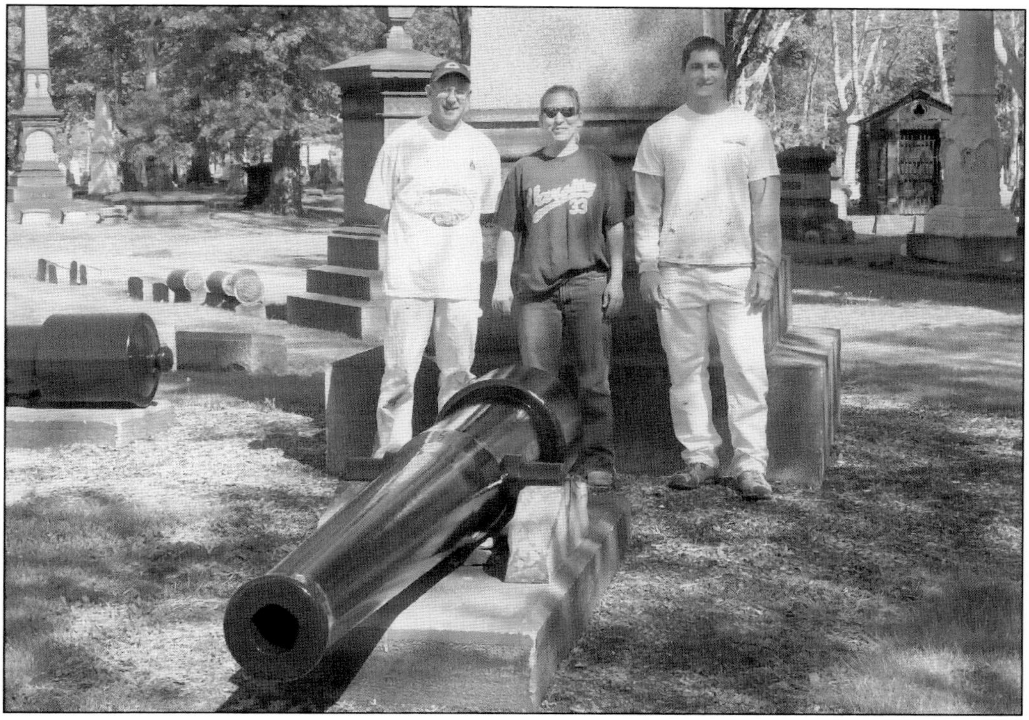

The Cannon Restoration Project was successfully achieved in 2009 after several students in an apprenticeship program with the International Union Painters of Allied Trades (IUPAT) took an interest in this once-in-a-lifetime project. After numerous attempts and many errors and setbacks, the students successfully restored the four historical Robert Parott Cannons that had been cast at the West Point Foundry for use in the Civil War. (International Union Painters of Allied Trades.)

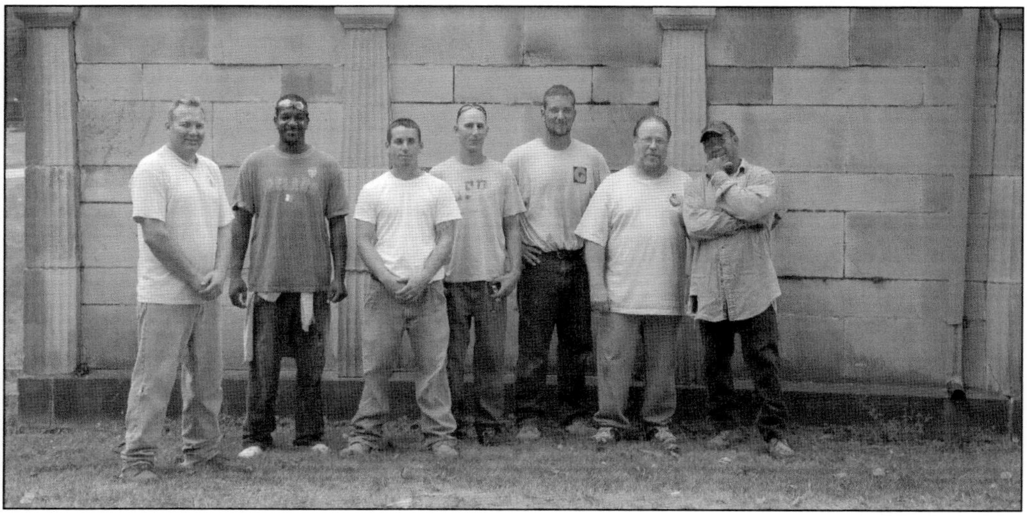

Woodland Cemetery welcomes and accepts skilled volunteer services to aid in repairs, install electrical items, or fulfill other requirements as identified. For example, the Roofers, Waterproofers and Allied Workers (RWAW) Local 44 enlisted (and assisted) their student apprentices with needed repairs on the flat-roof mausoleums, which had fallen into a state of deterioration over the years. (MAD.)

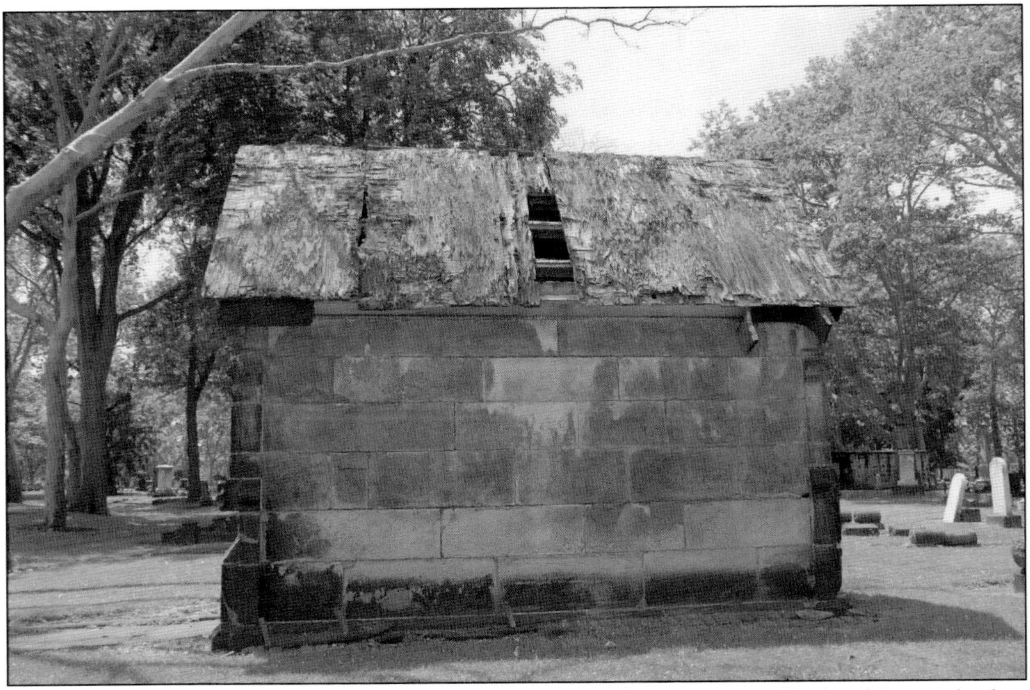

Martin B. Scott (1801–1872), a lineal descendant in the sixth generation of Richard Scott, the first American Quaker, became one of Cleveland's best-known businessmen. He opened an agency of the American transportation company of canal boats on the Erie Canal, built a steam elevator of brick, and invested in lake commerce. In 1861, he conveyed his confidence in the government by purchasing $5,000 in treasury notes, later known as war bonds. In 2009, the deteriorated mausoleum roof was replaced by volunteer Dean Murad. (MAD.)

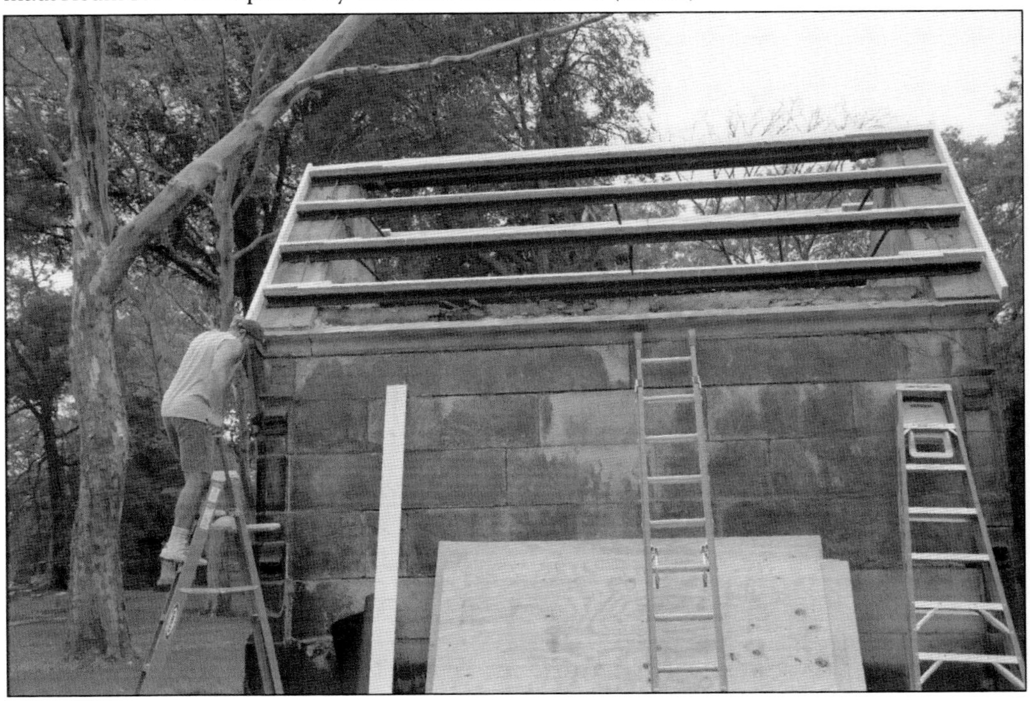

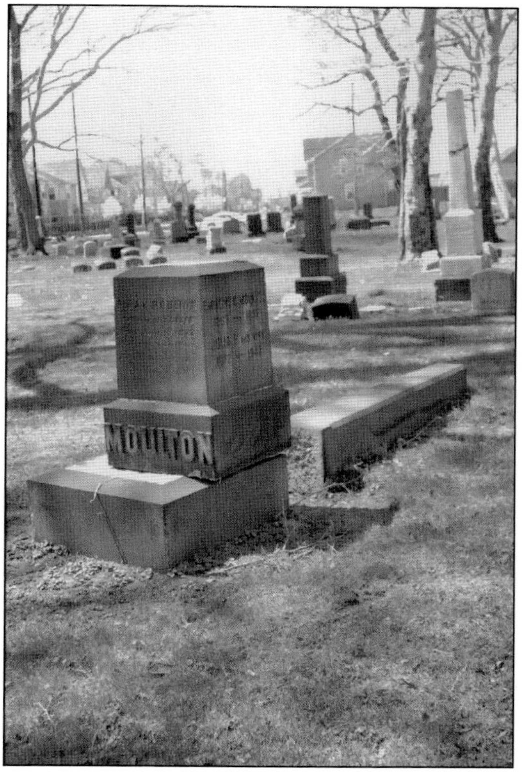

Rev. Albanus K. Moulton (1810–1873), born in Hatley, Quebec, became licensed as a reverend in 1837 during the Geauga Quarterly Meeting in Burton, where he had stopped on his way to the plantations of the South (as he was strongly against slavery). He traveled extensively as a preacher. On June 19, 1873, while walking on a railroad bridge with his wife, Julie, and a son, he tripped and fell to his death. (MAD.)

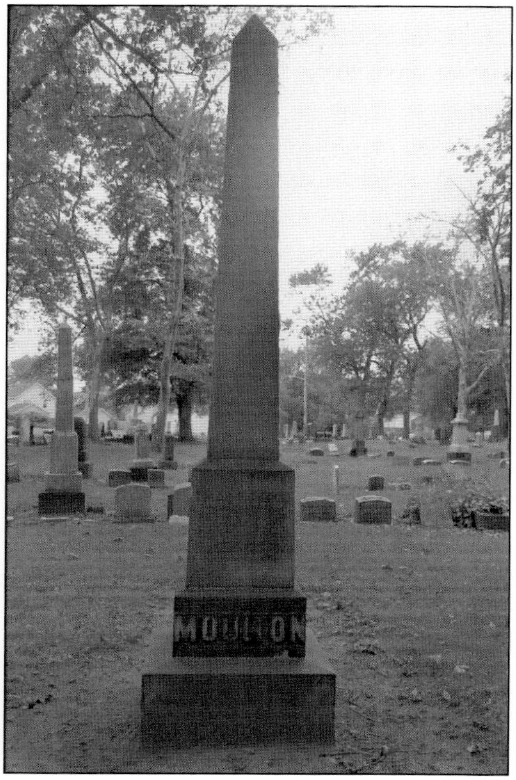

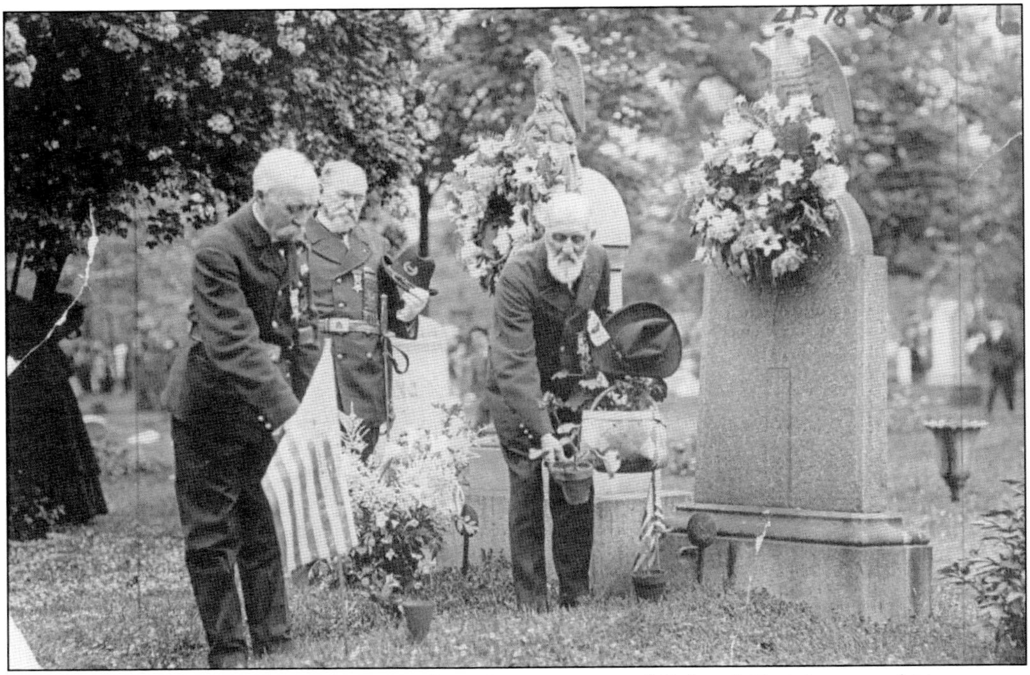

In August 2007, the eagles were restored on the gravesites of Colonel Creighton and Lieutenant Colonel Crane. Their gravesites were donated by the City of Cleveland in 1865, following the return of their bodies after both were killed at the Battle of Ringgold, Georgia. As a tribute to the hometown heroes, the City of Cleveland had their bodies laid in state at city hall. Since 1865, on every Decoration Day, their gravesites have been honored appropriately by veteran groups. During the latter half of the 1900s, the eagles disappeared. The foundation chose the replacement of the eagles as their first restoration project on the graves. Pictured here are the 7th Ohio Volunteer reenactors who participate at Woodland Cemetery every Memorial Day. (CPLPC/Carolyn Vigneulle.)

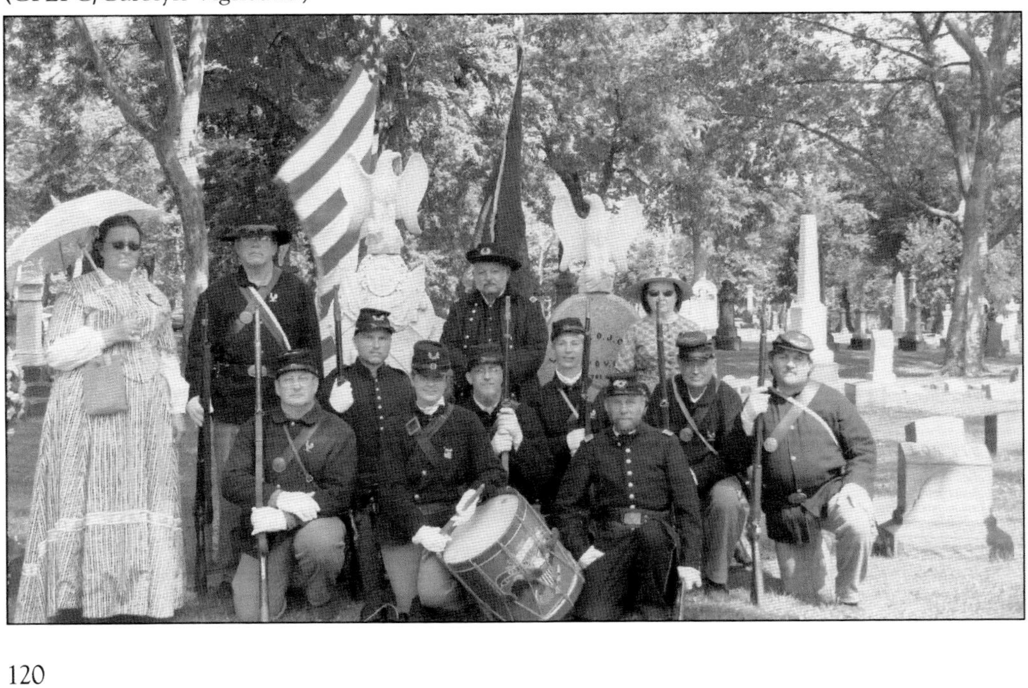

The records for Woodland Cemetery have been invaluable to David Borger in his genealogical research. Other civil and church records painted a conflicting or incomplete picture of Theobald's family. When David found his relatives all buried in the same lot at Woodland, everything came together. The inclusion of not only dates of death but also last addresses helped him be sure of the relationships. Unfortunately, even though the records showed that they were buried together, there was only a single, small marker for one of them, Mary Tupa, Theobald's younger sister. David decided that he wanted to see the entire family memorialized and, with the help of the cemetery foundation, was able to have this marker put in place. (David Borger.)

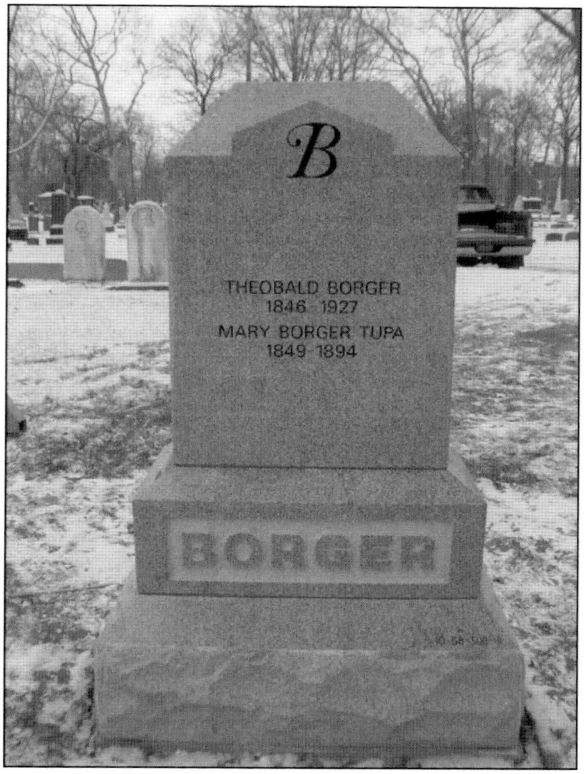

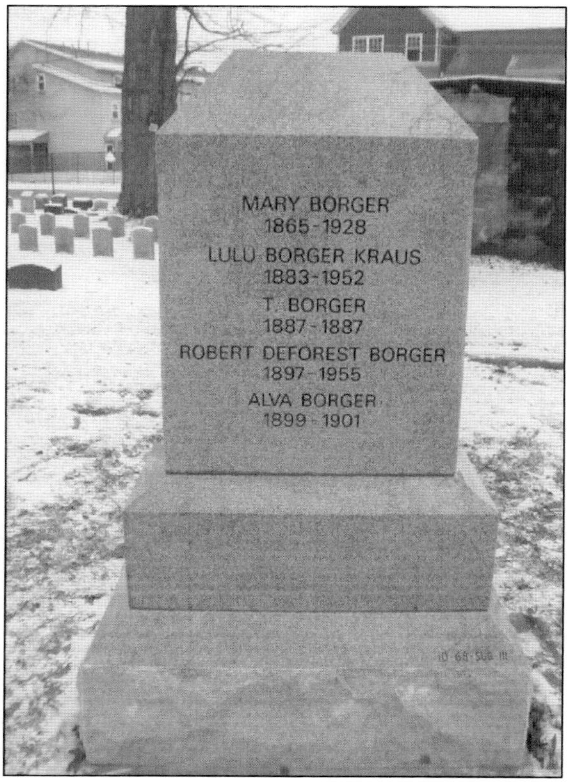

David's attention was first drawn to Woodland Cemetery when his research led him to the death certificate of his third great-grandfather, Daniel Borger (and Theobald's brother), who is buried in section 73. Along with Daniel, David found the graves of Daniel's wife and two of their sons and one of their daughters. (They had 11 children altogether!) Daniel's sister Elisabeth is also buried at Woodland along with their mother, Anna Mary (Mueller) Borger. Finally, from cemetery records, David discovered a great-aunt of whom no one in the family was aware. Although she died at five months, there is now a marker for her grave at Woodland.

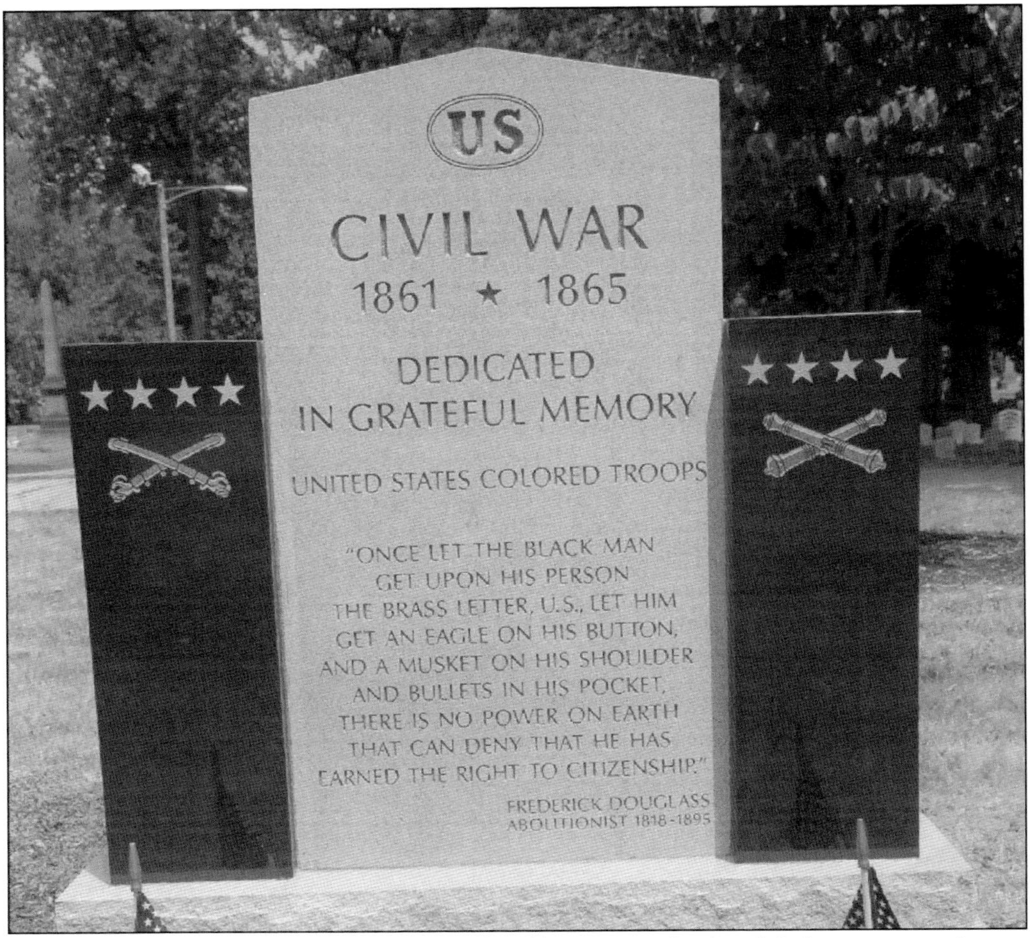

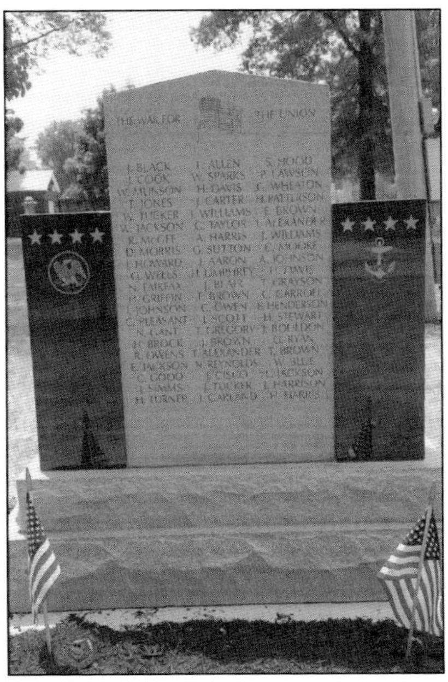

Black soldiers are credited with helping to turn the tide for the Union Army through their courage and sheer numbers, which amounted to about 10 percent of all Union troops. Approximately 80 veterans of the United States Colored Troops (USCT) are buried in Woodland Cemetery, many without headstones, as their contributions in the Civil War have often been overlooked throughout history. Every effort is being made to honor them, and on June 24, 2012, a monument dedicated to the USCT was unveiled. Currently, there are only 63 verified names inscribed on the monument, with space to inscribe additional names as they are confirmed. (MAD.)

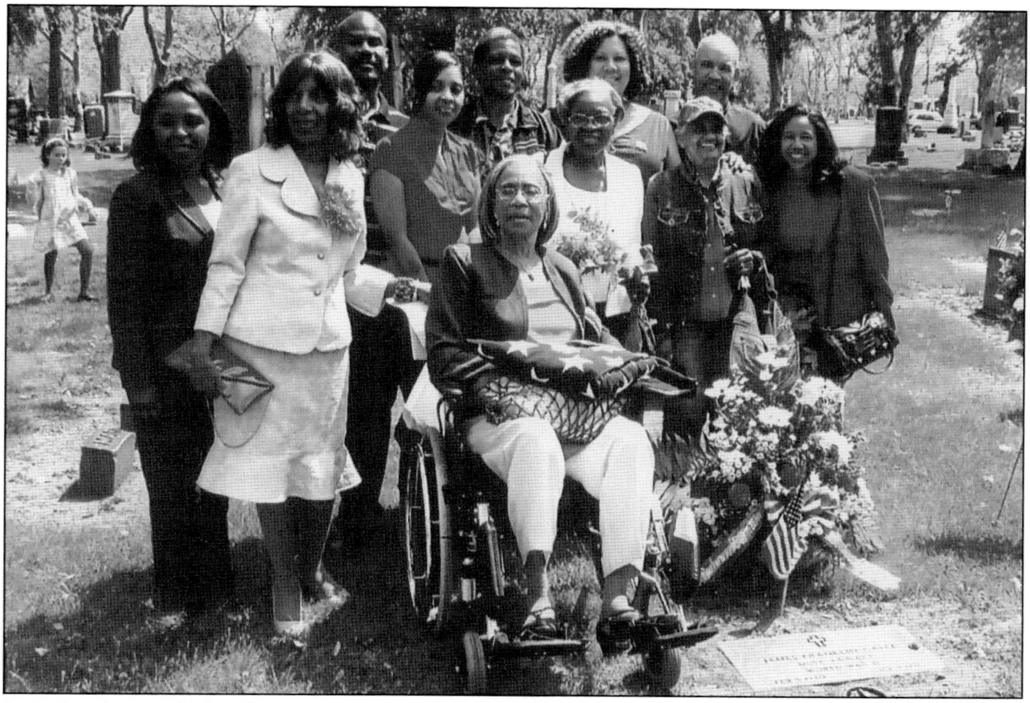

In 2008, the Gayle family came from across the United States to honor James Gayle. On September 1, 1943, at age 23, Jimmy enlisted in the US Navy as an apprentice seaman. In November 1943, he was classified as musician third class with the US Naval Band, and by June 1945 he was musician second class. After serving two years, Gayle was honorably discharged on December 9, 1945. He received the American Theatre Ribbon and the World War II Victory Medal while in the Navy. (Gina Gayle.)

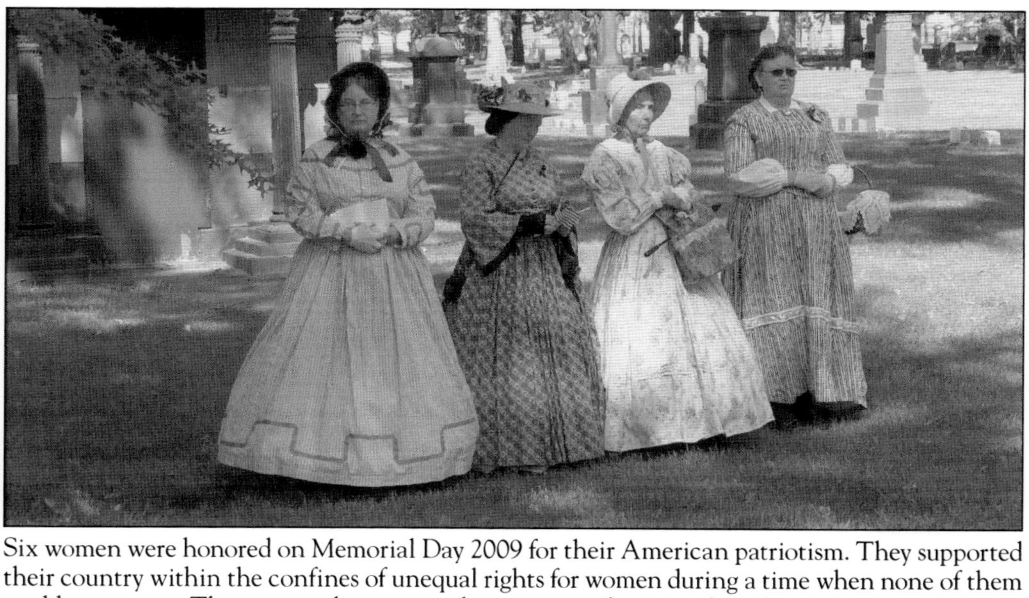

Six women were honored on Memorial Day 2009 for their American patriotism. They supported their country within the confines of unequal rights for women during a time when none of them could even vote. There were also many other women who contributed by nursing, organizing, gardening, or contributing whatever they could to help deal with the effects of war and the repercussions on the men who fought for them. (Carolyn Vigneulle.)

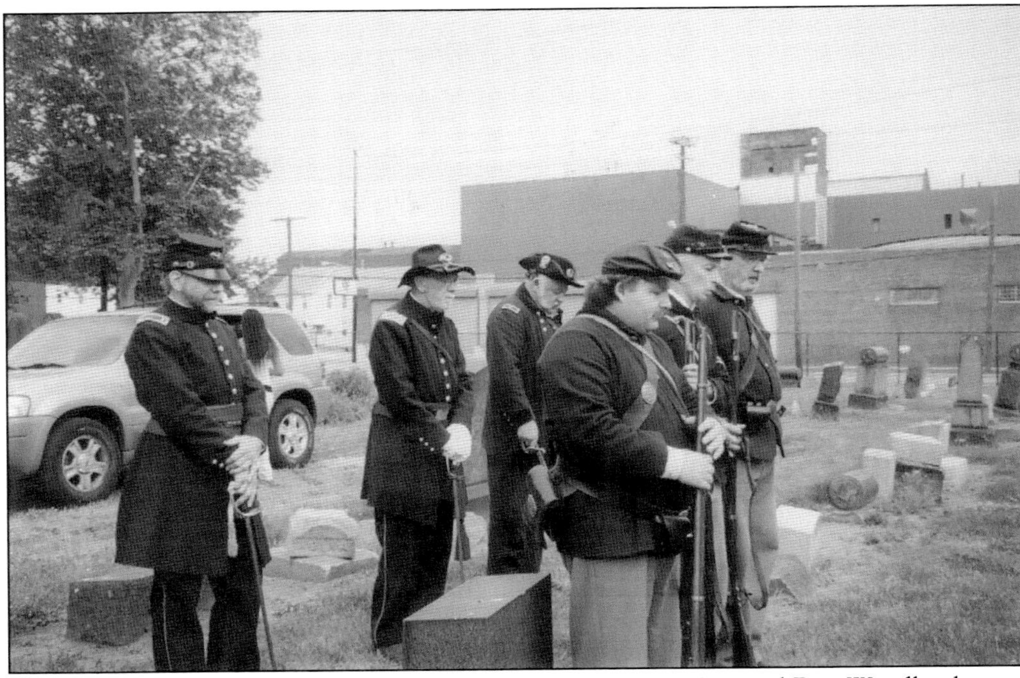

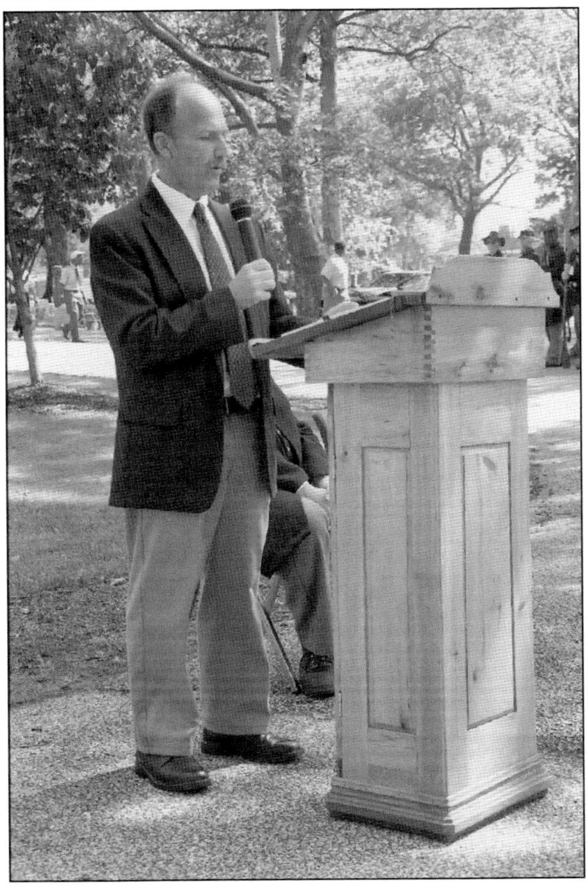

Every Memorial Day, Woodland Cemetery hosts an annual Decoration Day ceremony honoring those who died in the service of their country. Various veterans are chosen for this recognition. In 2010, Woodland honored four Vietnam veterans: George Early Jr., Ronald Hamilton, Eugene Nagy, and George White. The 7th Ohio Volunteer Infantry reenactors, seen here paying tribute to Eugene Nagy, have faithfully participated in these annual ceremonies. (Lynn Corbett.)

The sesquicentennial anniversary of the Civil War fell in 2011. In keeping with tradition of honoring the cemetery's veterans, this year's focus was on honoring the United States Colored Troops. Paul LaRue, who has researched and documented the black Civil War veterans in Ohio, was this year's keynote speaker. The event help lead the way for the WCF to install a monument dedicated to the members of the USCT who are buried in Woodland Cemetery. (MAD.)

Speaker E. Paul Morehouse Jr., archivist general of the General Society of the War of 1812 and registrar-genealogist of the Ohio Society of the War of 1812, Memorial Day keynote speaker, addresses the guests at Woodland Cemetery on Ohio's role in the War on the 200th anniversary of the War of 1812. Woodland is home to at least 25 War of 1812 veterans, including Ohio governor Reuben Wood, Gen. Donald McLeod, drummer boy Jarvis Hanks, William Jackson and many others. (MAD.)

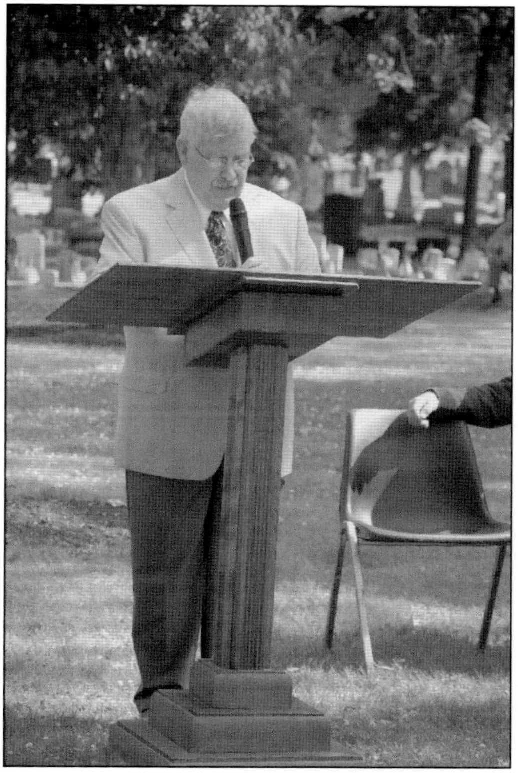

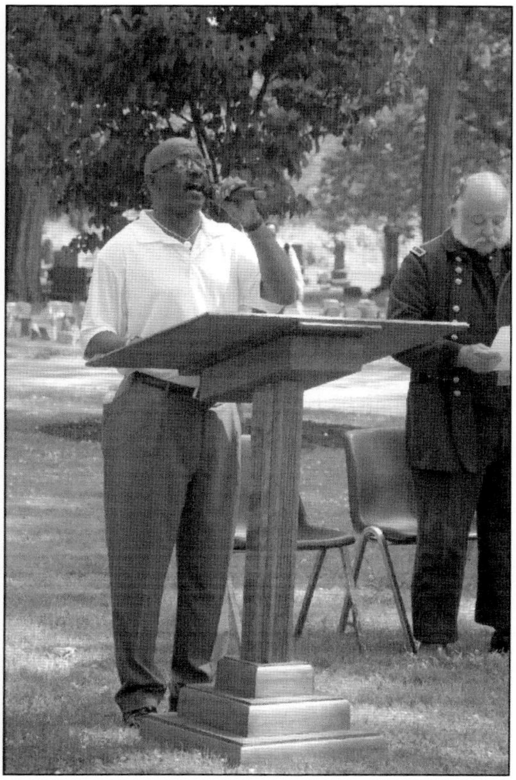

David R. Mitchell, manager of City of Cleveland Cemeteries, sings the national anthem during the annual Memorial Day service. David is responsible for 12 city cemeteries, the oldest dating back to 1826. The City of Cleveland is in charge of one of the largest cemetery operations in the state of Ohio. (MAD.)

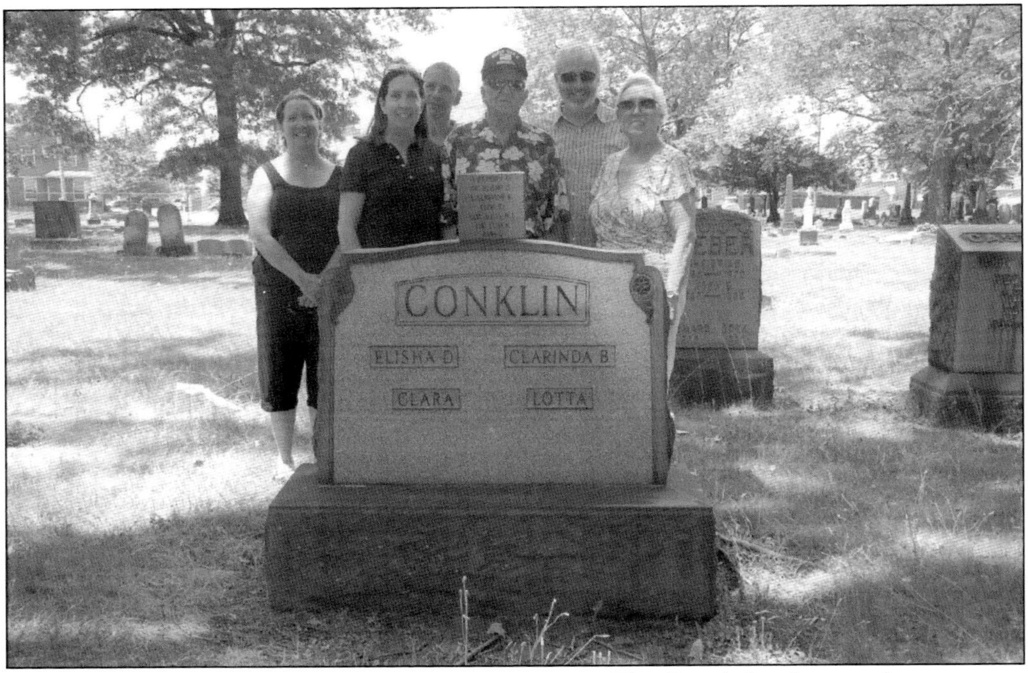

The Cusick family recently celebrated a family reunion in the area, coming from as far away as California and Ireland. While in Cleveland, a few from the group took time to pay respects at the resting place of their great-great-grandfather Elisha D. Conklin, who served during the Civil War as a lieutenant colonel in the Union Army from New York State. (MAD.)

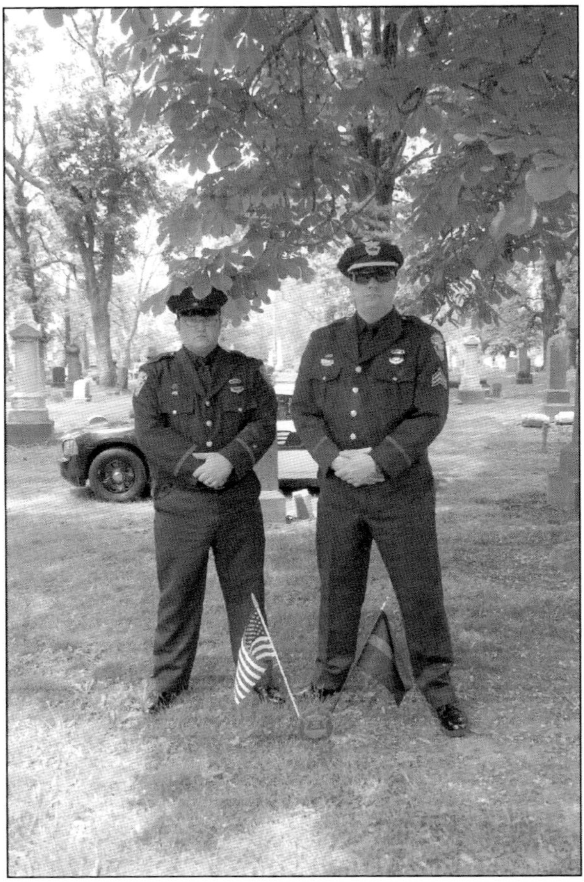

Woodland Cemetery is the final resting place of six fallen police officers. In 2012, the Greater Cleveland Peace Officers Memorial Society started honoring all the fallen officers listed on the Police Memorial in Cleveland. Standing at the unmarked grave of Henry Richter, Cuyahoga Metropolitan Housing Authority officers Sgt. James Neal and Ofc. John Smiddy visited the six officer gravesites to place memorial markers and flags during Police Week in May. (MAD.)

About the Foundation

In June 2007, in response to numerous public requests and the concerns of many individuals and organizations, the WCF was formed. Its purpose was to help restore the cemetery, owned and managed by the City of Cleveland, by relieving the city of the need to use critical public resources to do so.

The WCF was incorporated as an Ohio nonprofit on July 27, 2007, and is tax-exempt under Section 501(c)(3) of the Internal Revenue Code. The organization could now seek community support and involvement, as well as charitable donations and in-kind contributions to aid in the preservation of the cemetery. On May 5, 2008, the City of Cleveland Council passed an ordinance making Woodland Cemetery a Cleveland Landmark, which safeguarded the cemetery as a historical burial ground.

As mentioned elsewhere, one of the foundation's primary goals is to restore the 1870 Gothic Revival stone gatehouse that was systematically dismantled in the winter of 1995. Other projects include landscaping the grounds, installing sectional markers, assisting with funds and/or acting as volunteer contractors to repair headstones, monuments, and mausoleums and to improve roadways in the cemetery. Some restoration has already taken place, namely, the 7th Ohio Volunteer Infantry cannons, the 23rd Ohio Volunteer Infantry landscaping, new headstones, monument repairs, and a plan for the restoration of the gatehouse.

Although most of the lots in Woodland's 60 acres have been purchased, burials still occur and the cemetery remains active. Therefore, the WCF is committed to restoring Woodland's landscape to mirror its original design as a park-like location meant for quiet solitude, reflection, and contemplation.

Some mausoleum roofs have been repaired, an electrical outlet has been installed to enable microphone equipment to be used at special events, and technical additions have been made to the foundation's website to ensure accessibility to cemetery records. The Woodland Cemetery database (87,961 records) is available on our website, www.wcfcle.org, and can be searched by last name or burial date. The website has been invaluable in aiding WCF in its attempts to respond to the various requests received from around the world.

The WCF appreciates any financial support for any of its projects, and events as it continues its mission. Volunteers are welcomed and encouraged. Please check the website for information regarding memorial bricks, volunteer opportunities, meeting dates, or information regarding events. The foundation can also be reached at 216-319-2091.

The WCF is governed as an all-volunteer non-profit organization and is dedicated to preserving and honoring the past generations buried in Woodland Cemetery. In its effort to foster knowledge about the historical significance of the site, this book is a giant first step.